INTRODUCTION
TO QUEBEC LAW

REVISED

INTRODUCTION TO QUEBEC LAW

REVISED

Martin Franklin, B.A., B.C.L.,
Advocate, Bar of Montreal,
Assistant Professor, Department of Management,
Sir George Williams University, Montreal

David R. Franklin, B.A., B.C.L.,
Advocate, Bar of Montreal,
Lecturer, Department of Management,
Sir George Williams University, Montreal

Pitman Publishing

A Division of Copp Clark Limited
Vancouver Calgary Toronto Montreal

© *Martin Franklin and David Franklin 1972*
Revised 1976

Illustrations by Franklin Hammond
Cover and design by Brant Cowie

ISBN 0-273-04228-9
Library of Congress Catalog Card Number 72-89674

Pitman Publishing
517 Wellington Street West
Toronto M5V 1G1

Printed and bound in Canada

CONTENTS

PREFACE

This text is an introductory survey for students in which basic principles of Quebec civil and commercial law are examined.

Since this is probably the first law text used by the student, it concentrates on the general principles and necessarily excludes important and often interesting areas of law, including exceptions to the general rules. This work in no way pretends to provide the student with a body of professional knowledge, but rather attempts to acquaint him with some introductory knowledge of general legal principles, concepts, terminology and solutions to practical problems.

The names used in the examples and illustrations are fictitious and any similarity to actual persons living or dead is coincidental and unintentional.

M.F.
D.R.F.

INTRODUCTION

Chapter 1

INTRODUCTION

The purpose of this book is to present the student and layman with a broad introductory survey of the principles of Quebec law governing contracts, property and personal rights, and to familiarise them with the legal implications of their daily activities, more especially their rights and obligations arising out of the contracts they make.

WHY LAW?

Why law? Is law really necessary? Why lawyers and judges? Why not have several wise and honest men decide disputes between people? Why the volumes of textbooks and written laws? If a man is living alone on an island, never coming into contact with other persons, he is a law unto himself. No regulations, no prohibitions are needed and he can do as he wishes whenever he wishes and without anyone complaining. However, since man lives with others, be it in a complex modern society or in a tribe, he has to respect the rights of his fellow members, otherwise there will be social chaos. In the simple tribal community, the rules of conduct are usually unwritten but these customs are rigidly upheld, often because of the influence of taboos and religion. These types of laws are based on oral tradition and transmitted by the elders from generation to generation. When a society becomes more complex and literate, these prohibitions and taboos are formulated into rigid written law. Early examples are the Code of Hammurabi in Mesopotamia, the Ten Commandments of Moses and Roman law.

THE RULE OF LAW

Our Western democratic system of law provides that every

individual is free to act in any manner he wishes except when such conduct is prohibited by law. We are living not under the rule of men, but under the *rule of law*, which holds:

1. That *all* men are subject to the law. No matter how high a position a person may hold in society or government, if that person commits a crime, he is liable under the law.

2. That no man can be punished except for a breach of the law. A person can only be punished when the law specifically states that his act is a crime.

3. That every man is entitled to recourse to the courts. No man is excluded from the courts and all are subject to the judicial process.

WHY STUDY LAW?

Consider the ways you become involved in the daily operation of law regulations: you use the public transportation, purchase books, eat at a restaurant, buy clothes, live in a rented apartment. In fact most of your daily activities directly or indirectly involve or are circumscribed by the law. Surely it is important for you to be familiar with your rights and obligations in each of these situations.

When you enter into commercial contracts at work, you are committing yourself or the company you represent to possible serious financial consequences, and you should be aware of the legal consequences of your acts.

> *I sell you a TV set for $100 payable cash on delivery. You know you have to pay or else I won't deliver. Because the laws covering the sale of goods have been well defined, we both know that certain consequences will occur as a result of our entering into this contract.*

The law provides conduct guidelines and knowledge of the law enables you to foresee the legal consequences of your acts.

Not only should you be aware of what your rights

and obligations are, you should also know how to legally enforce them and how the law protects you through the system of courts.

WHAT IS LAW?

So far in our discussion of "why law" we have used the terms law, prohibitions, customs, written law, code, commandments, rights. These are all aspects of law. But what is law?

A definition of law is extremely complex. Law is not only a legal term but it is also a concept which has different meanings in different societies. In a formal legal sense, law may be defined as that body of principles and regulations enforceable in courts. In a broader sense, law includes a body of standards and rules, both written and unwritten, that governs the conduct and relationships among citizens and between citizens and the state. In a philosophical sense, law may be considered as an ideal—as justice, as morality, as universal unchanging principles of conduct, as natural law.

Law also has political and social significance. Governments pass new laws in response to political and social changes. In Canada, we have recently seen widesweeping changes in divorce, marriage and criminal law.

Although there is no adequate, single definition of law, in our discussion of commercial and civil laws perhaps we can define it as the body of rules that governs the legal relationships arising between persons in their dealings with one another.

SOURCES OF LAW

Where Is the Law Governing Contracts, Property and Personal Rights Found?

In the Province of Quebec, there are five sources of commercial and civil law:
1. The Civil Code of the Province of Quebec
2. legislation: statutory law

3. jurisprudence or court cases
4. the published works of legal experts
5. custom and usage

The Civil Code of the Province of Quebec

The main source of civil and commercial law in the Province of Quebec is contained in the Civil Code.[1] Quebec is the only province which has a unified Code of legal principles set out in 2,615 articles as its main source of law.

Prior to the British conquest of Quebec (New France) in 1759, the French law as it existed in France at that time, known as "The Customs of Paris," and modified by certain local laws, was in use in Quebec. In 1774, the Quebec Act guaranteed freedom of religion to Roman Catholics, made English and French the two official languages of the province and French civil law the law governing property, civil rights and contracts. From the British conquest until 1866, trade and commerce developed and certain English customs and practices were introduced into this French milieu. In 1866, one year before Confederation, this body of law, consisting of the existing law in the Province of Quebec with its sources in the old French law, the local laws passed by the Quebec Legislature and the English practice, was carefully reduced into one volume embodying law, both commercial and civil, entitled *The Civil Code of Lower Canada*. This compilation of Quebec law was patterned after the French Napoleonic Code of 1804. The French Code, commissioned by Napoleon Bonaparte, consolidated the old Roman law, French law and customs and the new law of the revolution which abolished special privileges and established equality of persons. Many Articles in the Quebec Code follow very closely, if not identically, those of the French Code.

1. Throughout the text, Articles of the Civil Code are cited in the abbreviated form "Art." followed by the number of the Article.

The Civil Code contains most of the commercial law used in the Province of Quebec and deals with such areas as persons, property, obligations, general rules governing contracts, contracts such as sale, lease, partnerships, loan, mandate, hypothecs. But it does not contain all the commercial or civil law. It is bilingual, the English generally being a translation of the French.

Legislation
Statutory Law

In 1867 the British North America Act divided legislative authority in Canada between the federal and provincial governments. Most of the areas we are going to examine fall within the powers of the Quebec provincial government. However, there are important areas of commercial and civil law governed by the federal government and applicable to all of Canada. They include bills of exchange, laws governing federal corporations, bankruptcy, trade mark, patents and copyright, fair trade practices, divorce.

Each year many new laws, called acts or statutes, are passed by both Ottawa and Quebec which amend, modify and sometimes radically change the body of civil and commercial law. From time to time Articles of the Quebec Civil Code are revised. For example, there have been recent changes in property law between husband and wife, and the age of majority was reduced from twenty-one to eighteen years.

There are other laws such as the Cities and Towns Act, the Highway Code, the Municipal Code, the Consumer Protection Act, the Bankruptcy Act, which came into effect after the Civil Code was established. These are bodies of law enacted by the Quebec National Assembly and by Federal Parliament. These laws are usually called statutes or acts and sometimes codes.

Jurisprudence or Court Cases

One of the principal sources of law are court case judgments called *jurisprudence* which interpret the law. In the other provinces, English law or *common law* has evolved through a lengthy series of these judgments, each built upon a previous similar case or *precedent*, until a well-defined principle is established. This principle of repeating and following previous decisions is called *stare decisis* (let the decision stand). However, the growing trend in the common law provinces is to reduce the vast number of court cases into written law.

In Quebec, the judges are not bound to follow previous court judgments but they generally do, especially decisions of the Appeal Court and Supreme Court. They examine the facts of each case, apply the relevant law, study similar previous court decisions and arrive at a judgment.

Writers

In Quebec an important source of law often referred to by the courts are legal writings by *jurists* from Quebec, other parts of Canada, France and England. A jurist may be a judge, lawyer or professor, who is knowledgeable in the law and who has written a book or an article in a legal journal.

Custom and Usage

When applicable, the courts will permit in evidence the common practice or custom in a certain locality or in a particular trade. For example, in a case involving personal injuries, it might be relevant to know whether it is the landlord or the tenant who customarily removes snow from stairways leading to apartment buildings.

CLASSIFICATION OF LAWS

Laws may be divided into international law, national law, substantive law and procedural law.

International Law

International law deals with relations between nations, in the form of treaties, conventions of the United Nations and other international bodies.

National Law

National law refers to the laws of Canada. Within Canada, law is divided into federal laws and provincial laws. In turn, provincial laws are subdivided into two levels: provincial laws and local municipal laws passed by cities, towns and municipalities (by-laws). *National law* may also be divided into subject matter: *public law* and *private* or *civil law.*

Public Law

Public law is the branch of law governing the relationship between the citizen and the government. Included in public law are criminal law, administrative law and constitutional law.

1. *Criminal law*: Canada has a federal Criminal Code applicable throughout the country which defines those anti-social acts which are illegal, prohibited and punishable by imprisonment and/or fine.

2. *Administrative law*: an appreciable amount of our law-making has been delegated by parliament and the provincial legislature to Boards, Commissions and administrative agencies which make detailed regulations on a specific area. For example, the Quebec Minimum Wage Board enacts detailed regulations concerning minimum wages in various trades.

3. *Constitutional law*: the British North America Act (1867) and its amendments (referred to as the B.N.A. Act) is our Canadian Constitution. Constitutional law deals with the structure of government, exercise of governmental power and the division of legislative powers between the federal and provincial governments. Canada has a federal system of government—both a central government as well as provincial governments—each with jealously guarded zones of authority.

The B.N.A. Act originally united four provinces, Ontario, Quebec, New Brunswick and Nova Scotia, and created a federal government with legislative powers distributed between the federal government in Ottawa and the provincial governments. Federal powers are largely set forth in Section 91 covering such areas as currency, weights and measures, bankruptcy law, company law, banks, divorce, bills of exchange, criminal law, interprovincial trade and customs and duties. Provincial powers are set out in Section 92, which includes direct taxation, administration of justice, and more particularly, property and civil rights (Section 92, subsection 13), by which each province is empowered to legislate on civil and commercial law. It is for this reason that each of the provinces has its own commercial laws although there is now a trend in the common law provinces towards a uniformity of legislation. For example, The Sale of Goods Act of Ontario is similar to that of the other provinces, except Quebec.

Private or Civil Law

Our Quebec civil law system is based on Roman law which in turn has been embodied in French and finally Quebec law. In the other provinces the source of law is the common law of England which is based on the rule of precedent, that is, previous court case judgments. The question is often asked, Are Quebec civil law and the common law different? There is a basic similarity between the two systems in that their social and economic frameworks are almost identical so that the manner of making contracts is the same. However, there are important differences in the law itself. Because of these differences, a legal problem in a particular area, e.g., sale, leases, property, offences and quasi offences, arising in Ontario might be decided differently in Quebec.

Civil law also means private law between citizens or businessmen rather than public law.

Substantive and Procedural Law

Law can be further classified as substantive and procedural.
1. Substantive law sets out the *substance* of the law—*what* your rights and obligations are in various areas of law and found principally in the Quebec Civil Code.
2. Procedural law states *how* to enforce your rights and is largely covered by the Quebec Civil Code of Procedure.

Legal Terminology

law
regulation
prohibition
custom
taboos
Code of Hammurabi
Ten Commandments
Roman law
the rule of law
justice
morality
natural law
The Civil Code
Quebec legislation
statutes
acts
British North America Act

division of legislative powers
Federal Parliament
jurisprudence
common law
court cases
precedent
stare decisis
jurist
usage
international law
national law
public law
civil law
criminal law
administrative law
constitutional law
substantive law
procedural law

Questions

1. Discuss why laws are necessary in society.
2. List three ancient written laws.
3. What is meant by the rule of law?
4. Why is a study of law necessary?
5. What is the meaning of law in its legal, philosophical, political and social contexts?

6. Give a definition of commercial law.
7. Describe the origin of the Civil Code.
8. What is the meaning of legislation?
9. What is the British North America Act?
10. What is meant by the division of legislative powers?
11. What is the meaning of jurisprudence?
12. What are legal precedents, and are they relevant in Quebec?
13. Who is a jurist?
14. What is custom and usage?
15. Define the following terms:
a. international law
b. national law
c. public law
d. criminal law
e. administrative law
f. constitutional law
16. Describe the differences between Quebec civil law and the commercial and civil law of the other provinces.
17. What is the difference between substantive and procedural law?

Problems

1. Suppose the Quebec National Assembly is considering passing legislation in the fields of bankruptcy and bills of exchange. Does it have the constitutional authority to do so?
2. You are called upon to draft a code of conduct governing the relationships between the students and the school. What areas of conduct would you cover and what penalties and punishments would you recommend?

What other groups and institutions are you a member of which have their own regulations? Obtain a copy of the rules and regulations governing one of them and after carefully examining these, give your opinions as to:
a. whether these regulations help make the institution function effectively;
b. what changes, if any, should be made in these rules.

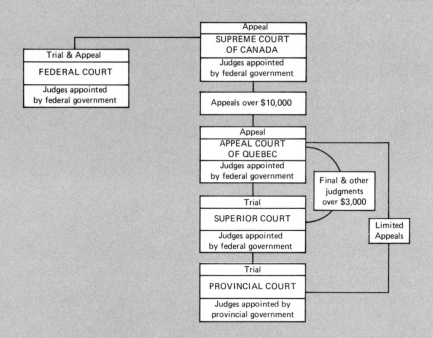

ADMINISTRATION OF LAW

Chapter 2

ADMINISTRATION OF LAW

Legal disputes are resolved before the courts of law. The B.N.A. Act divides authority over the courts and their officers between the federal and provincial governments. Quebec has a well-organised judicial system with a hierarchy of courts including courts of first instance (trial courts) and courts of appeal. Only the civil or commercial courts are considered in this text. It should be noted that there are other courts, such as the social welfare and criminal courts.

The civil court system found in Quebec is illustrated on the facing page.

APPEAL COURTS

The Supreme Court of Canada

This is the highest and final court of appeal in Canada. Its nine member bench sits in Ottawa and cases which have been previously decided before the Quebec Court of Appeal can be appealed to it. Generally speaking, permission for leave to appeal to the Supreme Court is obtained from the Supreme Court. The judges examine the court record including the proceedings and evidence made at the trial, the trial judgment and the Quebec Appeal Court Judgment, and the lawyers submit briefs and legal arguments.

The judges and court officials are appointed by the federal government. Judges hold positions until age seventy-five.

Court of Appeal

The Court of Appeal is the general appeal tribunal for the province. A losing party in a court case may appeal to this court concerning:

a. A judgment of the Superior Court where the amount involved is over $3,000.

b. A Provincial Court judgment where such court has exclusive jurisdiction under any Act other than the Civil Code of Procedure, e.g., cases involving contestation of elections.

c. A judgment of the Superior Court concerning injunctions, *habeas corpus* and other extraordinary remedies.

d. In other matters an appeal is permitted with prior written permission of two judges of the Appeal Court.

The Court of Appeal sitting on each case consists of three or five judges; no witnesses are heard. The Court examines the trial court proceedings and witnesses' evidence made at trial in the lower court and hears arguments of the lawyers. It then renders judgment. A majority opinion is sufficient to win the appeal. The Appeal Court may uphold, reverse or modify the judgment appealed from or it may order a new trial.

The judges are federal government appointees and hold office until age seventy-five.

TRIAL COURTS

The trial courts described here are presided over by one judge. His duty is to hear the evidence of witnesses and the arguments of the lawyers, to study and apply the relevant law to the issues and render a decision called a judgment. This judgment may be "off the bench," that is, verbal, made immediately by him after the trial, or his judgment may be written, rendered sometime after the trial.

The Federal Court

Formerly called the Exchequer Court and Admiralty Court, this court is under federal jurisdiction. It hears matters primarily involving disputes between the federal government and individuals and corporations, accidents occurring on federal government property, taxation disputes, as well as hearing appeals from decisions of federal administrative boards. Three federal judges sit as a bench on these appeals. Judges hold office until seventy years of age.

Superior Court

Throughout the province of Quebec the Superior Court hears all matters not assigned to other courts; this means that it has jurisdiction in most cases involving over $3,000; it also hears disputes between husband and wife including legal separation, divorce, alimentary allowance and custody, as well as bankruptcy cases.

The judge is a federal appointee holding office until the age of seventy-five. The court officials and staff are provincial employees.

Provincial Court

The Provincial Court is under sole provincial jurisdiction. One judge hears each case. He holds office "during good behaviour." Throughout the province the Provincial Court hears matters:

a. where the sum claimed is less than $3,000;

b. for the cancellation of leases when the rent and damages are less than $3,000;

c. for recovery of municipal and school taxes.

Generally speaking, and with several exceptions, there is no appeal.

Small Claims Court

This court is under sole provincial jurisdiction. One judge hears each case. There is no appeal.

As of September, 1972, the Province of Quebec established a Small Claims Court where a person can, by himself, sue and defend disputes in which the amount claimed is less than $300. Generally, the plaintiff and defendant must handle their own case at trial and cannot use a lawyer there. The purpose is to simplify the operation and costs of these small cases. Similar courts have been in operation for years in other parts of Canada and the United States.

Municipal Court

The provincial government delegates to many municipalities the right to operate local courts which handle local traffic offences and infractions against local by-laws, such as health, building, pollution, licences, taxes. In some municipal courts minor criminal cases are also handled, such as drunken driving, simple assault and disturbing the peace.

The provincial government nominates the judges. The court staff members are municipal employees.

JURY

Seldom in civil cases (but quite often in serious criminal cases) is trial by jury used. The jury consists of six persons selected from the public at large. Their duty is to decide on the facts only, that is, whether according to the facts the defendant is responsible. Their decision is the verdict. The judge's role is to direct the jury on points of law and to render a judgment.

LAWYERS

A lawyer or advocate is a professional whose role is to advise others concerning their rights or obligations under the law, and to represent them before the courts. For this purpose lawyers advise, draw up contracts, institute and defend court cases, interrogate witnesses and plead generally before the courts, etc. You do not require a lawyer to "go to court." You can handle your own case. But if you want someone to act on your behalf, you must choose a lawyer.

To practise law and to qualify to be a member of the Bar Association of a province one has to have a university law degree, B.C.L. or L.L.B., and pass provincial Bar exams. Each association keeps a vigilant administration over its members and the standard of professional conduct required of them is kept rigorously high. There is also a Canadian Bar Association to which lawyers across Canada may belong.

Lawyers are often called by the more formal term of advocate or attorney. In Quebec, as in the rest of Canada, a lawyer not only prepares the cases but also pleads them before the court. In England the profession is divided: solicitors prepare the case and barristers plead it before the court.

NOTARY

Quebec is the only province where notaries are a separate legal profession. In the other provinces lawyers perform the function of notaries. A notary's principal functions are the drafting and witnessing of certain important legal documents, for example, marriage contracts, real estate transactions and hypothecs (mortgages). They, as well as lawyers, also often act in the winding up of estates of deceased persons.

BAILIFFS AND SHERIFFS

A *bailiff* is a legal officer empowered to serve legal proceedings, to make seizures of property and to bring moveable property to sale in virtue of a judgment. A *sheriff* is a legal officer whose duties include bringing immoveables (land and buildings) to sale in virtue of a judgment.

COURT OFFICIALS

1. *A prothonotary:* a legal officer of the Superior Court who renders judgments in certain noncontested matters such as actions on cheques, actions for merchandise sold and delivered and who is also responsible for court records.
2. *Clerks of the Provincial Court:* legal officers whose duties are similar to prothonotaries of the Superior Court.
3. *Court reporters:* official stenographers who take down and transcribe into writing the evidence of witnesses.

4. A *Commissioner of Oaths:* a person authorised by the provincial government to take oaths and sworn statements.

LEGAL FEES

When an individual retains the services of a lawyer, he will be required to pay a fee. The amount of the fee depends on a variety of factors: the lawyer's experience, the complexity and amount involved in the problem, the time and effort spent. An attorney is entitled to charge at least a minimum collection fee on amounts collected when the claim is based on cheques, merchandise sold and delivered, rent, etc., as follows:

a minimum of 15 percent on first $500;

a minimum of 10 percent on excess up to $2,000.

You should always ask your lawyer to estimate what his total bill will be. Even if you are successful in your court action, legal fees are *not* collectable from the other party.

Legal aid is a free service provided by legal aid clinics, the Legal Aid Bureau of various Bar associations and by members of the Bar, both legal and notarial, for persons who cannot afford legal fees. The government pays the fees of a lawyer who accepts a legal aid case.

COURT COSTS

In civil matters, in order to institute proceedings and bring a case to trial, there are court costs to pay. The losing party has to reimburse the court costs to the other party's lawyer. These costs are set out in an official court tariff and vary according to the amount of the court case and the stage of the proceedings. Consequently, the lawyer in a successful case obtains a fee from his client and court costs from the losing party.

Before embarking on a court case it is always advisable to discuss with your attorney what the court costs would be if you lost your case.

You sue Smith for a $500 debt. He pays only after judgment and a bailiff's seizure. It will now cost him an additional $120 which includes court costs and bailiff's seizure expenses. When your lawyer accounts to you, he sends you $500 less 15 percent collection fee, or $425.

Legal Terminology

Supreme Court of Canada	barristers, solicitors
Trial Courts	Bar Association
Court of Appeal	notary
Federal Court	bailiff
Superior Court	sheriff
Provincial Court	prothonotary
Small Claims Court	clerk
Municipal Court	court reporter
jury	Commissioner of Oaths
judge	legal fees
lawyers, advocates, attorneys,	legal aid
	court costs

Questions

1. What is the highest court of appeal in Canada?
2. Which court hears cases concerning federal income tax?
3. Which government appoints judges to the Superior Court of Quebec?
4. Which courts does the Quebec provincial government have sole jurisdiction to organise and operate?
5. What is the role of the courts?
6. Describe the small claims court.
7. The Provincial Court hears what court cases?
8. What court cases does the Superior Court hear?
9. What is the function of the Court of Appeal?
10. What minister is responsible for administration of justice?
11. What is the role of the presiding judge?
12. What is the role of a jury?

13. What is the role of a lawyer or advocate?
14. What is the purpose of the Bar Association?
15. What are the prime functions of a notary?
16. What do the following officers do?
a. sheriff
b. bailiff
c. prothonotary and clerk of the court
d. court reporters
17. What are legal fees and how are they estimated?
18. What are court costs and who is liable for payment?
19. What is legal aid?
20. What is a Commissioner of Oaths?

Problem

Name the proper courts to hear the following matters:
a. legal separation
b. an automobile accident claim for $750
c. a final appeal from a judgment of $38,000
d. an action on a $1,000 N.S.F. cheque
e. a parking ticket
f. contestation of a municipal election

PROCEDURE IN A CIVIL ACTION

Chapter 3

PROCEDURE IN A CIVIL ACTION

What do you do when

a. John owes you money and refuses to pay you?

b. You were injured while a passenger in Robert's car when it was involved in a collision?

c. You accepted a cheque for $500 from Smith which the bank has returned N.S.F.?

CONSULT YOUR LAWYER

Although you may act on your own behalf before the law courts, it is not generally advisable to do so, since you just do not have the knowledge and skill necessary to prepare and present your case, especially when the facts and law are complicated. Also, you are not able to view your case objectively. There is an old saying that "a man who acts as his own attorney has a fool for a client."

Then what should you do? Arrange an appointment with a lawyer. Explain the facts to him. He will advise you as to the best possible course of action to take and of your legal rights.

If your lawyer tells you that you have a "good case," then you must decide whether or not to sue, that is, to take legal proceedings before the court. Even if you win and collect, you will still have to pay your lawyer a fee, which means that you will not be reimbursed all that is owing. Even if you win, you may not be able to enforce your judgment, if the debtor has no seizable assets, no property, no job, or if in the meantime he has left the country or gone into bankruptcy. If the amount involved is small, it may not be worthwhile taking proceedings, especially if there is some doubt as to the debtor's solvency, for if your lawyer cannot collect after judgment, he may ask you to pay to him the court costs, which the debtor would have paid if he had any seizable assets.

Often settlement out of court is arrived at through your lawyer. For instance, the debtor might make you an offer of 75 percent of your claim of $500 payable at $25 per week. You might instruct your lawyer to accept it. A case can always be settled at any stage in the proceedings.

INSTITUTION OF LEGAL PROCEEDINGS

You decide to sue Smith to recover the sum of $500 he owes you. The rules governing court procedure are set out in a separate code called the Quebec Civil Code of Procedure, which is a companion work to the Quebec Civil Code. Your lawyer will proceed as follows:

a. The first step will be the preparation and issuance of a *writ of summons.* This is a document issued by the court, at the instance of the plaintiff (you), ordering the defendant (Smith) to appear at the court house within ten days from the date he received the writ, to answer the claim. To this writ is attached a *plaintiff's declaration* setting out the basic facts and conclusions of your claim.

b. The writ and declaration are *served* on Smith by a bailiff. A copy of same is left either personally with the defendant or with a member of his family.

c. The defendant has the right to *appear* at court personally or through his own lawyer, who files an *appearance* at court on his behalf.

d. If Smith does not "appear" within ten days from the bailiff's service then the plaintiff may within a short delay obtain *judgment* against him *by default.* If the defendant does file an appearance he has ten days after his appearance within which to make his *defence* (plea). The bailiff serves a copy of the defence upon your lawyer. Your lawyer may prepare and serve an *answer to plea.* Both lawyers file at court the originals of these documents bearing the bailiffs' reports of service.

e. At this point the issues are joined in the contested case, that is, both parties have set out their side of the case, and the case is *inscribed for proof and hearing;* your lawyer will notify the court to put the case on the list of cases to be heard, (probably at least six months later).

f. In due course the court fixes a *trial date* and assigns a courtroom where the trial is to be held. Both parties and *witnesses* will go to court on that day. Your lawyer prepares *subpoenae* to be served by a bailiff, ordering the witnesses to appear in court.

g. *Pretrial Hearings*

There are proceedings which may be taken in your case before the trial date. For example, if the plaintiff's declaration is vague, the defendant's lawyer may make a motion to the court requesting *particulars*—more details of the allegations contained in the plaintiff's action—or he may question you under oath before the trial, or your lawyer may decide to question the defendant under oath most probably in order to obtain *admissions,* and thus help "make" your case. This examination of the parties is called an *examination on discovery* and is held in court with an official stenographer present to record the questions and answers. The *transcript* then goes into the court record.

In an action for bodily injuries the plaintiff may be examined by the defendant's doctor.

h. *The Trial*

The judge sits on a raised platform at one end of the room behind a large desk; below him at a table sits the clerk of the court. Next to this table is a box where the witnesses stand facing the judge to give evidence. Then at a lower level is a table where the lawyers for plaintiff and defendant sit. Their clients are permitted to sit beside them. Everyone else sits on the benches filling the rest of the chamber. The *clerk* calls the case and he will administer the *oath* to each witness called to testify. The lawyer for the plaintiff begins—he calls his first witness and after he is through questioning him the attorney for the defendant has a right to question (cross-examine) the witness. Each witness is questioned in this fashion. After all the witnesses are heard, the two lawyers then sum up their respective sides of the case, first the attorney for the plaintiff, then the attorney for the defendant. The judge may give *judgment* then and there, although this is not generally usual. More often the judge reserves judgment, that is, he does not render judgment verbally off the bench but instead renders a written judgment. In preparing his judgment, he will usually review the facts as brought out in the evidence, discuss the arguments made by the attorneys, consider and apply the relevant law and conclude in favour of one of the parties, including the awarding of *court costs,* which the losing party is ordered to pay to the other party's lawyer. The losing party can *appeal* the judgment to the Court of Appeal if the amount claimed is $3,000 or more, or with leave of the court if under $3,000.

i. *Execution*

Your lawyer advises you he has received a copy of the judgment, you have won your case and Smith has been ordered to pay you $500, plus costs to your lawyer.

Now your lawyer takes steps to enforce the judgment. There are several procedures that he can take: Smith can be summoned to appear in court to answer questions under oath as to his assets. If he fails to attend he may eventually be found guilty of contempt of court and sentenced to jail for up to a year or have to pay a fine of not more than $5,000.

A *writ of execution* can be obtained from court to make a seizure of the debtor's property and bring it to sale to satisfy the judgment debt and costs. A bailiff proceeds to the *seizure* of moveable property and the sheriff of the district to the seizure of immoveable property. Public notice is given of the sale and the property is sold by auction, for cash.

A *seizure* can be made of the debtor's property which is being held by a third party. For example, your lawyer may seize Smith's bank account in the hands of the bank or his salary in the hands of his employer, or money owing to him by a third party. However, there is certain property which is unseizable. The debtor may select and withdraw from the seizure clothing and bedding for himself and his family, household furniture and utensils to a value of $1,000, books and tools of his trade, family papers, alimony awarded by the court, retirement pensions.

Part of the debtor's salary is unseizable and the rules are as follows:

1. If the employee is single, the first $20 of his weekly salary is unseizable.

2. If he is married and has no more than one child as a dependant, $30 of his salary is unseizable. For each additional dependant, a further $5 of his salary is unseizable.

Consequently, if Smith is earning $100 gross a week, is married and has one child, $30 of his gross salary would be unseizable, leaving $70. The law provides that 70 percent of this remaining portion of his salary is unseizable. The result is that only 30 percent of $70 can be seized, being the sum of $21 a week. In time your lawyer will collect the amount owing to you, however, you must keep in mind that the debtor and his family, if he has one, are entitled to live and there are limits placed on your right to payment.

SPECIAL LEGAL REMEDIES

There are certain legal remedies available in particular situations.

Quo Warranto

This is an action against a person occupying a public office illegally. For example, if a person is acting as mayor of a municipality without having been elected, an elector can apply to the court for an order to oust him.

Mandamus

One can apply to the court for a *mandamus* ordering a person to perform a duty required by law, for example, the calling of an election, or the issuing of a city permit which is being unjustifiably withheld.

Habeas Corpus

Any person who is confined or deprived of his liberty, except by order of a court, may apply to a judge of the Superior Court for a *writ of habeas corpus* ordering the person detaining him to bring him before the court and show why he is being detained. This writ is sometimes used in civil cases involving minors, for example, in instances where a parent illegally takes a child away from the other parent who has custody and also in cases involving people allegedly being held illegally in mental institutions.

Injunction

An injunction is an order of the Superior Court, or of a judge thereof, enjoining a person, his officers, agents or employees, not to do or cease to do, or, in cases which admit of it, to perform a particular act or operation, under pain of all legal penalties.

> *A lime quarry adjacent to your house is sending clouds of lime dust into the air continuously, and your house is always full of dust. In such a case, the court might order issuance of an injunction ordering the quarry not to pile up or handle the lime in open air.*

Except in cases of public nuisance, the court will issue an injunction only if there is no other remedy available and if the damage being caused is irreparable and cannot be remedied by the payment of money.

Other proceedings are available in noncontested matters, such as correction of the records of birth or death, probating wills, appointing a tutor to a minor or a curator to a person who is incapable of handling his own affairs because of mental illness or drunkenness.

Legal Terminology

sue
legal proceedings
fee
judgment
assets
settlement out of court
writ of summons
plaintiff's declaration
appearance
service
bailiff
defence (plea)
answer to plea
inscribe for proof and
   hearing
trial date
trial
witnesses
subpoena
pretrial hearing

particulars
admissions
examination on discovery
transcript
judge
clerk
oath
cross-examination
court costs
appeal
execution
contempt of court
writ of execution
seizure
sheriff
unseizable property
special remedies
quo warranto
mandamus
habeas corpus
injunction

Questions

1. Why is an interview with a lawyer important when you have a legal problem, and what is taken into consideration before deciding whether to sue?
2. Describe briefly the institution of legal proceedings up to trial.
3. What is the purpose of a pretrial hearing?
4. Describe briefly how a trial is conducted.
5. How is a judgment enforced?

6. What is meant by the unseizable portion of a debtor's salary?

7. Describe briefly the following:

a. *quo warranto*
b. *mandamus*
c. *habeas corpus*
d. injunction

PERSONS
[Legal Separation]

Chapter 4

PERSONS

The first part of the Civil Code deals with the law of persons and the civil status of individuals. "Persons" legally includes human beings and artificial beings such as limited companies (see chapter 15 on "Business Organizations") and municipalities. This chapter will deal with the rights of individuals such as children, and husband and wife.

CITIZENSHIP

As a basic rule, any person born in Canada is a Canadian citizen. Generally, one may also obtain Canadian citizenship by applying to the government after residing here for five years. However, you do not have to be a Canadian citizen to enter into contracts. In Quebec there is complete freedom of contracting open to all persons (including corporations) regardless of nationality, religion or race. In fact, many of our major industries, both in Quebec and the rest of Canada, are owned and operated by foreign corporations.

RESIDENCE AND DOMICILE

Very often the words residence and domicile are used by laymen interchangeably. In law, however, they are quite different. Residence is a place where you are actually residing either temporarily or permanently. You may have two residences, for example, a house in the city and another in the country. A retired executive may have several residences. However, he has only one domicile—the place where he has his family roots. It is easy to change one's residence, it is far more difficult to change one's domicile.

A person can only have one domicile at a time.

John was born in Montreal, educated there and presently works there. He goes to Europe on vacation where he meets Jacqueline, a Parisian girl, and he marries her in Paris. At the time of his marriage where was John domiciled?

One of the fundamental principles of civil status depends on the law of the domicile of the person, for it is upon determining domicile that such matters as the distribution of assets upon death and property relationships between husband and wife are decided.

The Civil Code states:

Art. 79   The domicile of a person, for all civil purposes, is at the place where he has his principal establishment.

Art. 80   Change of domicile is effected by actual residence in another place coupled with the intention of the person to make it the seat of his principal establishment.

Art. 81   The proof of such intention results from the declaration of the person and from the circumstances of the case.

The essence of these Articles is that the *domicile of origin*, that is, the domicile of one's parents at birth, continues until it is conclusively changed by the establishment of a new domicile. A new domicile is effected by setting up residence in another place coupled with the intention of that person to make the new place his permanent establishment. Evidence of that intention is demonstrated by the written and verbal declarations of the person, and all the surrounding circumstances of his move from the old domicile to the new one, e.g., change of job, purchase of new home, participation in community affairs; in short, the putting down of new roots.

The rules relating to domicile generally play an

important part in determining the property relationships between husband and wife. The law of the domicile of the husband *at the time* of the marriage will determine the property rights of the husband and wife thereafter.

Returning to the problem on page 32, since John was domiciled in the Province of Quebec at the time of his marriage, the marriage law governing his property rights is the law of Quebec. Quebec law in this area is very different from that of the rest of Canada.

ACTS OF CIVIL STATUS

You were born, you may marry and someday you will die. These three events are major landmarks in your life and each gives rise to a series of rights and obligations. To evidence each of these events the Quebec Civil Code requires the maintenance of registers of births, marriages and deaths in duplicate by those civil officers or religious ministers specifically authorised by law to keep them. At regular intervals the clergyman or officer deposits duplicate books at the local court house. If you require a certificate you may obtain it from the church or court house at a nominal fee.

The three acts of civil status are as follows:

1. *Act of birth* (birth certificate). Article 54 states the contents of a birth certificate:

> Art. 54   Acts of birth set forth the day and the place of the birth of the child, that of its baptism, if performed, its sex, and the names given to it; the names, surnames, occupation and domicile, of the father and mother, and also of the sponsors, if any there be.

2. *Act of marriage* (marriage certificate). Article 65 states the contents of a marriage certificate:

> Art. 65   In this act are set forth:
>
> 1. The day on which the marriage was solemnized;

2. The names, surnames, quality or occupation and domicile of the parties married, the names of the father and mother of each, or the name of the former husband or wife;

3. Whether the parties are of age, or minors;

4. Whether they were married after publication of banns, or with a dispensation or license;

5. Whether it was with the consent of their father, mother, tutor or curator, or with the advice of a family council, when such consent or advice is required;

6. The names of the witnesses, and whether they are related or allied to the parties, and if so, on which side, and in what degree;

7. That there has been no opposition, or that any opposition made has been disallowed;

8. Whether the parties are married without a marriage contract; or, if they have entered into a marriage contract, the name and address of the notary before whom it was entered into.

3. *Act of burial* (death certificate). Article 67 sets forth the contents of a death certificate:

> Art. 67   The act of burial mentions the day of the burial and that of the death, if known; the names, surnames, and quality or occupation of the deceased; and it is signed by the person performing the burial service, and by two of the nearest relations or friends there present; if they cannot sign, mention is made thereof.

These various acts or certificates are called acts of civil status.

MARRIAGE

The laws governing marriage and the family include the

obligations between husband and wife, and the children born of that marriage. These obligations are rooted in the traditional view of the family as the basic social unit and are essentially financial in nature.

Requisites of Marriage

In order for a marriage to be valid in the Province of Quebec the following requisites must be observed:

1. The boy must be at least fourteen years of age and the girl at least twelve years of age.

2. Both parties must consent freely to the marriage. In theory a marriage can be annulled on the grounds of violence, fear and error, but such cases are very rare.

3. A person under the age of eighteen years must obtain the consent of his parents, otherwise a parent who does not consent to the marriage generally has the right to have the marriage annulled.

4. The parties must be either single or widowed. Bigamy would make the second "marriage" illegal.

5. The marriage must not be with a person who, by law, is in a prohibited degree of alliance by marriage or by blood. The law prohibits a person entering a marriage with the immediate members of his family and other relatives including uncle and niece, and other ascendants and descendants. However, first cousins are permitted to marry.

Celebration of Marriage

The solemnisation of the marriage must be performed by an authorised officer. Ministers of religious congregations, who are authorised to keep registers of civil status of marriage, are empowered to perform marriage ceremonies, but they are not legally obliged to marry a couple if it is against their conscience or religion to perform the marriage.

It is now possible to be married civilly at the Superior Court before a court officer authorised for that purpose.

A marriage performed outside the Province of Quebec in accordance with the law of that place is valid in Quebec. If you are domiciled in Quebec and you marry elsewhere in accordance with the legal formalities of that place, Quebec law will recognise the validity of that marriage provided you did not marry elsewhere to avoid Quebec law.

Obligations between Husband and Wife

The Civil Code outlines the respective rights and duties of husband and wife both towards each other and towards their children.

Art. 165 Husband and wife contract, by the mere fact of marriage, the obligation to maintain and bring up their children.

Art. 173 Husband and wife mutually owe each other fidelity, succor and assistance.

Art. 174 The wife participates with the husband in ensuring the moral and material control of the family, in providing for its maintenance, in bringing up the children and preparing their establishment in life.
The wife exercises these functions alone when the husband is unable to make his will known by reason of his incapacity, absence, remoteness, or other cause.

Art. 175 A wife is obliged to live with her husband, and must follow him and reside wherever he fixes the residence of the family. The husband is bound to receive her there.
When the residence chosen by the husband exposes the family to dangers of a physical or moral nature, the wife may, by exception, be authorized to take up for herself and her children another residence fixed by the judge.
Such authorization may be given upon a petition to a judge of the Superior Court, after service upon the husband.

Art. 176   A husband is obliged to supply his wife with all the necessities of life according to his means and condition.

Art. 177   The legal capacity of each of the consorts is not diminished by marriage. Only their powers can be limited by the matrimonial regime.

Art. 178   Each consort may give the other a mandate to represent him or her in the exercise of his or her rights and powers under the matrimonial regime.

Art. 179   A consort, although a minor, may give his concurrence or consent in all cases in which it is necessary.

Art. 180   A married woman has, under any regime, the power to represent her husband for the current needs of the household and the maintenance of the children including medical and surgical care.

Acts thus done by the wife bind the husband towards a third person, unless he has withdrawn from his wife the power to do such acts and the third person had knowledge of such withdrawal when he dealt with her.

LEGAL SEPARATION

A marriage breakdown resulting in legal separation can have serious financial consequences on both husband and wife. Legal separation results in two households instead of one and therefore additional expenses.

Separation as to bed and board must not be based simply on the mutual consent of the parties. The Code requires specific and precise causes to be alleged in the separation action, such as adultery, outrage, ill-usage and grievous insult on the part of either the husband or the wife, or the refusal of the husband to receive his wife and to furnish her and the children with all the necessities of life according to his financial means, rank and condition.

> *John and Mary are married and living together but*
> *there are serious difficulties in their marriage. John*
> *frequently assaults Mary, he often returns home late*
> *at night without explanation, he fails to support her*
> *adequately and insults her constantly. What are her*
> *rights?*

Effects of Separation

A judgment declaring the husband and wife separate as to bed and board does not dissolve the marriage. Neither party can marry so long as the other survives. However, it does have these positive effects:

1. Separation as to bed and board relieves the consorts from living together.

2. The wife may establish her own domicile.

3. Custody of the children is given to the parent who is best able to look after the child. If there are several children, custody may be divided between the parents, or, if it is in the best interests of the children, custody is given to a third party. The court decides on visiting rights and, when required, the amount of alimentary contribution by each consort. If the wife is working, her earnings are taken into consideration since she is also obliged to contribute to her own support and that of her children. If there is partnership of acquests or community of property, separation of property takes place and dates from the final judgment of separation as to bed and board (see the following chapter on "Marriage Covenants").

The parties may effect a reconciliation at any time, thus terminating the separation.

Alimentary Support

The law regards the family as an institution whereby each member is required to financially assist the others. Consequently, the husband is obliged to maintain his wife and the parents are obliged to educate and properly provide for the maintenance of their children. The wife, therefore, is entitled to claim financial assistance for herself and for her minor children from the husband before the courts. This financial support is called *alimentary pension* and the obligation between parents and children is reciprocal. Consequently, if the father and mother become incapable of supporting themselves either through age or sickness or otherwise, the children are obliged by law to support their needy parents.

In all cases of alimentary support the amount, if not settled by agreement between the parties, is determined by the court which considers the needs of the party requesting it and the ability of the party providing support.

> Art. 169   Maintenance is only granted in proportion to the wants of the party claiming it and the means of the party by whom it is due.

> Art. 170   Whenever the condition of the party who furnishes or of the party who receives maintenance is so changed that the one can no longer give or the other no longer needs the whole or any part of it, a discharge from or a reduction of such maintenance may be demanded by means of a petition to a judge of the Superior Court.

The wife who is deprived of maintenance can also file a nonsupport charge under the Criminal Code.

When you marry you are also legally obliged to support your father-in-law and your mother-in-law if they are in need! This obligation is reciprocal.

DISSOLUTION

A marriage is dissolved either by death or divorce. A marriage may also be annulled and declared by the court as non-existent, e.g., if one of the parties is already married.

The purpose of a divorce action is to end the marriage.

The grounds for divorce are contained in Sections 3 and 4 of the Divorce Act:

3. Subject to section 5, a petition for divorce may be presented to a court by a husband or wife, on the ground that the respondent, since the celebration of the marriage,

(a) has committed adultery;

(b) has been guilty of sodomy, bestiality or rape, or has engaged in a homosexual act;

(c) has gone through a form of marriage with another person; or

(d) has treated the petitioner with physical or mental cruelty of such a kind as to render intolerable the continued cohabitation of the spouses.

4. (1) In addition to the grounds specified in section 3, and subject to section 5, a petition for divorce may be presented to a court by a husband or wife where the husband and wife are living separate and apart on the ground that there has been a permanent breakdown of their marriage by reason of one or more of the following circumstances as specified in the petition, namely:

(a) the respondent

(i) has been imprisoned, pursuant to his conviction for one or more offences, for a period or an aggregate period of not less than three years during the five year period immediately preceding the presentation of the petition, or

(ii) has been imprisoned for a period of not less than two years immediately preceding the presentation of the petition pursuant to his conviction for an offence for which he was sentenced to death or to imprisonment for a term of ten years or more, against which conviction or sentence all rights of the respondent to appeal to a court having jurisdiction to hear such an appeal have been exhausted;

(b) the respondent has, for a period of not less than three years immediately preceding the presentation of the petition, been grossly addicted to alcohol, or a narcotic as defined in the *Narcotic Control Act,* and there is no reasonable expectation of the respondent's rehabilitation within a reasonably foreseeable period;

(c) the petitioner, for a period of not less than three years immediately preceding the presentation of the petition, has had no knowledge of or information as to the whereabouts of the respondent and, throughout that period, has been unable to locate the respondent;

(d) the marriage has not been consummated and the respondent, for a period of not less than one year, has been unable by reason of illness or disability to consummate the marriage, or has refused to consummate it; or

(e) the spouses have been living separate and apart

(i) for any reason other than that described in subparagraph (ii), for a period of not less than three years, or

(ii) by reason of the petitioner's desertion of the respondent, for a period of not less than five years, immediately preceding the presentation of the petition.

(2) On any petition presented under this section, where the existence of any of the circumstances described in subsection (1) has been established, a permanent breakdown of the marriage by reason of those circumstances shall be deemed to have been established.

Section 5 of the Divorce Act refers to jurisdiction for institution of divorce proceedings:

5. (1) The court for any province has jurisdiction to entertain a petition for divorce and to grant relief in respect thereof if,

(a) the petition is presented by a person domiciled in Canada; and

(b) either the petitioner or the respondent has been ordinarily resident in that province for a period of at least one year immediately preceding the presentation of the petition and has actually resided in that province for at least ten months of that period.

Either party may request payment of an alimentary pension for the maintenance of the petitioner and/or the children, either by periodical payments or in one lump sum.

CHILDREN

Children are either born issue of a marriage in which case they are called legitimate, or born out of wedlock in which case they are called illegitimate or natural children. Legitimate children are those who are conceived or born during the marriage. Illegitimate children are legitimised by the subsequent marriage of the parents. Legitimate children bear the name of their father and the birth certificate or baptismal certificate is proof of the affiliation and age of the child. Illegitimate children have the right to obtain support from their mother and their father. They have no right to inherit from their father unless he mentions them in his Will.

Minors

A person who is under the age of eighteen years is considered by law to be a minor and is subject to certain incapacities in his abilities to make contracts. A full discussion of this is found in chapter 9 entitled "Contracts in General."

Adoption

The Adoption Act of Quebec allows the adoption of children by an adoptor. The child then takes the name of the adoptor and obtains all the rights and obligations of a legitimate child.

Interdiction

A person who is insane may, by court order, be declared *interdicted*. This is done by a petition from a member of the family on the advice of a family council, composed of at least seven persons of the immediate family or, in default, friends, which is then approved by the court. When a person is interdicted, a curator is appointed to him and all contracts and other legal matters must be made through the curator.

If a person is not insane, but is of weak intellect and there is a fear that he will dissipate his property, then a judicial adviser may be appointed to assist him.

Legal Terminology

persons
individuals
nationality
residence
domicile
civil status
domicile of origin
birth certificate
marriage certificate
death certificate
marriage
solemnisation of marriage
obligations
legal separation

separate as to bed and
  board
alimentary support
alimentary pension
reciprocal obligations
reconciliation
legitimate children
illegitimate children
natural children
minors
adoption
interdiction
family council
curator
judicial adviser

Questions

1. What is meant by the term persons?
2. What are the legal rights of foreigners in Canada?
3. Distinguish residence from domicile.
4. Define domicile. How is it changed?
5. Discuss domicile in determining the property relationships between husband and wife.
6. Describe briefly the three acts of civil status.
7. What are the requisites for marriage?
8. How is marriage legally celebrated in Quebec?
9. What are the obligations arising from marriage?
10. What is meant by a legal separation and what are its effects?
11. What is meant by alimentary support? How is it determined and to whom is it due?

12. What are the grounds for divorce?
13. What are the rights of legitimate children and illegitimate children?
14. At what age does the law consider a person to be a minor?
15. What are the rights of an adopted child?
16. What is meant by interdiction?

Problems

1. Robert decides to change his domicile from Montreal to Toronto. What must he do to establish a new domicile?
2. John, who at the time of his marriage is domiciled in Quebec, marries Mary in Montreal. Two years after the marriage they experience serious marital difficulties, because of John's drinking problem. They have an infant son. What are Mary's legal rights?

MARRIAGE COVENANTS
[The Marriage Contract]

Chapter 5

MARRIAGE COVENANTS

John is domiciled in Montreal. While on a trip in France he meets Jacqueline and they marry soon after in Paris. What law governs the property relationships between them?

The law of the domicile of the husband at the time of the marriage governs their property relationships. Since John was domiciled in Montreal at the time of the marriage the Quebec law applies.

When a couple marry they have to decide whether the general law of the Civil Code will determine the property arrangements between them or whether they are going to make a marriage contract in notarial form, stipulating the property relationship between them. Basically, their choice is between two systems—the legal system provided by the Civil Code and the conventional system agreed upon in a marriage contract.

THE CIVIL CODE

If a couple were married before July 1, 1970, and did not have a marriage contract, the legal system applicable to them is called *community of property*. Under the system most of their property acquired both before and after marriage forms a community, where both have equal shares, the main exception being real estate owned before marriage which remains their private property.

On July 1, 1970, a new system called *partnership of acquests* was introduced for couples getting married from that date who do not have a marriage contract. This new system is based on the theory that marriage is a partnership commencing at the date of marriage and consequently, property owned by the consorts before marriage remains their own individual property, whereas most property acquired after marriage forms a community of acquests where both parties have an equal share.

MARRIAGE CONTRACTS

If the parties do not wish to be governed by the provisions of the Civil Code, then they must enter into a *marriage contract.* This contract will probably provide that the future consorts will be married under the regime of separation as to property, that is, the property acquired before and after the marriage will remain their individual, separate property and there will be no partnership or community.

Therefore, under Quebec law there are three main systems of property relationships:
1. community of property
2. partnership of acquests
3. separation as to property

Community of Property

If a couple were married before July 1, 1970, and the husband was then domiciled in the Province of Quebec, and if they did not sign a notarial marriage contract before their marriage, their property rights are governed by the property relationship called community of property. This means generally that the moveable property possessed by both parties before and after the marriage and all the immoveable property acquired after the marriage forms a community which at the time of dissolution of the marriage, by death, divorce or legal separation, is divided equally between both parties.[1] The husband has substantial administrative rights but requires the wife's consent as follows:

1. Salary and savings earned by a wife from her work remain her own property during the marriage, but at dissolution of the marriage form part of the community.

Art. 1292 (in part)   The husband alone administers the property of the community subject to the provisions of article 1293 and articles 1425a and following.

He cannot sell, alienate or hypothecate without the concurrence of his wife any immoveable property of the community but he can, without such concurrence, sell, alienate or pledge any moveable property other than a business or than household furniture in use by the family.

The husband cannot, without the concurrence of his wife, dispose by gratuitous title *inter vivos* of the property of the community, except small sums of money and customary presents.

Therefore the husband requires the wife's consent:
a. to sell the house, household furniture or a business, etc.;
b. to make substantial gifts.

Partnership of Acquests

For all marriages taking place after July 1, 1970, if the husband is domiciled in the Province of Quebec at the time of marriage and there is no marriage contract between the parties, the parties are presumed to be married under the regime entitled *partnership of acquests.*

Under this regime each consort remains owner of all property, both moveable and immoveable, that he or she possessed at the time of the marriage. Generally, all property acquired after the marriage belongs to the consort acquiring it.

On the dissolution of the partnership of acquests, which occurs on death, legal separation and divorce, there is an equal partition between them of all the property acquired and realised by both of them during the marriage. Property possessed by the consorts before the marriage or acquired after the marriage by gift, remains private property and is not subject to partition, nor are effects of a personal character such as souvenirs and tools, equipment and books used in a trade or profession. However, all other property and revenues arising out of work are subject to partition.

Consequently, during the marriage the consorts are basically separate as to property and it is only upon dissolution that the property of the partnership is divided.

Under this regime each consort retains the entire control of his property and remains fully responsible for his debts. However, each consort contributes according to his means to the needs of the household.

In conclusion, therefore, if you do not obtain a marriage contract you will be under the system of partnership of acquests.

Marriage Contracts

Many husbands-to-be are reluctant to be under the partnership of acquests system and one reason is that if there is a divorce or legal separation, his wife may obtain half of his property. Consequently, marriage contracts are often established.

What is a marriage contract? If the husband-to-be is domiciled in any of the provinces of Canada, except Quebec, the law provides that the property arrangement between husband and wife is *separation as to property.* This means that, except in Quebec, there is no partnership of property, each consort remains separate both as to property possessed before marriage and after marriage, and when there is a dissolution of the marriage there is no property to be divided. He keeps his property, she keeps hers.

This system of separation as to property is also available to Quebeckers by signing a marriage contract, usually before marriage, although it is now possible to make one, with some inconvenience and expense, after marriage. The marriage contract is in notarial form and invariably stipulates that the parties shall be separate as to property, that is:

1. What belongs to the parties before the marriage remains their own property.

2. What they each acquire during the marriage remains their own individual private property.

3. Each consort is liable for his or her own personal debts acquired before and during marriage.

BEFORE MTRE.   ANDREW JACKSON   the undersigned
Notary for the Province of Quebec, practising in the City
and District of Montreal

APPEARED:

JOHN BROWN

OF THE FIRST PART:

AND:

MARY SMITH

OF THE SECOND PART:

Who in view of the intended marriage which is to be solemnized between them, have entered into the following contract and agreement:

The said future consorts shall be married under the regime of Separation as to Property and neither consort shall be responsible for any debts contracted by the other previous to or during the said intended marriage.

The First Party shall himself bear and pay all household expenses, including the necessary personal expenses of the Second Party, and the maintenance and education of the child or children that may be born of the said intended marriage, and furthermore donates unto his said future wife, hereto present and accepting:

A.   The sum of   twenty thousand dollars ($20,000)
to be paid at any time during the said marriage as he sees fit, the First Party hereby constituting himself Debtor of the Second Party to the extent of the said sum. The Donor, however, reserves the right at any time to pay the whole or any part of the said sum, either in cash or by the transfer of property, moveable or immoveable. But should the said sum not have been paid during the existence of the marriage and he predeceases her, she shall have the right to demand payment of this sum or the part thereof then unpaid or unsatisfied from his succession.

B.   As an irrevocable donation "inter vivos," household furniture, moveable property and effects to an amount and value of five thousand dollars ($5,000)
which he binds and obliges himself to deliver to the said future wife within a delay of ten (10) years from the date hereof and in such manner as that there shall at all

A Marriage Contract

times thereafter be furniture, goods, moveables and effects to that extent and value, whether those which may be originally furnished as forming part of this donation or others being renewals or additions thereto, so that such amount and value shall be maintained and shall continually form the present donation.

It is expressly agreed, that should the future wife predecease her future husband or should the said intended marriage be dissolved by competent authority before the above-mentioned gift of the sum of   five thousand dollars ($5,000)

has been fully completed by payment, the said future husband shall be under no obligation to complete the payment of the balance of the said gift then unpaid or unsatisfied.

It is hereby stipulated that the aforesaid sum of money or the property or investments representing the same, and the revenues which may at any time be derived therefrom and the said household furniture, moveable property and effects and all replacements thereof, have been thus given for the alimentary support and maintenance of the said future wife, and the same shall, in consequence, not be liable to seizure or attachment for any debts which she may contract or for any other cause or reason, the said Donor hereby expressly exempting all the foregoing from seizure or any liability whatsoever; but nothing herein contained shall prevent the future wife voluntarily alienating, hypothecating or disposing of the property hereby given to her or performing any other acts of ownership in reference thereof.

EXECUTED at the said City of Montreal on this   6th   day of   July   One thousand nine hundred and seventy -two   under the number

of the original Notarial Minutes of the undersigned Notary.

AND AFTER DUE READING HEREOF the parties have signed with and in the presence of the undersigned Notary.

John Brown

Mary Smith

Andrew Jackson

4. The husband usually undertakes to make gifts to his wife of a specified value during the marriage, often of household furniture and effects. When the wife receives the gifts they will become her absolute property, and will not be subject to seizure by the husband's creditors (unless he gave her these gifts in order to avoid payments to his creditors). This gift protects the household furniture from seizure by her husband's creditors up to the amount of the gift stated in the contract. For example, the husband promises to give his wife a gift of furniture in the value of $5,000 during the first five years of marriage. The husband's creditors (except the landlord) cannot seize the first $5,000 worth of furniture.

COMMUNITY OF PROPERTY (AT DISSOLUTION)

WIFE'S OWN PROPERTY immoveables before marriage	COMMUNITY OF PROPERTY moveables before and during marriage immoveables during marriage	HUSBAND'S OWN PROPERTY immoveables before marriage

PARTNERSHIP OF ACQUESTS (AT DISSOLUTION)

WIFE'S OWN PROPERTY property acquired before marriage	PARTNERSHIP OF ACQUESTS property acquired after marriage	HUSBAND'S OWN PROPERTY property acquired before marriage

SEPARATION AS TO PROPERTY (MARRIAGE CONTRACTS)

WIFE'S OWN PROPERTY property acquired before and after marriage	HUSBAND'S OWN PROPERTY property acquired before and after marriage

Another gift that is often made in a marriage contract is one that takes effect upon the death of the husband. The clause is worded so that the husband has the option of making the gift during the marriage. This gift usually allows the husband to transfer immoveable property into his wife's name. This type of gift clause protects the wife in the event of the husband's death. In the event that the husband were to make a last will leaving his estate to a third person, the marriage contract gift on death clause must be paid off in full before the heirs under the will receive any assets.

The marriage contract may be altered by a notice in the newspapers advising creditors of said change effected before a notary and ratified by the court.

Legal Terminology

community of property   *separation as to property*
partnership of acquests   *dissolution*
marriage contract   *gift*

Questions

1. What persons are under community of property and what does the community consist of?
2. How is partnership of acquests established, who controls the assets and how are the partnership assets divided at dissolution of the marriage?
3. What is a marriage contract and how does one obtain it? What are the general provisions contained in a marriage contract?
4. What are the main advantages of a marriage contract?
5. What are the basic differences between legal community, partnership of acquests, separation as to property and marriage contracts?

Problem

You are in business for yourself in Montreal and are about to get married. What are the advantages of obtaining a marriage contract?

PROPERTY AND OWNERSHIP
[Servitudes]

Chapter 6

PROPERTY AND OWNERSHIP

DISTINCTION OF PROPERTY

What Is Property?

All property is either moveable or immoveable. Moveable property may be either corporeal or incorporeal. Similarly, immoveable property may be either corporeal or incorporeal.

PROPERTY IS EITHER

MOVEABLE Corporeal or Incorporeal	OR	IMMOVEABLE Corporeal or Incorporeal

Corporeal property can be perceived by the senses, e.g., an automobile or a house. *Incorporeal* property cannot be perceived by the senses; it consists of legal rights to a thing. A right is moveable if its object is moveable, and immoveable if its object is immoveable.

Bill owns shares in a limited company. He does not own the assets of the company directly but his share certificate is a right of participation in the total assets of the company. This share is an incorporeal moveable.

John has a right of passage allowing him to cross Bill's land. John does not own the path, but has a right to use it. His right is an incorporeal immoveable.

Immoveables

The distinctions drawn between immoveables and moveables are important to know, since the laws governing immoveables are often quite different from the laws governing moveables. For example, you can have a hypothec upon an immoveable (often called real property or real estate), but not upon a moveable. Municipal, school and real estate taxes are levied on immoveables.

Some contracts involving immoveables, such as a hypothec, must be prepared in a formal manner by a notary. Contracts involving moveables are often prepared by the parties themselves.

Property is immoveable either by nature or by its destination. Property may also be immoveable by reason of the object to which it is attached (incorporeal immoveable, right of servitude), or by *determination of law* (seldom encountered).

Immoveable by Nature

Art. 376   Lands and buildings are immoveable by their nature.

Land is really the only property truly immoveable by its very nature.

What are buildings? Buildings include not only houses and factories, but all constructions of any kind incorporated or attached to the soil, such as bridges, dams, gas and water mains, because they form part of and are one with the land. They are immoveable because of their incorporation with the land. The buildings need not be constructed for permanency nor does the person who erected the building have to be the owner of the land; therefore, incorporation and attachment to the land are essential parts of the state of being immoveable by nature. Booths erected at a fair are not immoveable by nature because they are not constructed with physical attachment to the soil.

Furthermore,   immoveable   by   nature   includes

moveables serving to complete a building, even though they may be readily detached without injury to the thing itself or to the building, e.g., balconies, heating and plumbing systems, pipes, boilers. Therefore, an air furnace and accessories, elevators, refrigeration systems are held to be constituent parts of the building and are not merely accessory. Without these objects the building would be incomplete. The key, therefore, is that the moveable becomes immoveable by nature if it is attached to an immoveable in such a way that it becomes an integral, indispensable part of the immoveable.

Immoveable by Destination

Moveable things which an owner has placed on his real property permanently or which he has incorporated there are immoveable by their destination, so long as they remain there, e.g., all utensils necessary for manufacturing are considered by law to be immoveable. These objects are moveable *per se,* but are declared immoveable by law. They are accessories serving the land. There are certain conditions for a moveable to become immoveable by destination:

1. The moveable must be placed on the immoveable by the owner of the immoveable.
2. The moveable must belong to the owner of the immoveable property.
3. It must be placed on the land for a permanency or incorporated therewith.

Permanency or *incorporation* is determined not only by what the proprietor of the land says, but by the nature of the immoveable property, the purpose of placing the moveable on the land, and the intent of the use of the moveable. For example, heavy machinery is immoveable by destination because it is the means by which the industry is carried on.

> *John owns a furniture factory which contains lathes and wood cutting machines belonging to him. Although these machines are easily removable, they are immoveable by destination.*

However, moveables placed for a permanency may be taxed as immoveable regardless of whether the owner of the moveable also owns the immoveable or not.

MOVEABLES

What is a moveable? Property is moveable either by nature or by law.

Moveable by Nature

All bodies which can be moved from one place to another, either by themselves (e.g., animals), or by extrinsic force (e.g., automobiles, machinery) are moveable by nature.

Moveable by Law

Shares in all types of corporations, even in real estate companies, are moveable by law.

> In his Will, John's father leaves his son all of his "moveables." The father has shares in Moon Real Estate Co. John is heir to these shares, which are moveables.

OWNERSHIP

Ownership is a legal relationship between a person and a thing, moveable or immoveable. It is "the right of enjoying and of disposing of things in the most absolute manner, provided that no use be made of them which is prohibited by law or by regulation" (Article 406). As our urban society becomes more and more complex, ownership rights become increasingly restricted in order that owners of property do not use it in such a way as to injure other parties.

Who Owns Property?

Art. 399   Property belongs either to the crown, or to municipalities or other corporations, or to individuals.

Crown

Land and property owned by the provincial or federal government is called *Crown property*. In addition to the laws contained in the Civil Code, Crown property is also governed by public or administrative law. Crown property includes roads maintained by the state, rivers, seashores, ports, military places.

Municipalities

Municipalities include cities, towns, villages. Municipalities are governed by municipal law contained in the Municipal Code and in the Cities and Towns Act as well as by the terms and provisions of their individual municipal charters granted by the provincial government. Large cities such as Montreal and Quebec City each have a charter which varies their powers.

Corporations

In law, a corporation or limited company is a separate legal person which can own property, sue and be sued. In addition to being regulated by the Civil Code, companies are governed by:
a. the Companies or Corporation Act (either federal or provincial) under the provisions of which the company was incorporated;
b. the charter that the government issues to the company;
c. the internal by-laws of the company and resolutions passed by the directors.

Individuals

A person can own property alone or with others. He is governed by the Civil Code and other laws referring to individuals and persons.

The Theory of Absolute Ownership

In theory, ownership is absolute. The owner can do with his property what he pleases. In fact, however, he is subject to numerous limitations in the interest of individuals and of the public generally. In theory, ownership is exclusive. The owner can prevent others from interfering with the thing he owns.

The owner exercises his right of ownership:

1. By physical acts: he occupies the house, builds on his land, cultivates his farm.
2. By legal acts: he sells the land, transfers it by gift or by Will, leases it or hypothecates it.

What then are the elements of absolute and complete ownership? They are expressed in three Latin words:

a. *Usus:* the owner can use the thing he owns.
b. *Fructus:* the owner can take the fruits of the thing, e.g., rents and revenues it produces.
c. *Abusus:* the owner can dispose of the thing as he may think proper. He may clear his land by cutting down trees, then cultivate it; he may leave it fallow; he may grant rights to others upon the land; he may lease it, sell it or give it away.

John owns his own house which is on a large lot. He lives in it with his family, rents the basement to a teacher, builds an extension to the house, and sells a part of the land to a neighbour. John has entered into a number of contracts which indicate his wide powers of ownership.

The Difference between Complete and Incomplete Ownership

The owner can exercise all of the powers in the preceding example when his ownership is complete. Ownership is the sum of all the rights in a thing. Yet, the owner's right is not always complete. It is incomplete when the thing owned is subject to a right in favour of another.

Limitations of Ownership

The following are examples of limitations of ownership:

1. Expropriation: the government, either federal, provincial or municipal, can expropriate your land and buildings "in the public interest" for public use, e.g., to build roads or public housing projects.

2. Municipal by-laws: these may impose limitations on heights and types of building construction, and provide zoning regulations.

> *John, who lives in a residential area of Montreal, requests a permit from the city to open a chemical factory on his property. The city refuses as the area is zoned for residences only.*

3. Abuse of rights: you have the right to enjoy your property, but you must allow your neighbours to enjoy and use their own property. You cannot use your rights and property so as to damage or inconvenience your neighbour's property. If, in using your property to excess you injure your neighbour's property or deprive him of the normal use of his property, you may be sued in damages or be ordered to cease doing these acts by means of an injunction (see chapter 3 on procedure).

How far does this rule of noninterference go? You cook supper outdoors on your patio; your neighbour does not like the odour of charcoal-broiled steak. Can he take proceedings to prevent you from cooking? No. The cases hold that "everyone is bound to submit to reasonable inconvenience which the neighbourhood brings with it." What is "reasonable inconvenience"? This largely depends on the character of the neighbourhood. What might be tolerable in a manufacturing district would be intolerable in a residential district.

The monetary damage is determined by assessing the excess of damage beyond what is considered "reasonable," after taking into consideration the circumstances of the time and place, the quantity of annoyance and the relations of the adjoining properties to each other.

> R. lived on the waterfront where he owned some
> property and the Black Coal Co. installed a coal
> apparatus on a nearby dock, which made a great deal
> of noise. R. sued for damages but the court dismissed
> his action maintaining that he lived on the harbour
> area and could expect such noise, since the area was
> no longer residential but was a commercial and manu-
> facturing centre.

> Seventy years ago D. owned a stable on St. Denis
> Street, in Montreal, which at the time was a residen-
> tial area. His neighbour sued for damages for nuisance
> caused him by the noise of horses pawing the floor
> and odours. The court held that D. was liable for
> damages resulting from his operating a stable in a resi-
> dential district. It is worth noting that D. was operat-
> ing with a city permit and his stable was well
> constructed.

4. *Usufruct:* the word *usufruct* is derived from the two
Latin words *usus* and *fructus* already explained. A *usufruct* is
often established by a Will in which a husband gives ownership of a property to his children and the *usufruct* to his surviving wife. Obviously, there is a great limitation on the
children's right of ownership. The children have the right to
sell the property but subject to the mother's right of full use
and enjoyment of it, usually for life.

5. Servitudes:

> You own a country house near, but not fronting on, a
> beautiful lake surrounded by private property. Do
> you have a legal right to cross your neighbour's prop-
> erty and swim in the lake? The answer is found in the
> law governing servitudes.

Art. 499   A servitude is a charge imposed on one real estate for the benefit of another (real estate) belonging to a different proprietor.

The law imposes upon both your property and that of your neighbour certain mutual restrictions and benefits which are called *servitudes.*

Essentials of Servitudes

1. There must be two lands. The land which benefits from the servitude is called the dominant land. This is the land that has the right. The other land which is subject to the servitude is called the servient land. It is charged with the servitude.
2. The lands must belong to different owners.
3. The charge is upon one land for the benefit of the other. For example, drawing water from a well, not building above a certain height, the right of passage, the right of view.

Types of Servitudes

Art. 500   A servitude arises either from the natural position of the property, or from the law, or it is established by the act of man.

Both natural and legal servitudes are created by law alone. Conventional servitudes are created by a written agreement between property owners. All three may or may not be either positive or negative; they may prohibit certain acts; they may be continuous or discontinuous servitudes (Article 547 enables the holder of the right to do some act); or they may be apparent or unapparent (Article 548).

Art. 547   Servitudes are either continuous or discontinuous. Continuous servitudes are those the exercise of which may be continued without the actual intervention of man; such are water conduits, drains, right of view and others similar. Discontinuous servitudes are those which require the actual intervention of man for their exercise; such are the rights of way, of drawing water, of pasture and others similar.

Art. 548   Servitudes are apparent or unapparent.

Apparent servitudes are those which are manifest by external signs, such as a door, a window, an aqueduct, a sewer, or drain, and the like.

Unapparent servitudes are those which have no external sign, as for instance the prohibition to build on a land or to build above a certain fixed height.

Positive and Negative Servitudes

A positive servitude entitles the owner of the dominant land to obtain certain services from the servient land, e.g., the right to draw water from it, to pasture cattle, to cut timber. A negative servitude deprives the owner of the servient land of certain advantages that he otherwise would enjoy as owner of his property, e.g., a servitude restricting the height of buildings which the owner of the servient land may build.

Natural Servitudes

Art. 501   Lands on a lower level are subject towards those on a higher level to receive such waters as flow from the latter naturally and without the agency of man.

The proprietor of the lower land cannot raise any dam to prevent this flow. The proprietor of the higher land can do nothing to aggravate the servitude of the lower land.

Natural servitudes arise from the geographical lay of the land, e.g., since water flows downhill, the lower land must receive the water (rain, snow, stream) coming from the higher neighbouring land. The dominant landowner cannot aggravate the situation by adding waste to the natural waters, and conversely, the servient landowner cannot raise a dam to prevent the flow.

Legal Servitudes

A legal servitude is one established by law and has for its purpose either public or private utility. Servitudes for public utility include footpaths along the banks of navigable rivers, and the construction or repair of roads or other public works.

Servitudes for private utility subject property owners to different obligations with regard to one another.

> *Each neighbour is mutually obliged to construct the roof of his house in such a manner that the rain and snow on them fall upon his own land and not upon the land of his neighbour.*

There are numerous other legal servitudes; the most important ones are those dealing with windows and rights of passage. There are two different types of views from windows, direct and indirect (oblique).

Windows

Art. 536   One neighbour cannot have direct views or prospect windows, nor galleries, balconies or other such like projections overlooking the fenced or unfenced land of the other; they must be at a distance of six feet from such land.

Art. 537   Nor can he have side openings or oblique views overlooking such land, unless they are at a distance of two feet.

John owns a semidetached house with a garage beneath the livingroom. The other half of the semidetached house is built exactly the same way. In both houses there are windows in the front facing the street and windows in the back facing the backyard.

Direct View

In the preceding example the garage and windows look directly onto city property (streets and sidewalks) and onto the neighbour's property in the back. The law requires that these garage door openings and windows be at least a minimum distance of six feet from the property line. A municipal by-law may require a greater minimum distance.

Indirect View

The window and garage openings on the semidetached house look indirectly onto each other, that is, each owner would have to turn sideways in order to see his neighbour's house. These openings must be at least two feet from the property line or common wall separating the two houses.

Thus, the windows and garages directly facing the street and indirectly facing each other must be at least six feet from the property line in front and two feet from the property line separating the two neighbouring properties.

Right of Passage

You have a country property which is separated from the public road by another property owned by Smith. Can you legally oblige Smith to give you access across his property so that you can travel from the public road to your property? Generally, yes. But you have to pay for any damage and loss you cause to Smith's property. This right to access is a legal servitude comprising a right of passage.

> Art. 540   A proprietor whose land is enclosed on all sides by that of others, and who has no communication with the public road, may claim a way upon that of his neighbour's for the use of his property subject to an indemnity proportionate to the damage he may cause.

Art. 541   The way must generally be had on the side where the crossing is shortest from the land so enclosed to the public road.

Art. 542   It should however, be established over the part where it will be least injurious to him upon whose land it is granted.

The above Articles refer to land which is cut off from the public road. In such a case the owner is entitled to a servitude of *right of passage.*

Conventional Servitudes

John's country house borders the public highway but his neighbour's house is between his and the lake. Is John legally entitled to access to the lake across his neighbour's property? No.

John's property has access to the public road. If there is no conventional servitude in John's favour, his neighbour Bill can prevent John from crossing. Or conversely, if there were a conventional servitude in John's favour, he would be entitled to access.

Art. 545   Every proprietor having the use of his rights, and being competent to dispose of immoveables, may establish over or in favour of such immoveables, such servitude as he may think proper, provided they are in no way contrary to public order. The use of the extent of these servitudes is determined according to the title which constitutes them, or according to the following rule if the title be silent.

An owner of property may, in writing, agree to allow his neighbour certain rights over his property. These agreements are generally executed before a notary and registered at the court house deed registry office.

Refer back to the example on page 65: What if the garage doors and windows are very close to the neighbour's property line—so close that they are within the prohibited distance? Is this allowed? Yes, if there is no contravention of a municipal by-law and the property owners have a written agreement, called a *conventional servitude,* in which each grants to the other a reciprocal servitude permitting both to have a garage door opening, let us say, eight inches away from the line. If there were not such an agreement between the two owners, then that part of the garage door opening that came within two feet of the property line could be ordered closed by the other owner and vice versa.

There are many examples of one neighbour creating a servitude on his property in favour of another:

a. direct window views within six feet of the property boundary;

b. pathway access to a lake allowed by a neighbour;

c. cutting of wood, or drawing of water from a neighbour's property.

Once this conventional servitude is created, it continues forever, unless it is for a specific period, or unless the two owners agree to terminate it or unless it is not used for thirty years. It is very important before buying a property to examine the deeds to see whether any servitudes exist on or in favour of the property.

Prescription

Another situation limiting ownership is prescription. There are two types of prescription: acquisitive (or possession) and extinctive (or negative).

Acquisitive (or Possession)

If a person possesses, detains or enjoys the immoveable property of another then after a certain length of time he may become the owner of the property. The length of time depends on whether his possession was in good faith or bad faith. Bad faith possession means that the possessor had no legal title to the property, that is, he is a "squatter." He must be in possession for thirty years in order to become owner.

If, on the other hand, the possessor believed that he had good title to the immoveable property, but in fact his title was defective, the period necessary for his becoming owner is ten years. In both cases, one can see that the true owner may be deprived of his ownership.

Further, both cases must conform to qualifications:
1. Possession must be continuous: an interruption of possession is a loss of possession and the prescriptive period must start all over again from the very beginning.
2. Possession must be peaceable: the possessor must have taken and continued possession by peaceful means and not by acts of violence.
3. Possession must be public: this is hardly possible to avoid. The fact that he possesses the property and is actually living there is sufficient.
4. Possession must be unequivocal.
5. The possessor must hold as owner: he must hold as though he were himself owner of the thing possessed, e.g., a tenant who pays rent while he is in possession is not possessing as an owner and he cannot prescribe ownership.

For over thirty years John's country property has been occupied continuously by a farmer who represented himself as owner without John's knowledge. Can the farmer now claim ownership? Yes.

Extinctive (or Negative)

Brown owes you $350 which he refuses to pay; Jones damaged your automobile and you had it repaired at a cost of $200; you slipped on the city sidewalk and injured your wrist. These are three different claims and each is subject to different periods of time within which you must sue in order to exercise your legal rights.

Extinctive prescription is that area of the Civil Code which deals with time limitations imposed by law on the institution of court actions.

Ownership includes the right to institute legal proceedings for the recovery of sums of money owed or actions in damages for breach of contract or bodily injuries; the law states, however, that legal action to enforce your rights must be instituted within a certain period of time or satisfactory settlement to be·reached as follows:

1. All commercial actions must be instituted within five years, e.g., merchandise sold and delivered, work done.

2. All actions based on cheques, promissory notes, drafts and acknowledgements of debt must be instituted within five years.

3. Actions for recovery of property damage must be instituted within two years from the date of the cause of the damage, e.g., from the date of the accident.

4. Actions based on bodily injuries or resulting in death must be instituted within one year from the date of the accident. When the claim is against a municipality or city a registered letter must be sent immediately and an action must be taken within six months of the date of the accident.

If the proposed action does not fall into the above categories, the general rule is that the prescription of an action is thirty years. If no settlement is obtained, in order to protect your rights it is necessary that a court action be instituted within the time limit.

You are involved in an automobile accident on September 1st, 1972; you suffer a broken arm. You must sue within one year—before September 2nd, 1973, if settlement has not been received.

Emphyteutic Lease

An *emphyteutic lease* or *emphyteusis* is a contract by which the proprietor of an immoveable conveys it for a time to another, the lessee subjecting himself to make improvements, to pay the lessor an annual rent, and to such other charges as may be agreed upon. The duration of emphyteusis cannot exceed ninety-nine years and must be for more than nine. During the term of the contract the lessee enjoys all the rights of ownership including alienation, transfer and hypothecation, without prejudice to the rights of the lessor. At the end of the lease, the lessee must give up, in good condition, the property received from the lessor, as well as the buildings he obliged himself to construct. This type of lease is used in the development of commercial property.

Limitation of Ownership
Due to Incapacity

Some persons such as interdicts and minors have ownership but not the right of disposal. This is further discussed in chapter 9 on "Contracts in General."

Legal Terminology

property	usus
moveable	fructus
immoveable	abusus
corporeal	*expropriation*
incorporeal	*municipal by-laws*
right	*abuse of rights*
immoveable by nature	usufruct
immoveable by destination	*servitudes*
permanency	*dominant land*
incorporation	*servient land*
moveable by nature	*right of passage*
moveable by law	*possession*
ownership	*prescription*
Crown	*emphyteutic lease*
absolute ownership	*emphyteusis*

Questions

1. Into what categories is property divided? Describe each.
2. Define the term immoveable by nature.
3. What are the requisites for a moveable to be considered immoveable by destination?
4. Describe moveable property.

5. Define ownership.

6. Who owns property and what laws govern them?

7. What is meant by the theory of absolute ownership and what is meant by incomplete ownership?

8. Discuss abuse of rights.

9. What is *usufruct*? Give one common example of its use.

10. What is a servitude and what are its essentials?

11. Describe the three types of servitude and give one example of each.

12. What are the qualifications for possession?

13. What is meant by prescription? Give two examples.

14. In what way is emphyteusis a limitation of ownership?

OBLIGATIONS

Chapter 7

OBLIGATIONS

An obligation can be defined as a duty of one person to another to give, to do or not to do something. An obligation can bind a person in conscience and/or in law. In order for the person to be bound in law there must have been an intent that the undertaking (obligation) be legally binding. For example, if a friend invites you to a movie and later cancels the date, he would not be responsible to you as there was no intent by either party to be legally bound. An example of an obligation to give occurs in a contract of sale where the seller is obliged to deliver the thing bought; an obligation to do occurs, for example, when a garage undertakes to repair your car; an obligation not to do imposes a duty on you not to cause injury to another person, for example, and if you do, you will be held responsible.

SOURCES OF OBLIGATION

A person can be obliged to another:

1. By contract: in a contract of sale the seller must deliver the thing bought to the buyer.

2. By quasi contract: your neighbour is absent, his house is on fire, you rush in and save some of his property, but in doing so singe your clothing. There is a tacit agreement between you that he will pay the damages to your clothing.

3. By delict:

> Art. 1053   Every person capable of discerning right from wrong is responsible for the damage caused by his fault to another, whether by positive act, imprudence, neglect or want of skill.

Every person capable of knowing right from wrong is responsible for all damages he intentionally causes to another person by his fault; for example, if a person strikes another, he is responsible for damages.

4. By quasi delict: for damages caused to another unintentionally, as in an automobile accident.

5. By operation of the law solely: obligations result in certain cases from the sole and direct operation of law, without the intervention of any act, and independently of the will of the person obliged or of him in whose favour the obligation is imposed, e.g., the obligation of children to furnish the necessaries of life to their indigent parents (Art. 1057).

In contracts, the obligations are generally bilateral—there are obligations on both sides. If one party fails to perform his obligations as required, he cannot call upon the other party to perform what he has undertaken. When a party attempts to enforce his rights in court it must be in good faith and he must have fulfilled all his then due obligations to the other party. If, for example, he is suing for the price of goods, he must allege that he has sold and delivered the goods.

INEXECUTION OF OBLIGATIONS

In the case of breach of contract the aggrieved party can assert the following rights before the court:

1. Cancellation of the contract: this means that he seeks to be relieved of the duty to perform his own obligations, while recovering the monetary value of those obligations which he has already performed and financial compensation (damages) for losses caused to him by the other party's default.

> *A tenant refuses to pay his rent. The landlord is entitled to ask for cancellation of the lease, payment of the arrears of rent, and damages. (See chapter 12 on "Leases.")*

2. Specific performance: he may ask the court to order the

other party to perform his obligations under the contract, e.g., in a contract of sale he may ask for delivery of the thing bought. If the situation warrants, the court may grant an injunction ordering the party not to do something.

> *Bill gave John an exclusive agency to sell his products but he is now selling through Jack, too. The court will order that Bill stop dealing with Jack.*

3. Damages: in every case where one party is in default to fulfil his obligations the innocent party is entitled to damages. These damages will consist of the actual monetary loss suffered, injuries sustained, profits of which the innocent party was deprived and expenses incurred. Whether the damages are the result of a breach of contract or an automobile accident, their purpose is to compensate and restore the innocent party to the position in which he would have been if the contractual obligation had been fulfilled or if the accident had not occurred.

> *Sam, a pedestrian, is hit by an automobile and his leg is broken. He is entitled to claim for his medical and hospital expenses, loss of salary, pain and suffering, and an amount for temporary and permanent incapacity.*

Damages due the landlord for breach of contract by a tenant include:
a. an amount to cover the time necessary to lease the premises to another tenant (generally the equivalent of three months' rent);
b. if the tenant has physically damaged the premises, the cost of repairs.

> *You are a lumber dealer. In a contract of sale you have purchased a large quantity of specially cut wood from Smith Lumber Mills, but Smith fails to deliver. You would be entitled to claim the difference you had to pay to later purchase the specially cut wood from another mill.*

*After you had made the contract with Smith Lumber
Mills you entered into a contract with your clients,
Jackson, Arthurs and Brown to deliver wood to
them, which you were unable to do because of
Smith's failure to deliver. You are unable to purchase
the wood elsewhere. You are entitled to claim from
Smith your loss of profit on the contract with your
said clients.*

The claim for damages might be combined with either a claim
for cancellation of the contract or with an action for specific
performance.

DIFFERENT KINDS OF OBLIGATIONS

There are various types of obligations. We'll discuss conditional obligations, obligations with a term, joint and several
obligations, and penal clauses.

Conditional Obligations

Art. 1079   An obligation is conditional when it is
made to depend upon an event future and uncertain,
either by suspending it until the event happens, or by
dissolving it accordingly as the event does or does not
happen. When an obligation depends upon an event
which has actually happened, but is unknown to the
parties, it is not conditional. It takes effect or is de-
feated from the time at which it is contracted.

An obligation is conditional when it is made to depend on an
event which is future and uncertain. The obligation may be
suspended until the event occurs (suspensive conditon), or
cease to exist if the event occurs, or does not occur as the
case may be (resolutive condition). For example, John's
father promises to pay his son $100 if he passes his exams.

Obligations with a Term

When an obligation is made with a term, its performance is delayed until the term has expired. A common obligation with a term is the commercial invoice marked "net thirty days," which means that the buyer has the obligation to pay at the end of the term of thirty days.

Joint and Several Obligations

Art. 1103   There is a joint and several obligation on the part of the codebtors when they are obliged to the same thing, in such manner that each of them singly may be compelled to the performance of the whole obligation and that the performance by one discharges the others toward the creditor.

Art. 1105   An obligation is not presumed to be joint and several; it must be expressly declared to be so.

This rule does not prevail in cases where a joint and several obligation arises of right by virtue of some provision of law.

Nor is it applicable to commercial transactions, in which the obligation is presumed to be joint and several, except in cases otherwise regulated by special laws.

A joint and several obligation is that in which two or more debtors are each liable to their creditor for the *entire* debt. The creditor, at his option, may sue one or some or all the debtors for the entire debt, and after judgment enforce payment partly against one debtor and partly another, or all from one. Such a debtor cannot say to his creditor that he is only liable for half of the debt, or whatever his share might be. A joint and several debtor is liable for the whole debt, but can recover from his codebtors. Partners in a commercial partnership are jointly and severally liable to those with whom they contract. There is a presumption in commercial transactions that the debtors are jointly and severally obligated.

> *Al and Bill are partners in a grocery store. Smith is a creditor for $500. He may, at his option, sue one or both parties and upon judgment collect all from one partner or part from one and the balance from the other. Al cannot say to Smith, "Bill and I are equal partners and you can only collect one-half of the debt from me." If Smith collects in full from Al, then Al can claim one-half of what he paid from Bill.*

Joint Obligations

The opposite of a joint and several obligation is a joint obligation. This means that each debtor is liable to the creditor only for his share, therefore, three debtors would each be liable for one-third. This is the situation in a residential lease unless there is a clause indicating joint and several liability.

> *Betty, Jane and Mary sign an apartment lease and do not pay. The lessor can collect only one-third from each.*

Penal Clauses

Art. 1131   A penal clause is a secondary obligation by which a person, to assure the performance of the primary obligation, binds himself to a penalty in case of its inexecution.

Art. 1134   The penalty is not incurred until the debtor is in default of performing the primary obligation or has done the thing which he had obliged himself not to do.

Art. 1135   The amount of penalty cannot be reduced by the court. But if the obligation has been performed in part to the benefit of the creditor, and the time fixed for its complete performance be not material, the penalty may be reduced; unless there is a special agreement to the contrary.

The following is an obligation by a debtor to pay not only the amount of the debt but also an amount as penalty should he fail to perform his obligation.

Al borrows $1,000 from Jack and agrees that if he does not repay within two months he will pay an additional $100 as penalty. If he is in default to pay, Jack can claim $1,100.

EXTINCTION OF OBLIGATIONS

An obligation can be terminated in various ways, the most important of which are payment, payment with subrogation, release, compensation, impossibility of performance, prescription and novation.

Payment

This is the most common method of extinguishing an obligation.

Art. 1139   By payment is meant not only the delivery of a sum of money in satisfaction of an obligation, but the performance of any thing to which the parties are respectively obliged.

In a contract for the repair of Ralph's automobile, payment of the obligation of the garage is made when the work is finished. Payment of Ralph's obligation is discharged when he has paid the account.

Art. 1141   Payment may be made by any person, although he be a stranger to the obligation, and the creditor may be in default by the offer of a stranger to perform the obligation on the part of the debtor, without the knowledge of the latter, but it must be for the advantage of the debtor and not merely to change the creditor that the performance of the obligation is so offered.

Payment may be made to the creditor by someone other than the debtor but to constitute payment it must be for the advantage of the debtor and not simply to substitute one creditor for another.

> Art. 1152   Payment must be made in the place expressly or impliedly indicated by the obligation. If no place be so indicated, the payment, when it is of a certain specific thing, must be made at the place where the thing was at the time of contracting the obligation.
>
> In all other cases payment must be made at the domicile of the debtor; subject, nevertheless, to the rules provided under the titles relating to particular contracts.

Payment must be made at the place stipulated, either expressly or implied, in the contract.

Payment with Subrogation

Subrogation occurs when a creditor has been paid by a third party and the creditor transfers all his rights against the debtor to the third party. The third party may now exercise the rights of the original creditor against the debtor.

> *John borrows $100 from Peter. Harry pays Peter the $100 and becomes John's new creditor. John now owes $100 to Harry who has been subrogated in the rights of Peter. Harry now has all the rights previously held by Peter against John.*

Release

An obligation may be extinguished by the creditor releasing the debtor, either:

a. expressly, when, for example, the creditor gives the debtor a written statement that the debt is extinguished; or

b. impliedly, when the creditor voluntarily surrenders to the debtor the documents proving the creditor's claim.

> *John borrows $100 from Peter and gives him written acknowledgement of the debt. Peter returns the written statement to John when the debt is paid.*

Compensation

Compensation occurs when two people are mutually debtor and creditor to each other. Both debts are extinguished by compensation up to the amount of the smaller debt.

> *John owes Peter $100 and Peter owes John $55. The two debts are compensated in the amount of $55 and John still owes Peter $45.*

For compensation to operate the two debts must be exigible and liquidated, that is, both ascertained and due, owing and demandable, and both must be payable in money.

Impossibility of Performance

When the thing which is the object of an obligation perishes or delivery becomes impossible, the obligation is extinguished provided that the debtor of the obligation is not at fault.

Prescription

The law stipulates that an obligation will be extinguished by a certain lapse of time. The length of time necessary for prescription varies according to the nature of the obligation.

John owes $75 to the local department store for merchandise he purchased. The store's claim will be prescribed after the lapse of five years from the date of purchase.

Sam is personally injured in an automobile accident. He must sue within one year from the date of the accident for bodily injuries, otherwise, his claim will be prescribed. He has a two-year period to claim for the damages to his car.

Prescription is interrupted:

a. by the creditor instituting legal proceedings against the debtor;

b. and might be in certain circumstances by the debtor making payments on account of the debt.

If you have a claim against someone be certain as to the prescriptive period of your claim. You must sue or receive from the debtor a satisfactory settlement within this time limit; otherwise, your claim will be extinguished.

Novation

An obligation may be terminated by novation which is effected:

1. when the debtor contracts towards his creditor a new debt which is substituted for the ancient one, and the latter is extinguished, e.g., a debtor signs a new promissory note and the old one is torn up.

2. when a new debtor is substituted for a former one who is discharged by the creditor, e.g., a son agrees to be substituted for his father as debtor.

3. when by the effect of a new contract, a new creditor is substituted for a former one toward whom the debtor is discharged, e.g., by a new contract a new landlord is substituted for a former landlord who releases his former tenant.

In all cases, novation is not presumed and must be evident from the writings between the parties.

Legal Terminology

obligation
contract
quasi contract
delict
quasi delict
reciprocal obligations
inexecution of obligations
damages
specific performance
conditional obligations

term obligations
joint and several obligations
joint obligations
penal clauses
extinction
payment
subrogation
release
compensation
prescription
novation

Questions

1. What is an obligation?
2. What are the sources of obligations?
3. What kinds of obligations are there?
4. What is the difference between a conditional obligation and an obligation with a term?
5. What does joint and several mean?
6. What are the available recourses when there is inexecution of an obligation?
7. When is special performance ordered?
8. How is an obligation extinguished?
9. How does subrogation operate?
10. Discuss prescription.
11. Give three instances of novation.

CIVIL RESPONSIBILITY

Chapter 8

CIVIL RESPONSIBILITY

1. John has a violent argument with Jack and strikes him in the face with his fist, breaking Jack's nose.

2. John loses control of his car and hits a pedestrian, injuring him. The car swerves and hits another car, injuring its occupants.

3. John's employee, Bill, while on the job, accidentally damages property belonging to Smith.

4. John's pet dog bites the postman severely in the leg.

In each of the above examples John is responsible for the act causing damage and he is obliged to compensate the victim by paying him for the damages sustained.

Damages are the financial injury and loss incurred; thus, in example 4, John would be obliged to pay the postman all his medical expenses, the cost of damaged clothing, loss of salary, an amount for pain and suffering, and for disfigurement and disability, if any.

FAULT

The basic rule governing negligence and damages to person and property is contained in Article 1053.

> Art. 1053 Every person capable of discerning right from wrong is responsible for the damage caused by his fault to another, whether by positive act, imprudence, neglect, or want of skill.

There is a legal obligation to act with care and attention. The person who does not act prudently and causes damages or injury to another, is obliged to compensate the claimant.

In all cases based on *fault,* which includes accidents, assaults, breach of contract, abuse of rights, personal injuries, damages to property, honour and reputation, the court examines the standard of care of the defendant as follows.

1. Was the defendant at fault by acting negligently or carelessly?

2. Did the defendant do everything that could be expected from a prudent and reasonable man?

Acts of carelessness are either offences (delicts) or quasi offences (quasi delicts). An offence occurs when the act causing the damage is done intentionally; a quasi offence occurs when the act causing damage is done unintentionally. Example 1 is an example of an offence. Examples 2, 3 and 4 are quasi offences.

VICARIOUS RESPONSIBILITY

Example 3 deals with vicarious responsibility. John did not cause the damage himself, his employee did. The law considers that in certain cases, a person is responsible not only for his own fault but that of others under his control. In this case, the injured party can claim from the employee under Article 1053 and from the employer under Article 1054.

> Art. 1054 He is responsible not only for the damage caused by his own fault, but also for that caused by the fault of persons under his control and by things he has under his care;
>
> The father, or, after his decease, the mother, is responsible for the damage caused by their minor children;
>
> Tutors are responsible in like manner for their pupils;
>
> Curators or others having the legal custody of insane persons, for the damage done by the latter;
>
> Schoolmasters and artisans, for the damage caused by their pupils or apprentices while under their care.

The responsibility attaches in the above cases only when the person subject to it fails to establish that he was unable to prevent the act which has caused the damage;

Masters and employers are responsible for the damage caused by their servants and workmen in the performance of the work for which they are employed.

A father is not responsible for the acts of his minor children when the father is "unable to prevent the act which has caused the damage." The courts have interpreted this to mean that the father will be liable if he failed to give the child a good education and moral upbringing or neglected to exercise a degree of control that would be reasonably expected from a father.

> *John's son Tim, who is nine years old, takes his father's gun, which John left in the den, and accidentally shoots a playmate causing severe injury. Is John liable? Yes.*

An employer is responsible for damages caused by his employees if the following facts are established:
1. that the employee is working for the employer;
2. that the employee was in the performance of the work for which he is employed at the time of the accident. For example, Joe, a crane operator, strikes and damages a parked car in the street while operating a crane and boom at a building demolition site.
3. that the damage is a result of the fault of the employee;
4. that the act complained of caused damages. The cost of repairing a car is $350 and that is the amount of damages claimed by the owner.

Art. 1055 The owner of an animal is responsible for the damages caused by it, whether it be under his own care or under that of his servants, or has strayed or escaped from it.

He who is using the animal is equally responsible while it is in his service.

The owner of a building is responsible for the damage caused by its ruin, where it has happened from want of repairs or from an original defect in its construction.

Article 1055 concerns the responsibility of the owner of an animal. In the fourth example, John is liable for the damages caused by his pet dog.

The owner of a building is responsible for the damage caused by its ruin, either due to want of repair or from an original defect of construction, e.g., a brick falls off a building hitting a pedestrian. The only defence of an owner is to show that the damage was caused by an act of God, or a fortuitous event, such as a storm of extraordinary and unexpected force, or a severe flood.

Art. 1056 In all cases where the person injured by the commission of an offence or a quasi offence dies in consequence, without having obtained indemnity or satisfaction, his consort and his ascendant and descendant relations have a right, but only within a year after his death, to recover from the person who committed the offence or quasi offence, or his representatives, all damages occasioned by such death.

Article 1056 concerns the right of action by certain relatives to recover compensation from the person who caused the damage within one year after death. Within that time, the wife and children and parents of a person fatally injured by an accident, may sue the responsible party.

MUNICIPAL LIABILITY

The Municipal Code, the Cities and Towns Act and the Charters of large cities state the liability of that city concerning property owned by it. For example, the city is responsible for the maintenance of streets and sidewalks. As a general rule, in a claim against a municipality it is important to immediately send to the city a registered letter holding it responsible and to institute proceedings within six months if no settlement has been reached.

OTHER PROVISIONS OF THE CIVIL CODE

See chapter 12 on "Leases" concerning the liability of the tenant for fire damages.

Architects and builders are responsible according to Article 1688.

> Art. 1688   If a building perish in whole or in part within five years, from a defect in construction, or even from unfavourable nature of the ground, the architect superintending the work, and the builder are jointly and severally liable for the loss.

Innkeepers are responsible according to Article 1814.

> Art. 1814   Keepers of inns, of boarding-houses and taverns, are responsible as depositaries for the things brought by travellers who lodge in their houses.

Carriers of goods are responsible according to Article 1675.

> Art. 1675   They are liable for the loss or damage of things entrusted to them, unless they can prove that such loss or damage was caused by a fortuitous event or irresistible force, or has arisen from a defect in the thing itself.

OTHER LEGISLATION

In addition to the above Articles of the Civil Code there are several other important relevant Acts. (See also the Workmen's Compensation Act in chapter 17.)

The Quebec Highway Code sets forth provision for the licensing, registration and use of automobiles and penalties for operating an automobile without due care and attention.

The Highway Victims Indemnity Act

The Highway Victims Indemnity Act concerns the liability of owners of automobiles. Basically, an owner of an automobile is responsible for all damages caused by his automobile unless he proves one of the following:

1. that the damage is not due to any fault on his part or on the part of a person in the automobile or of the driver;

OR

2. that at the time of the accident the automobile was being driven by a third party who had stolen it;

OR

3. that at the time of an accident that occurred elsewhere than on a public highway, the automobile was in possession of a third party for storage, repair or transportation.

The driver of an automobile is also responsible unless he proves that the damage is not due to any fault on his part.

> *John lends his car to Paul. Paul hits a stationary truck. John is liable as owner and, of course, so is Paul as driver.*

When two persons are liable they are held to be *jointly and severally liable* which means that each person is liable for payment of the full amount of the damages.

In Quebec, automobile insurance is not compulsory. If you are involved in an automobile accident and you do not have insurance amounting to at least $35,000 subject to a deduction of $200 from all damage to the property of others, you will be obliged to show "financial responsibility" by (1) furnishing evidence of automobile liability insurance of at least $35,000 or (2) by producing a bond of an approved bonding company or (3) making a deposit in cash or bonds of

$35,000. If you do not have insurance and cannot furnish the required financial guarantees and if you are found responsible for damages, your licence will be suspended until the damages are paid.

If you are involved in an accident and the other party is at fault but has no insurance or if he is not known (as in a hit and run) you may claim against a government body called the Highway Indemnity Fund. The fund will pay personal injury claims over $100 and property damages (automobile) over $200 up to the legal financial responsibility limit, currently $35,000.

Minors must furnish proof of financial responsibility before an automobile can be registered in their name and automobile dealers before being granted a dealer's licence.

How To Act in an Automobile Accident

1. Stop immediately. It is a serious criminal offence to hit and run. Show the other party your car registration and driver's licence.
2. Offer aid to injured persons. However, you could be responsible for aggravating the injuries. Call a doctor.
3. Call the police.
4. Do not move the automobile until after the police arrive, unless you are endangering traffic. Place warning signs, to avoid further accidents.
5. If the damages are under $100 the police are not obliged to make a report. Take down all the details including:
a. The name and address of the other side, both owner and driver.
b. The name of the insurance company and the policy number of the other side.
c. The date, place and location of the accident.
d. The numbers of both the owner's permit and the driver's licence of the other side.
e. Names and addresses of witnesses and passengers, and if possible, a written statement from the witnesses.
6. Do not admit responsibility. Tell the police only the facts

of the accident and do not give your opinion as to the fault. Do not sign any statements nor accept or make any settlement but leave this to your insurance company or lawyer.

7. Make a diagram and take relevant measurements of positions of vehicles and of skid marks, etc.

8. In case of arrest, consult a lawyer.

9. Always advise your own insurance company, even in cases where you think you are not responsible. If you do not advise it immediately, you may be in financial difficulty with both the other side and with your insurers. If the insurers have to pay, they might be able, under the terms of the policy, to sue you for the moneys they paid to the other side.

10. See a doctor if you are personally injured so he may assess your claim.

11. See a lawyer. If you are sued and are insured, your insurance company will defend you. If you have a claim to make against the other party, you must seek your own attorney.

12. Finally and most important—
Do not drink alcohol before you drive, or if you do—
take a taxi to your destination.

Drunken driving is itself a serious offence and often leads to the commission of other offences such as hit and run, injuring or even killing, a pedestrian. The police are legally entitled to request you take a breathalyser test. Should you refuse this raises a presumption of guilt against you.

The Crime Victims Compensation Act

The Crime Victims Compensation Act went into force on March 1, 1972, and is applied by the Workmen's Compensation Commission. In the event a person is injured or killed in Quebec during the commission of a serious criminal act, e.g., murder, rape, robbery, assault, the victim will be compensated by the government. A crime victim is defined as any person killed or injured in the province of Quebec:

a. by reason of the act or omission of any other person

occurring in or resulting directly from the commission of an offence, the description of which corresponds to the criminal offences mentioned in the schedule to this Act;

b. while lawfully arresting or attempting to arrest an offender or suspected offender or assisting a peace officer making an arrest;

c. while lawfully preventing or attempting to prevent the commission of an offence or suspected offence, or assisting a peace officer preventing or attempting to prevent the commission of an offence or suspected offence;

d. the dependant of a victim killed as a result of the above circumstances.

However, the benefits under this Act shall not be granted:

a. if the victim is killed or injured in circumstances giving recourse to the Workmen's Compensation Act, either in his favour or in that of his dependants;

b. if the victim, through his gross fault, contributed to his injuries or death;

c. to a dependant who was a party to the offence which caused the death of the victim.

A crime victim, who is disabled and unable to work, receives 75 percent of his salary up to $129.81 per week. A victim with over 10 percent disability is entitled to a life pension. Those with less than 10 percent incapacity receive a lump sum depending on the degree of disability. When a crime results in death, the dependants receive a cash allocation to cover the funeral expenses and a monthly pension for the widow of at least $142.80 or more if she has children.

All applications for compensation must be made to the Workmen's Compensation Commission within six months following the crime.

Legal Terminology

civil responsibility	*fault*
damages	*standard of care*
obligation	*negligence*
injury	*imprudence*
compensate	*offence*

quasi offence
delict
quasi delict
vicarious responsibility
Highway Code
Highway Victims Indemnity
  Act

financial responsibility
joint and several liability
insurance
Crime Victims Compensation
  Act
Workmen's Compensation
  Commission

Questions

1. What is meant by damages?

2. What is the basic rule governing damages to persons and property?

3. On what basis does the court examine the standard of care of the defendant in a damage action?

4. What is the difference between offences and quasi offences?

5. What is the meaning of vicarious responsibility and discuss the liability of the employer for acts of his employee, as well as the responsibility of a father for his minor child.

6. Discuss the responsibility of the owner of an animal.

7. Discuss the responsibility of an owner of a building.

8. If you have a claim against a municipality, what should you do?

9. Discuss the responsibility of an owner of an automobile involved in an accident.

10. What are the implications of not having insurance if you are involved in an accident?

11. What recourses does a victim have in a hit and run accident?

12. What should you do in the case of an automobile accident?

13. What is the purpose of the Crime Victims Compensation Act and what government body administers it?

Problem

Tim, who is fifteen years old, is a delivery boy for Sam's Grocery Store. With permission, he borrows his father's car to make the deliveries and while doing so, he hits Mary, a pedestrian. Who can Mary sue? Give reasons.

CONTRACTS IN GENERAL
[Fraud and Lesion]

Chapter 9

CONTRACTS IN GENERAL

Virtually every business transaction involves some kind of contract. When a person buys a machine or car, he has entered into a contract of sale; everytime he leases an apartment, borrows money, enters into partnership, hires a salesman, insures his goods, he makes a contract. Therefore contracts cover a wide area of commercial law. All of these contracts have certain elements in common—they all have the same general rules.

A contract may contain any agreement to which the parties may voluntarily agree. The only prohibitions are that "no one can by private agreement, validly contravene the laws of public order and good morals" (Article 13) or contravene specific mandatory provisions of the law.

Once the contract is made it is the "law between the parties." The parties may make agreements in a contract which the law does not ordinarily require of them, but if they agree to do so, they are bound.

> *The law does not require a tenant to be responsible for repairs to the roof of his rented house. But if in the lease he accepts that responsibility, then he is obliged.*

> *A used car dealer does not have to warrant (guarantee) against apparent defects in the cars he sells by law. However, if he agrees to in the contract of sale, then he is legally bound.*

Here are some terms which are used in discussing contracts:

1. Contracts: contracts are the most common source of obligations. A contract is distinguished from other sources of obligations in that in every valid contract there must be agreement between the parties as to their respective obligations.

2. Quasi contracts: in a quasi contract there is no express agreement between the parties, however, they are bound just as if (quasi) there were. For example, if Al voluntarily undertakes to do something for Bob, even without Bob's knowledge or consent and Bob benefits, Bob incurs the obligation to reimburse Al for his expenses.

> *Al extinguishes a fire in Bob's house, while Bob is on vacation. Al incurs expenses in doing so (burnt clothing, etc.). Bob must pay Al these costs. There is an implied contract that Bob would have authorised Al to do what he did do.*

3. Unilateral obligations: a unilateral obligation occurs where only one party of the parties has an obligation to perform. The other clearly benefits. For example, he receives a gift. The donor has the obligation of giving, while the beneficiary (donee) benefits without any obligation on his part.

4. Bilateral obligations: a bilateral obligation occurs where both parties have obligations. In a sale the vendor has the obligation to deliver and the purchaser has the obligation to pay for the object sold.

FREEDOM OF CONTRACTING

A contract is formed by mutual agreement after an exchange of offer and often counter offer has been made between the parties. The negotiations must be between independent and capable persons.

However, there are instances where the parties do not expressly agree to all the terms of the contract. Unless the parties have expressly agreed to otherwise in the contract, the law obliges the parties to perform certain obligations and duties in each specific contract. For example, in leases the parties might not have specifically outlined what are landlord and tenant repairs. In absence of this type of contractual agreement, the Code states the duties of each party.

The parties are at liberty to add to, diminish or cancel the obligations imposed by law, unless doing so is against public order or good morals or unless there are obligatory statutory conditions.

Although the law presumes that each party is free to negotiate the terms of a contract, in fact, many contracts are offered on a "sign it or leave it" basis. Many contracts are printed on so-called standard forms which put one party inevitably in the stronger bargaining position so that he can insist that either the whole contract be accepted or else no contract is made at all. Most utility contracts, e.g., electricity, hydro, telephone, gas, are highly standardised leaving little scope for negotiation. These are called *contracts of adhesion.*

FORMATION OF CONTRACTS

In order for there to be a binding contract, there must be a "meeting of minds" on all of the essential conditions and terms of the contract. For example, in the contract of sale, the contracting parties must agree on the object, the price and the terms of payment. Unless there is a clear meeting of the minds, there is no contract; there might have been negotiations or offers, but no completed contract. How, then, is a contract completed?

Offer and Acceptance

To form a contract, first of all an offer must be made. For example, Jones (the offeror) offers to sell you (the offeree) his auto for $1,000 payable immediately. If you accept his offer without qualification, a contract has been formed and this legally obliges him to deliver the car to you on immediate payment of $1,000. If, however, after hearing Jones's offer you say, "I accept your offer to sell me your auto for

$1,000, however, I want to pay the $1,000 thirty days from now and not immediately," then the contract has not been completed. His offer to sell was met by your new conditions. What you have made is really a new offer or a counter offer. Now Jones must accept or reject your offer to buy his car for $1,000, payable in thirty days. Because you have not accepted the terms of his offer, Jones's offer is revoked by your counter offer. If Jones accepts your offer to purchase unconditionally, a contract is formed and he is obliged to deliver the car and you, the buyer, are obliged to pay thirty days after delivery. Once an offer is accepted, it cannot be withdrawn. A contract has been made and both parties are bound to respect their obligations.

An offer may have a time limit within which the offeree may accept. This is called an *option.*

> *Al offers to sell Bob his car, giving him an option of one week to purchase. Bob does nothing and the one week expires. Al may then sell the car to a third person. But if Bob had accepted the offer to sell within the one-week period, then Al would have had to sell to Bob.*

If there is no time limit prescribed for the acceptance, the offer may be terminated (before acceptance) by withdrawing the offer after it has been available for a reasonable period of time. If the offer has not been withdrawn, it may be accepted. What determines a reasonable delay will depend on the circumstances. Once the acceptance has been communicated, it cannot be withdrawn—a contract has been made.

In order for a contract to have been completed, the offer and acceptance must contain all the essentials of the contract, e.g., in a contract of sale a seller, buyer, description and quantity of the goods and price must be outlined.[1]

---

1. There are certain offers which are not really offers but "invitations." Newspaper advertisements and promotional catalogues which list goods and are circulated to the public at large do not make offers, but invite the public to make offers for the goods described, the store being at liberty to accept or reject such offers.

Does this form a contract?
"Want to buy a car," says John.
"Yes," says Bill.

FORM OF CONTRACTS

Unless there is a specific stipulation in law, all contracts may be either written or verbal.

Written Contracts

A written contract may be handwritten, typed or printed. Generally, no special form, no formalities, no witnesses are required. The contract may be either a formal legal document or it may be the result of correspondence by letters between the parties. All that is necessary is that the parties clearly state all the terms of the contract. Verbal evidence will not be accepted to vary or contradict the terms of a valid written contract.

Marriage contracts, hypothecs (mortgages) and deeds containing gifts must not only be in writing, but must also be in notarial form.

Since verbal contracts are binding, is there any real advantage to having written contracts? Clearly, yes, for a well-drafted written contract sets down all the terms and conditions so that there can be no doubt as to the agreements made between the parties. Furthermore, although verbal contracts are binding, they are very difficult to prove in court. The rules of evidence state that generally in all civil, noncommercial matters, there must be a written contract in order for testimony to be admissable. Therefore, if two private individuals enter into a verbal contract of sale for an automobile, and one of the two parties wishes to cancel the contract before the car is actually delivered or any evidence in writing of this contract is given, it would be virtually impossible for the other party to successfully sue him.

It may be necessary in some commercial matters, and in most noncommercial matters, in order for the testimony of witnesses to be permitted, in cases of fifty dollars or more, that there be a "commencement of proof in writing" emanating from the other party, e.g., a receipt, a written contract, an offer, a cheque—all must be signed by the other side. Only then will verbal evidence before the courts be admissible. For this reason it is advisable to obtain a written purchase order from a buyer, rather than merely accepting his verbal order.

Contracts by Correspondence

Problems may arise as to the completion of a contract when negotiations are carried out over long distances and in particular, when the offer and acceptance are made in two different provinces.

Jack lives in Montreal and makes an offer to purchase a piece of land belonging to Ross who lives in Toronto. Jack gives the offer by hand to Al, who is Ross's agent. Ross mails his acceptance from Toronto, but Jack states he never received the letter and withdraws his offer. Has a contract been formed?

John, who lives in Montreal, mails a letter containing an offer to purchase a machine belonging to George, who lives in Toronto. George sends his acceptance by return mail. John states he never received the letter and withdraws his offer. Has a contract been formed?

In the first example, can the post office be considered Jack's agent to receive Ross's acceptance? No. Jack sent his offer by messenger, therefore, the acceptance of the offer should have been made either by the same messenger or by some other means so that it could be conclusively proved that Jack did receive the acceptance.

In the second example, since John mailed his offer to George, he constituted the post office as his agent of communication. The mailing of the acceptance by George completes the contract, even if John does not receive the letter. The post office, as John's agent, has received George's acceptance and John is bound.

The rule in contracts by correspondence is that when the offeror elects to use a certain type of agent, be it the post office or messenger, the contract is made the moment the acceptor communicates the acceptance to that same authorised agent, even though in fact the offeror is unaware of the acceptance. Therefore, if the offer was mailed, the contract is complete when the acceptance is placed in the mail box. The mailing of the acceptance must be proved by the acceptor. If the acceptor uses another means of communicating the acceptance, the contract is only formed if the acceptor can prove that the acceptance actually reached the offeror. Also, if the acceptor uses a different agent he risks the chance that before the acceptance reaches the offeror, the offeror will revoke his offer by a quicker means.

The place where there has been a valid and binding acceptance is the place where the contract has been made and consequently the contract will be governed by the law of that place.

INVALID CONTRACTS

If a contract does not contain all the essentials, then it is an invalid contract. The following terms will be used in discussing contracts which are invalid:

1. Null and void: from a legal standpoint a contract that has no legal effect and is nonexistent.
2. To annul: to have a contract declared null and void, that is, to have it declared never to have been validly in existence.
3. Voidable contract: a contract which a party may either enforce or cancel at his option.
4. To cancel: one of the parties wishes to end a valid contract because of the nonperformance of an obligation by the other; or cancellation can be by mutual agreement.
5. Unenforceable contract: a contract that cannot be enforced by legal action before the courts because of a technical defect. For example, a marriage contract must be made by a notary, and if it isn't, it cannot be enforced.
6. Illegal contract: an illegal contract is prohibited by law

and it is null and void. For example, it is illegal for unauthorised persons to sell drugs.

THE VALIDITY OF CONTRACTS

There are certain legal grounds on which a contract can be set aside and annulled and therefore held not legally binding.

Legal Formalities

Certain contracts, such as marriage contracts and hypothecs, must be made by a notary, otherwise they are not binding.

Four Requisites to the Validity of a Contract

Art. 984   There are four requisites to the validity of a contract:
1. Parties legally capable of contracting;
2. Their consent legally given;
3. Something which forms the object of the contract;
4. A lawful cause or consideration.

The absence of any one or more of these four essentials makes a contract null and void.

LEGAL CAPACITY TO CONTRACT

The parties to a contract may either be natural or artificial persons (corporations). The capacity of natural persons is dealt with in various parts of the Code: the capacity of a corporation is found in the Companies Act under which it was incorporated; the capacity of a city is dealt with in its charter and in the Cities and Towns Act.

The general rule is that all persons are capable of contracting except the following:

Art. 986 Minors in the cases and according to the provisions contained in this code;

Interdicted persons;

Those who, by special provisions of law, are prohibited from contracting by reason of their relation to each other, or of the object of the contract;

Persons insane or suffering a temporary derangement of intellect arising from disease, accident, drunkenness or other cause, or who by reason of weakness of understanding are unable to give a valid consent.

Minors

A person who is under eighteen years of age, male or female, remains a minor until that age is reached. Actually, a minor is able to contract, but the important point is that he is able to avoid the consequences of his contractual obligation, under certain conditions.

There are two types of minors: unemancipated and emancipated. An *unemancipated minor* is a minor who is unmarried or has not been emancipated by court order. The unemancipated minor has full capacity to contract; he can bind others. The contract is valid, but he can avoid his obligations by showing:

1. that he is a minor; and
2. that he has suffered an unfair and unequal obligation, which is called *lesion.*

Lesion occurs when either the minor cannot financially afford the object even though it is worth its value or when the minor can afford it but it is overvalued. Of course, a case where a minor could not afford an overvalued object would also be lesion.

> *John is seventeen years old, a student with little income. He purchases a secondhand car for $2,000 (its actual value is $800). He makes a down payment of $100 and writes out a series of postdated cheques for the balance. Can John set aside the contract?*

Lesion can only be raised by the minor himself. This means that the store or person with whom he has contracted cannot cancel the contract merely on the basis that they have sold to a minor; the contract is binding against the adult (the store, businessman, etc.).

A minor who can validly plead lesion may do so when he is sued by the store for payment. His claim would be that he could not afford the purchase price or that he was taken advantage of because of his inexperience as a minor. Or the minor may take the initiative by suing the store for cancellation of contract. The fact that a minor falsely states that he is of the age of majority does not necessarily prevent him from pleading lesion, except if his false declaration amounts to fraud. Therefore, the risks in doing business with a minor are quite evident.

A minor cannot claim lesion in the following instances:

1. Unforeseen event: a minor is not relievable for cause of lesion, when it results only from a casual and unforeseen event (Article 1004).

> *John, a minor, buys a television set which he can afford and is reasonably priced. Soon after buying it, the federal sales tax is abolished which results in similar sets being sold at a much lower price. John cannot cancel the contract due to this "unforeseen event."*

2. Offences and quasi offences: a minor is not relievable from obligations resulting from his offences and quasi offences. Article 1053 states that every person capable of discerning right from wrong is responsible for the damage caused by his fault to another by positive act, imprudence, neglect or want of skill. This Article binds only those who are capable of distinguishing right from wrong. Therefore, an infant cannot commit an offence. Consequently, as long as a minor knows the difference between right and wrong he is responsible for damages caused by his acts. In the chapter on

"Civil Responsiblity," the question of the liability of the father for acts of his minor children is discussed.

3. Ratification: a person is not relievable from a contract made by him during minority, when he has ratified it since attaining the age of majority (Article 1008). In the example on page 105, John could plead lesion. But if on attaining the age of eighteen he signs a document ratifying the contract, he is bound. Merely continuing to use the car after attaining the age of majority would not constitute ratification.

4. When aided by a tutor or curator: in any contract that is executed by a tutor for a minor, the contract is valid and not subject to lesion, except in certain instances, e.g., granting hypothecs or sale of land, when the tutor must obtain prior approval of the court. A *tutor* is a court-appointed guardian to an unemancipated minor; if the minor is emancipated, the court appoints a *curator.* When a minor institutes or defends legal proceedings a tutor (or curator) generally represents him.

5. All contracts for necessities of life: these include reasonable rent, clothing, groceries, etc.

Emancipation of a minor is effected either by a court order or by his marriage. Such a minor cannot plead lesion in the following cases, in addition to the ones listed under unemancipated minors:

1. All contracts for necessities for life, including rent, grocery bills, clothing for himself, his wife and children.

2. Acts of administration of his property, e.g., grant leases for terms not exceeding nine years.

3. All contracts directly arising from or for the purposes of his business. A minor engaged in trade is reputed of full age for all acts relating to such trade (Article 323).

> Art. 1005   A minor who is a banker, trader or mechanic is not relievable for cause of lesion from contracts made for the purposes of his business or trade.

Therefore, if a travelling salesman who is a minor buys a car, the sales contract is binding upon him even if he cannot afford it. But if he bought a television set he could annul the contract, after proving that the need for a TV does not arise from his work and that he suffered lesion.

4. Obligations arising from marriage, e.g., he owes support to his wife and children.

> Art. 1006   A minor is not relievable from the stipulations contained in his marriage contract, when they have been made with the consent and assistance of those whose consent is required for the validity of his marriage.

Interdicted Persons

A person of full age (over eighteen) or even an emancipated minor who is in an habitual state of imbecility or insanity, may upon application made by his family to the court be declared to be an interdict—he is legally declared incapable of contracting.

Contracts made by an interdicted person are null and void even if entered into during a lucid interval.

Similarly a prodigal—one who commits acts of prodigality which give reason to fear that he will dissipate his assets—may be interdicted. So, too, habitual drunkards or drug addicts may be interdicted even for acts they commit while sober. These interdicts have curators appointed to manage their affairs. The interdicted person can plead lesion.

Other Persons Incapable of Contracting

Incapacity also arises out of the relation of the parties to each other, or to the object of the contract.

> Art. 1484   The following persons cannot become buyers, either by themselves or by parties interposed, that is to say:

Tutors or curators, of the property of those over whom they are appointed except in sales by judicial authority;

Agents of the property which they are charged with the sale of;

Adminstrators or trustees of the property in their charge, whether of public bodies or of private persons;

Public officers, of national property, the sale of which is made through their ministry.

The incapacity declared in this article cannot be set up by the buyer; it exists only in favour of the owner and others having an interest in the thing sold.

Art. 1485 Judges, advocates, attorneys, clerks, sheriffs, bailiffs, and other officers connected with courts of justice, cannot become buyers of litigious rights which fall under the jurisdiction of the court in which they exercise their functions.

Insane Persons

Persons insane or suffering temporary derangement, drunkenness, etc., are unable to give a valid consent.

John sells his car while he is in a drunken state. If John can prove that he was unable to give his consent due to his drunken condition, the contract would be cancelled.

General Rule Concerning Contracts Made by Incapables

A contract made by an incapable is voidable at the option of the incapable person if he can prove his incapacity at the time of the contract. The contract remains valid until it is cancelled.

CONSENT OF THE PARTIES LEGALLY GIVEN

Consent is either expressed or implied. It is invalidated by:
a. lesion
b. error
c. fraud
d. violence or fear.

These causes of nullity must be proved in order for the contract to be cancelled. If proved they give a right of action by the aggrieved person to annul the contract or to defend an action based on the invalid contract.

Error

Error occurs when a party consents to a contract in the mistaken belief that a set of facts are true.

> Art. 992   Error is a cause of nullity only when it occurs in the nature of the contract itself, or in the substance of the thing which is the object of the contract, or in some thing which is a principal consideration for making it.

1. Error in the nature of the contract: John enters into a contract which is really a sale of his auto. However, he mistakenly believes he is leasing the auto. He is in error as to the nature of the contract. He never would have consented to selling his auto.
2. Error in the substance of the thing which is the object of the contract: John buys what is reported to be a race horse. In fact, it is a work horse and not a race horse—error in object.

Bob buys a painting represented to him as an original Picasso. In fact it is only a good reproduction—error as to the substance.

Al buys what the seller Smith honestly believes to be silver candlesticks. They are later discovered to be made of brass.

Even though Smith is in good faith, this does not prevent Al from raising the ground of error to set aside the contract.

3. Error in something which is a principal consideration for making the contract: Jones enters into a contract with you to paint his portrait. You have represented yourself as John Brown, the famous artist. In fact, you are another John Brown. Jones's principal consideration for entering into the contract is the skill of the famous John Brown—there has been error as to identity.

The error must be an important error—a principal reason for making the contract. The general rule is that contracts are valid and upheld unless the party can clearly show error as defined in its narrow legal sense. The mere fact that a person could have bought it cheaper elsewhere is not considered as error.

Fraud

Art. 993   Fraud is a cause of nullity when the artifices practised by one or with his knowledge are such that the other party would not have contracted without them. It is never presumed and must be proved.

What is fraud? Fraud is a manoeuvre, trick, artifice or ruse, used by one person to deceive another person.

Al knowingly falsely represented the print as an original Picasso to Bob, willfully leading him into error. If Bob acts upon this false representation he may have the contract of sale annulled. If Al got Bob drunk before getting him to sign the contract of sale, Bob could claim that since he was drunk he did not know what he was signing and was in error as to its true import. He could also claim that he signed because of the fraudulent manoeuvres of Al. Therefore, fraud and error are closely associated grounds of nullity.

Violence or Fear

Art. 994   Violence or fear is a cause of nullity, whether practised or produced by the party for whose benefit the contract is made or by any other person.

Bill signs a deed agreeing to buy a house from Ron. But Ron is holding a gun at Bill's head. This is a threat of violence. If Bill can prove by showing the circumstance and by his immediate repudiation of the contract that Al used threat of violence to force his consent, then the contract can be annulled.

The contract is null whether Al threatened Bill or whether a third party, Charles, held the gun and forced Bill to sign. Violence or its threat destroys liberty and freedom to give or withhold consent. However, the contract between Bill and Al, the seller, stands valid until Bill successfully challenges its validity. It is a voidable contract.

> Art. 994   The fear whether produced by violence or otherwise must be a reasonable and present fear of serious injury. The age, sex, character and condition of the party are to be taken into consideration.

> Art. 996   Fear suffered by a contracting party is a cause of nullity whether it is a fear of injury to himself or to his wife, children or other near kindred, and sometimes when it is a fear of injury to strangers, according to the circumstances of the case.

In order to annul the contract, Bill must prove that the fear he experienced and which caused him to sign was (a) a reasonable and (b) present fear of (c) serious injury. For example, if Al had said only, "Well, I will be annoyed if you don't sign" and Bill signed, an actual present fear could not be proved. The age, sex, character and condition of the party complaining are considered by the court in determining whether the fear was reasonable.

Al might have forced Bill to sign by threatening, "You had better sign. My pal has a pistol and is in the next room with your son and it will be too bad for your son if you don't sign." To save his son, Bill would sign; this is a valid cause of nullity.

> Art. 997 Mere reverential fear of a father or mother, or other ascendants, without any violence having been exercised or threats made, will not invalidate a contract.

Suppose Bill's father says, "I demand that you buy the house from Al." Bill feels a sense of duty to respect his father's wishes and he signs. Bill cannot later succeed if he raises this reverential fear as a reason to set aside the contract.

The Effect of Setting Aside a Contract

When a contract has been annulled on the basis of error or fraud or violence and fear of lesion, the parties revert to the position they were in previous to the forming of the contract. The legal ties are severed.

If no obligations have yet been performed before the annulling, then parties are released from these obligations. If obligations have been performed then each party must hand back all that he received from the contract. The party who acted in good faith is not obliged to return profits, revenues, or rents he collected from the property. He restores only the property. The party that was aggrieved (defrauded, etc.) may also claim damages.

THE OBJECT OF THE CONTRACT-

What Is an Obligation?

An obligation is a legal tie or bond by which a person is bound toward another to give, to do or not to do. Legal obligations are sanctioned by law to enforce the performance of an obligation (see chapter 7 on "Obligations").

Art. 1058   Every obligation must have for its object something which a party is obliged to give, or to do, or not to do.

The transfer of ownership of a house fulfils the obligation to give. The act of building a house fulfils the obligation to do—the house is the object.

The object of a contract must be lawful, otherwise it is an invalid and unenforceable contract. What objects are illegal?

1. Those things which are not objects of commerce (Article 1059).

2. Objects forbidden by statute, e.g., the private sale of liquor or drugs by unauthorised persons. Also certain contracts made on Sunday are illegal.

3. A contract to commit an offence, e.g., John agrees to pay Jack $100 if he beats up Carl. Jack cannot collect.

4. Contracts contrary to public order and good morals (Article 1062), e.g., John agrees to pay Mary ten dollars a week if she does not marry.

5. Objects which are impossible, e.g., John sells land on Mars to Jack.

Art. 1060   An obligation must have for its object something determinate at least as to its kind.

The quantity of the thing may be uncertain, provided it be capable of being ascertained.

The object must be determinate as to kind: I sell your next year's potato crop. The contract is determinate as to kind but the quantity and quality are uncertain. However, they will be ascertained next year.

Art. 1061   Future things may be the object of an obligation.

John undertakes in a contract to sell to Wilson the next TV cabinet he makes at his workshop.

CAUSE OR CONSIDERATION

Art. 989   A contract without a consideration, or with an unlawful consideration has no effect; but it is not the less valid though the consideration be not expressed or be incorrectly expressed in the writing which is evidence of the contract.

Art. 990   The consideration is unlawful when it is prohibited by law, or is contrary to good morals or public order.

Art. 13   No one can by private agreement, validly contravene the laws of public order and good morals.

Valuable Cause or Consideration

Cause (or consideration) is the reason or the purpose for which the parties contracted, and the obligation of one party is the cause of the other party. For example, I sell you my auto for $1,000. Your consideration for entering into the contract is to become owner of the auto, and my obligation is to transfer ownership and deliver the auto. My consideration is to obtain $1,000 from you and your obligation is to pay the $1,000. To sum up, my consideration is the price; your cause is to obtain ownership of the auto.

In a contract of loan of money, the consideration for the lender is the payment by the borrower of interest. The obligation of the borrower is the repayment of the sum of money loaned. Because there is a material or monetary object in these examples, the cause is *valuable*. [2]

---

2. Quebec law also recognises certain natural or moral obligations, a discussion of which is outside the scope of this text.

THE EXTENT OF
CONTRACTS

Between the Parties

Contracts have effect only between the contracting parties and cannot effect or bind third persons who were not parties to the contract. A person cannot, by a contract in his own name, bind anyone but himself, his heirs and legal representative (Article 1028). He can however stipulate for the benefit of a third person (Article 1029) without the third person being a party to the contract. For example, a life insurance policy is a contract between the assured and an insurance company to pay a third person, e.g., his wife.

Rights of Creditors

A creditor who is not a party to the contract can intervene and exercise the rights of his debtor when the latter prejudicially refuses or neglects to do so. Furthermore, a creditor may have contracts made between his debtor and a third person cancelled if the creditor is being defrauded as a result of them. This is called a *Paulienne Action* and originates from Roman law.

> *Tom is a creditor of John. John transfers his assets to his brother thereby defrauding Tom of his recourses to collect his debt. Tom may take action to cancel the transfer of property.*

Assignment

Assignment of a contract occurs when a contract has been transferred or sold to a third person who steps into the shoes of the assignor. A third person may obtain rights under an assigned contract and/or be liable thereunder.

> *John owns an apartment building and has rented apartments to twenty-five people. He sells the*

building to Tom and also assigns his interests in all the leases. Tom now is the landlord and has the right to collect the rent, and the tenants are liable to Tom for the payment of the rent, once they are notified of the assignment.

REMEDIES FOR BREACH OF CONTRACT

Recourses for breach of contract fall into several main classes of remedies. The aggrieved may sue for:
1. cancellation
2. damages
3. specific performance
4. injunction.

Cancellation

When one party breaches the contract, the other party who is not in default in performing his own obligations may by legal means cancel the contract, without prejudice to his rights to claim damages also, for example, a landlord may cancel the lease when his tenant fails to pay the rent.

Damages

An innocent party may always sue the other party who has breached the contract for damages. Damages are a monetary condemnation to compensate the injured party for financial losses that he is able to prove to the court were directly attributable to the breach of contract.

A purchaser of goods who is obliged to buy goods elsewhere at a higher price, when the vendor neglects to deliver, may recover the difference in cost.

The term *liquidated damages* means that the parties have prescribed the amount payable in the event of a breach of contract.

Specific Performance

Generally, when there is a breach of contract the court will only award damages. In some cases, the court may order the defendant to actually perform the obligation undertaken in the contract, e.g., specific performance would be granted where the defendant sold a piece of land to the plaintiff but refused to sign the notarial deed. The court would order the defendant to either sign the deed or the judgment of the court would itself constitute the deed.

Injunction[3]

An order restraining the defendant from doing something contrary to an undertaking in a contract, is called an injunction.

> *John agreed in his written employment contract with his employer Tom not to work for a period of two months with a competitor of Tom's after he left Tom's employ. Immediately after leaving Tom, John got a job with Jack, a competitor. Injunction could be sought against John.*

DISCHARGE OF CONTRACT

A contract may be discharged (terminated) ending all its obligations as follows.

By Agreement

A person cannot unilaterally terminate a contract, but both parties that made the contract may mutually agree to cancel it, and release each other from further obligation. The parties may also make a new contract cancelling the first contract.

---

3. See chapter 3 on "Procedure in a Civil Action."

By Performance

The contract is discharged if all the terms are fulfilled by each party. For example, a loan is discharged when full payment is made.

By Breach

A contract may be cancelled if one of the parties fails to perform his obligation under the contract. However, when performance of an obligation has become impossible, without any act or fault of the debtor and before he is in default, the obligation is extinguished and both parties are liberated (Article 1202).

In various contracts to be discussed, we shall examine what recourses a party has if the other does not fulfil his obligations, e.g., when
the tenant refuses to pay the rent;
the vendor neglects to deliver the goods;
the agent fails to execute his mandate.

By Prescription

After a certain lapse of time a contract may be unenforceable. Generally speaking, if a person has rights to enforce under a contract he must do so within thirty years; actions on commercial contracts and upon cheques and other negotiable instruments must be taken within five years.

SIGNING A CONTRACT

Once a contract is made, the parties are bound. It is therefore wise to exercise a certain degree of caution *before* signing.
1. You should thoroughly examine the object you are about to purchase and compare it with others available on the market.
2. Whenever possible, verify the reputation and trustworthiness of the other party. If the other party is dishonest or insolvent, you are looking for trouble if you deal with him.

3. In signing an important contract, consult a lawyer. If you are hesitant about his fees, ask him in advance what his total fees will be. Often a lawyer will save you much more money than the cost of his fees. This might be your first important contract; the lawyer has advised many on similar contracts.

4. Read the contract. Once it is signed you are bound. You are responsible for all of the clauses of the contract, even the ones in fine print or the so-called "standard clauses." If you do not understand a clause, do not sign until you are fully satisfied as to its meaning. If you do not like a particular clause, negotiate to change it.

5. The written contract contains all of the agreements between the parties. Verbal representations cannot contradict or vary the terms. Fill in all the missing blanks in a printed form.

6. Add clauses to protect yourself against uncertain future events such as escape clauses so you will not be liable in the event of strikes, or events beyond your control, or add liquidated damage provisions in the event of nonperformance of the other party.

7. Keep a copy of the contract!

INTERPRETING A CONTRACT

Despite all of this good advice, many persons sign contracts with clauses which are not clear as to their meaning. The role of the courts is often to interpret the intention of the parties and to make the contract effective.

Certain rules of interpretation are set forth in the Code:

Art. 1013   When the meaning of the parties in a contract is doubtful, their common intention must be determined by interpretation rather than by an adherence to the literal meaning of the words of the contract.

Art. 1014   When a clause is susceptible of two meanings, it must be understood in that in which it may have some effect rather than in that in which it can produce none.

Art. 1015   Expressions susceptible of two meanings must be taken in the sense which agrees best with the matter of the contract.

Art. 1016   Whatever is doubtful must be determined according to the use of the country where the contract is made.

Art. 1017   The customary clauses must be supplied in contracts, although they be not expressed.

Art. 1018   All the clauses of a contract are interpreted the one by the other, giving to each the meaning derived from the entire act.

Art. 1019   In cases of doubt, the contract is interpreted against him who has stipulated and in favour of him who has contracted the obligation.

Art. 1020   However general the terms may be in which a contract is expressed, they extend only to the things concerning which it appears that the parties intended to contract.

Art. 1021   When the parties in order to avoid a doubt whether a particular case comes within the scope of a contract, have made special provision for such case, the general terms of the contract are not on this account restricted to the single case specified.

CONTRACTS IN GENERAL AND CONSUMER SALES[4]

This chapter has discussed the general rules applicable to contracts. However, under the Consumer Protection Act, which deals with sales between merchants and consumers, certain sections derogate from the general rules normally applicable to contracts.

1. *Making Contracts*

Contracts in general: consent alone completes the contract; there is a "meeting of minds."

Consumer sales:

a. The contract must be in writing and in duplicate.

b. The merchants must first sign the writing duly filled out and give it to the consumer and grant him sufficient delay to understand its terms.

c. The contract is entered into when all the parties have signed it.

d. The contract is executory (enforceable) only when each party possesses a duplicate of such writing.

2. *Contents of the Contract*

Contracts in general: the parties may agree to any provisions not against public order and good morals or specifically provided otherwise by law.

Consumer sales: the parties are *obliged* to set forth details of the cost, cost of credit, terms of payment, etc.

3. *Evidence*

Contracts in general: verbal evidence may not contradict or vary the terms of a contract.

Consumer sales: the consumer may make proof by testimony, even to contradict or vary the terms of a writing, when the Act has not been complied with.

4. *Lesion*

Contracts in general: only minors and interdicts can plead lesion.

---

4. See also chapter 21 on "Consumer Protection."

Consumer sales: every consumer whose inexperience has been exploited by a merchant may demand the nullity of the contract or a reduction in his obligations if they are greatly disproportionate to those of the merchant.

5. *Penalties*

Contracts in general: if one of the parties breaches a contract, the other party may sue in cancellation and damages. There is no governmental supervision or fines.

Consumer sales: if the merchant violates the Consumer Protection Act, he is liable to fines up to $25,000 and imprisonment. The Act is supervised by the Consumer Protection Bureau.

Legal Terminology

public order and good
   morals
contracts
quasi contracts
unilateral obligations
bilateral obligations
contracts of adhesion
meeting of minds
offeror
offeree
offer
counter offer
option
invitation
written contracts
contracts by
   correspondence
agent
acceptance
acceptor
invalid contracts
null and void contracts
to annul
voidable contracts

to cancel
unenforceable contracts
illegal contracts
requisites
capacity
incapacity
minors
unemancipated minors
lesion
unforeseen event
offences
quasi offences
ratification
tutor
curator
emancipated minors
interdicts
prodigal
error
fraud
violence or fear
object
obligation
cause or consideration

valuable cause
Paulienne Action
assignment
breach of contract
cancellation
damages
liquidated damages

specific performance
injunction
discharge
agreement
performance
prescription
interpretation
consumer sales

Questions

1. What is the importance of contracts in business?
2. What agreements may be contained in contracts?
3. What is meant by a quasi contract?
4. Outline two exceptions to the rule of freedom of contracting.
5. What is the meaning of "meeting of minds"?
6. Discuss the formation of a contract by offer and acceptance.
7. Why is it advisable that contracts be written?
8. Discuss how a contract is made by correspondence through the mails.
9. Distinguish between annulling and cancelling a contract.
10. What are the four requisites to the validity of a contract?
11. What persons are capable and what persons are incapable of contracting?
12. What is an unemancipated minor and what is an emancipated minor?
13. Explain lesion.
14. When can a minor not plead lesion?
15. What persons can be interdicted?
16. What persons are unable to contract because of their relationship to each other?
17. What is meant by temporary derangement of the intellect concerning contracts?
18. What is meant by error?
19. What is the meaning of fraud?
20. What are threat of violence and fear as they apply to contracts?

21. What is the effect of setting aside a contract on the ground of fraud?

22. What is a legal obligation?

23. What characteristics must the object of the contract have?

24. What is meant by cause or consideration?

25. What is the effect of the contract between the parties and third persons?

26. What is meant by assignment?

27. Outline the remedies for breach of contract.

28. List the ways a contract may be discharged.

29. What should you be careful of when you sign a contract?

30. How does the Consumer Protection Act differ from the rules of contracts in general?

MANDATE

Chapter 10

MANDATE

You are rebuilding the back porch of your home. You instruct John to go to the local hardware store for some lumber and nails, and you tell him to charge the cost to your charge account. At the store, John advises the store clerk that he is buying the merchandise for you and that the price is to be charged to you. This is done. Suppose you later refuse to pay, can the store collect from you? Is John liable for payment? What is the legal relationship between you and John? If John had not advised the store clerk he was buying for you, would John then be liable to pay? If you discovered that the wood was rotten, could you claim against the store clerk?

This problem and its solutions are based upon the law governing the contract of mandate, or as it is often called, the contract of agency.

Our daily lives are becoming increasingly complex and we require the help of others to look after our personal needs as well as the needs of our business. We must delegate work to others. This brings risks because others are doing work for us and we may be responsible for their acts.

AGENTS AND EMPLOYEES

To keep your home in shape, you may hire employees on a part-time basis, such as a gardener, handyman, painter and a cleaning woman, who act under your directions and control. Do they negotiate for you and enter into contracts with other persons on your behalf, making themselves your agents? No. They are not agents. They are employees only.

You appoint lawyer Williams to sue your neighbour Jones for damages caused to your home when his son Willie hurled a rock through the front window. The lawyer is not your employee since he does not work under your direct control and authority, rather, he is your agent—a special kind of agent often called an *attorney*. He is acting with considerable latitude on your behalf in relation to Jones and his proceedings bind you.

Each time you appoint an agent you enter into a contract of mandate with him. There are two parties to this contract: you, as the principal, and the agent.

Applying the above principles to the following example let us determine who are employees only, who are employees as well as agents and who are agents only.

You start a small grocery store. You hire a delivery boy, John, to deliver the groceries to your customers' homes. You hire a butcher, a salesman, a cashier and a bookkeeper. You also obtain insurance from an insurance broker and legal advice from a lawyer. John proves to be so competent that you often leave the store to his entire management. He is then taking your place and is dealing with customers and others in your name.

When John is out delivering groceries or sweeping up the store, he is an employee only. He is not negotiating with third persons.

John uses your delivery truck to make deliveries. As such he is your employee. He takes the truck to a garage for repairs and in so doing, he is acting also as your agent. However, when he acts as manager he functions as both your employee, that is, he is under your direction and control, and he is also your agent. He represents you in relation to third persons and exercises his discretion with a certain latitude. An employee, pure and simple, just does what he is ordered to do and does not deal on your behalf with third persons.

What distinguishes the agent from the employee is the

function being performed. The same person may at one time be an employee and another time an employee as well as an agent.

DEFINITION OF
MANDATE

Mandate is the Quebec term for *agency*. It is a contract by which one person called the mandator (principal) appoints another person called a mandatary (agent) to act for and on his behalf. It is the quality of *representation* that distinguishes mandate from all other contracts.

The definition of mandate is contained in Article 1701:

> Art. 1701   Mandate is a contract by which a person called the mandator commits a lawful business to the management of another, called the mandatary, who by his acceptance obliges himself to perform it.
>
> The acceptance may be implied from the acts of the mandatary and in some cases from his silence.

There are three parties involved in this relationship. Going back to the example on page 127:
1. You are the mandator (principal).
2. John is the mandatary (agent).
3. The hardware store is the third party.

In practice, the words principal and agent are used rather than mandator and mandatary. The contract itself is called a contract of mandate or a contract of agency.

The words of the Code, "commits a lawful business to the management of another," refer to all situations in which the principal delegates authority to the agent—from appointing a manager to run your store to sending John to buy wood.

All organizations including commercial, industrial, government, charitable, and even "one man" business operations must rely on this mandate contract to operate effectively.

The shareholders of the business corporation annually elect a board of directors to manage the business affairs of the company and this board delegates specific wide agency powers to top ranking employees called officers. For example, whoever is appointed vice-president, sales, will usually have the authority to sell the company's manufactured goods, and to hire and fire sales personnel.

You decide to take John into partnership in your grocery store. The law presumes that each partner has authorised the other partner to act as agent of the partnership. Thus both you and John can make contracts which bind both of you (see chapter 15 on "Business Organizations").

The last paragraph of Article 1701 means this: You tell John to go purchase the wood. He says nothing but he does follow your instructions. By his conduct, he has agreed to enter into the contract of mandate with you.

Capacity

The agent represents the principal. So long as the principal is legally capable of contracting then he can appoint anyone to act as his agent. Since the agent becomes clothed with the capacity of his principal, it does not matter if the agent himself is incapable of contracting; for example, an agent can be a minor. When the agent acts, he puts into motion the legal personality and capacity of the principal and thereby contractually binds the principal with the third party.

The agent who is himself an incapable may at his option claim that his contract of agency with the principal is voidable because, he, as a party to the agency contract, is incapable of contracting.

Representation

You go shopping at a department store where you deal with Ross, the salesman. While it might seem that he is playing an active role and that the store is in a passive position, in actual fact, it is the store you are dealing with through its agent Ross. Although his charm and salesmanship are important reasons why you agree to buy, this does not alter the fact that you are contracting, not with Ross, but with the store. If you later have a complaint about the merchandise, you go back to Ross, who may say, "I'm sorry, I'm only a salesman here and I don't deal with complaints. Please see the complaint department."

The principal delegates to the agent authority to act in a specific instance or, more broadly, in a specific area of activity. So long as the agent acts within the limits of his delegated authority, he is not personally liable.

If he goes beyond his representative powers, then he may be held personally liable for his unauthorised acts.

> *Jones is general purchasing agent for a large department store and as such he is authorised to purchase clothing from suppliers. The store is liable for all these purchases. But, if Jones suddenly tried to sell store fixtures to Lamb, this would clearly be beyond his authority and the store would not be contractually bound to Lamb. However, Lamb has a claim in damages against Jones because he exceeded his authority, thus making himself personally liable for such acts.*

SOME TYPES OF AGENTS

There are various types of agents. Some are full-time employees working for one employer who instructs them to carry out specific agency functions, e.g., travelling salesmen. This type of agent is called a *special agent.*

A *general agent* is one who is employed to carry on the administration of a business for a principal. He is authorised to perform any administrative act necessary to operate the business including buying and selling stock, hiring and firing staff, signing cheques and making bank deposits.

When transactions are unusual and out of the ordinary, the principal must provide the agent, even a general agent, with specific written authority.

> *Smith Corporation wants to purchase a building for $150,000 from Jones. Its board of directors specially authorises one of its officers, Wilson, to sign the contract of purchase. Unless Jones sees this written authorisation, he will not be certain whether Wilson is empowered to act.*

The agent Wilson should insist on being authorised in writing in order to protect himself against the possibility that his company might later deny that he was given authority to sign the contract. In that event Jones might try to claim damages against Wilson.

A *power of attorney* is a written document signed by the principal empowering the agent with specific powers.

> *John is in the hospital and during his period of hospitalization, he delegates to his wife, Alice, wide powers of administration over his property including the right to collect rents, sign cheques against his bank accounts, deposit moneys into the bank.*

THE INDEPENDENT CONTRACTOR

You own and operate a restaurant. You make a contract with Jack, a building contractor, to build an extension onto your restaurant for $50,000, in accordance with your specifications. Is Jack your employee or agent? Neither. He is an independent contractor who directs his own building operations and only he decides how and by whom the work is to be done. He must fulfil the contract within the delay agreed upon.

FORMATION OF THE CONTRACT OF MANDATE

A contract of mandate does not have to be expressed in writing, and if it is, it does not have to be in any particular form. Mandate is subject to the general rules of contract (see chapter 9 on "Contracts in General"). The contract may be implied by the acts of the agent and in some cases even from his silence.

Most contracts of agency are oral. For example, few people working in middle management positions, such as production managers, sales managers, marketing managers, etc., have written contracts. They are paid monthly or bi-monthly by cheque. They are advised of their duties by their "boss." Their superiors rarely set down in writing the detailed specifics of the job. Sometimes the job title, such as vice-president, sales, indicates the degree of authority but not necessarily. For example, the powers of a comptroller vary greatly from one company to another.

> *Rogers, personnel manager of Smith Consultants, advises you by phone that you have been hired as assistant manager, credit department, and that you start work tomorrow. You say nothing about your accepting the job but you go to work. Your acceptance of the contract is implied by your conduct.*

Obligations of the Parties

Let's look back at the example on page 127. What are the obligations of:
1. the principal (you) toward the agent (John)?
2. the agent (John) toward the principal (you)?
3. the agent (John) toward third parties (the hardware store)?
4. the principal (you) toward third parties (the hardware store)?

Obligations of the Principal
to the Agent

Art. 1702   Mandate is gratuitous unless there is an agreement or established usage to the contrary.

The law considers that the undertaking of a mandate by an agent is one of friendship and therefore is free and gratuitous. Unless you and John decide otherwise, John is not entitled to be paid for getting the lumber for you.

You ask Andy, who operates a garage, to sell your car on your behalf. Andy sells it to Bill for $500. Is Andy entitled to claim a commission from you?

In this case, since there was no agreement as to commission, Andy would not be entitled to a commission. However, he is entitled to a reimbursement of actual expenses, e.g., the cost of gas he put in your car so that Bill could take a test drive.

However, members of certain professions are legally entitled to claim agents' fees or commissions from their principals even though there was no prior agreement covering their remuneration. Lawyers who collect money, stockbrokers who sell shares, real estate agents who handle property sales, have recognised tariffs they are entitled to charge their clients for work done.

For example, a lawyer is entitled to charge his client a collection fee of 15 percent upon collection of $500 from a debtor.

Usually an agent is entitled to claim commission only if he was instrumental in bringing about a contract between the principal, whom he represents, and the third party. If the agent does nothing to bring about the sale, he is not entitled to a commission, salary or remuneration. However, if he is appointed as an exclusive agent, he is entitled to the agreed commission even though he did nothing to complete the contract. The most usual example of the exclusive agent is the real estate agent.[1]

On May 1, you place your home for sale with Jones Realty Company under an exclusive listing, for a

1. In a real estate transaction an agent is not entitled to a commission unless he is a registered, licensed broker or salesman, under the Real Estate Brokerage Act.

three-month period. On May 24, Bob purchases your home directly from you, that is, not through the real estate agent. The real estate agent is entitled to a commission even though he did not introduce you to Bob.

Agents' Expenses

The agent is entitled to receive from the principal all expenses incurred in carrying out the mandate as well as all salary and commissions due him.

If, through no fault of his own, the agent is unable to accomplish the task he is given, he is still entitled to his expenses. He may deduct them, as well as his remuneration, from the moneys he receives from third parties. If the agent's calculations do not agree with the principal's and if he deducts too much, the principal may sue the agent for an accounting. Likewise, an agent is entitled to retain objects belonging to his principal until he obtains payment of what is due to him.

Obligations of the Agent to the Principal

1. To carry out the mandate with diligence and not to exceed the limits of his authority.
2. To account to the principal for all money and other property received.

Carrying Out the Mandate

The purpose of the contract of mandate is the entrusting by the principal to the agent of a task or tasks to be performed by the agent which he must perform diligently, and honestly, with "reasonable skill and prudence," and he is liable for damages if he acts negligently.

> Art. 1710   The mandatary is bound to exercise, in the execution of the mandate, reasonable skill and all the care of a prudent administrator.

Nevertheless, if the mandate be gratuitous, the court may moderate the rigor of the liability arising from his negligence or fault, according to the circumstances.

Although the agent must use reasonable skill and prudence, if he is not paid for his work and, through his imprudence, the principal suffers damages, the court may lessen the amount of his financial liability since he was acting gratuitously.

The "Double Agent"

An agent owes his principal devotion and loyalty, that is, he must not serve two masters who have conflicting interests.

> *John appoints Adam as his agent to sell his house. Bill is looking for a house to buy and he appoints Adam as his agent to locate a suitable house. Adam directs him to John's house, which Bill buys. Adam never advised either Bill or John that he was acting for both.*

Adam is secretly acting for two principals who have conflicting interests, that is, one wants to get the highest price and the other wants to pay the lowest price. He has an obligation to inform both of them of his double mandate.

> *A court judgment has held that, "It is now well established that while the acceptance of a double mandate by a real estate agent is not* per se *immoral or illegal it will be so regarded in the absence of it having been established that the agent's duties were discharged with perfect honesty after full and complete disclosure to the principal and that there has been no sacrifice of the latter's interests."*

Consequently, the agent's claim for commission was dismissed.

To Account for Moneys

The agent is obliged to account for all moneys received by him, even if they were not due.

The "Kickback"

Barnett is employed as senior purchasing agent for Smith's Department Store. He reports directly to Johnson, Vice-President, Purchasing, and he regularly buys merchandise from Jones Manufacturing. Every few months Jones gives Barnett gifts of money, sometimes up to $250 cash, and Barnett accepts this money and does not tell Johnson.

Is Barnett legally obliged as agent to disclose to his principal the fact that he is receiving these gifts? An agent must not receive any personal benefits from the third party since he owes complete loyalty to his principal. He should have refused to accept these moneys. If, however, he did take them he should have revealed the existence of these gifts and all moneys received should be given to his employer. Why? His company pays for the cost of any gifts Barnett receives, since one presumes that the cost to the supplier of such gifts is included by the supplier in the price of the merchandise charged to the store. By the giving and accepting of these moneys, both Barnett and Jones may be parties to the commission of the criminal offences of corruption and bribery.

Obligations of the Agent towards Third Parties

Art. 1715   The mandatary acting in the name of the mandator and within the bounds of the mandate is not personally liable to third persons with whom he contracts.

The agent, acting for and on behalf of his principal and within the limits of his authority, is not personally liable to third parties.

Art. 1716   A mandatary who acts in his own name is liable to the third party with whom he contracts, without prejudice to the rights of the latter against the mandator also.

Where an agent deals in his own name with the third party and does not disclose he is acting as an agent:
a. the agent is personally liable to the third party;
b. the third party retains his rights to proceed against the undisclosed principal;
c. the undisclosed principal has no rights under the contract between the agent and the third party.

The undisclosed principal who suffers injury may have a claim against his agent. Thus it is important for the agent to advise the third party that he is acting as agent, otherwise the agent will be personally liable to the third party. Very often the situation itself clearly indicates to the third party that he is dealing with an agent even though the agent does not say so.

> *You shop at a large department store. It is obvious that Ross who is selling you the merchandise is a salesman acting on behalf of the store. He is not personally liable if the merchandise later turns out to be defective. You claim against the store.*

Turn back now to the example on page 127 and try to answer the various questions raised.

Rights of the Undisclosed Principal to Sue

> *Smith, representing himself as lessor, made a contract to lease with a tenant, Jones. The house is actually owned by Mrs. Smith and it is she who is in fact the lessor. Jones did not pay the rent and Mrs. Smith sued him. In his defence the tenant claimed that the wrong party was suing him, that he had always considered Smith as landlord.*

*The court held that the undisclosed principal (Mrs.
Smith) does not have the right to sue a third party
who has entered into a contract with her agent Smith.
Mrs. Smith had no dealings with Jones. All matters in
connection with the lease including the negotiations
were handled by her husband who had a verbal mandate to manage her property. Mrs. Smith's action for
rent was consequently dismissed.*

Agent Exceeding Mandate

Since mandate is a contract of representation for a specific
purpose, an agent who exceeds the bounds of his authority is
personally liable to third persons.

> Art. 1718   He is not held to have exceeded his
> powers when he executes the mandate in a manner
> more advantageous to the mandator than that speci-
> fied by the latter.

The agent is not held to have exceeded his powers
when he executes the mandate in a way which is more ad-
vantageous to his principal. For example, the principal instructs his agent to buy 1,000 TV sets for $125 each. He
buys them for $95 each.

Agent's Signature

When an agent signs a contract he should clearly indicate his
agency position. For example, the end of the contract should
read something to the following effect, "John Smith, agent,
acting only for and on behalf of his principal, William
Brown."

Obligations of the Principal towards Third Persons

The principal is liable for all acts of his agent which
a. are done in the execution and within the scope of the
mandate;

b. exceed the agent's powers, but which the principal has approved either expressly or tacitly;
c. are done with ostensible authority.

> Art. 1730   The mandator is liable to third parties who in good faith contract with a person not his mandatary, under the belief that he is so, when the mandator has given reasonable cause for such belief.

> *Smith is employed as general manager of a used car lot owned by Brown. Smith, in Brown's name, bought William's car. Brown tried to set aside the purchase, claiming that Smith had no authority to buy and that only he, Brown, had that right. But to Williams it had always appeared that Smith had the apparent, ostensible authority to transact with him, for after all, Smith was the general manager. Since William's belief was a reasonable one, Brown would be bound by Smith's act.*

Furthermore, the principal is bound toward third parties for all damages caused by the acts of fault of the agent arising out of the performance of his work, (see chapter 8 on "Civil Responsibility").

> *Jones is employed as a travelling salesman working for Smith Steel Co. While driving his own car on company business, he hits a parked auto. The accident is entirely his fault. Since Jones was on "company business" in the performance of the work for which he was employed, on his way to visit a customer, his employer is liable.*

TERMINATION OF MANDATE

Art. 1755   Mandate terminates:
1. By revocation;
2. By the renunciation of the mandatary;

3. By the natural death of the mandator or mandatary;

4. By interdiction, bankruptcy, or other change in the condition of either party by which his civil capacity is affected;

5. By the cessation of authority in the mandator;

6. By the accomplishment of the business or the expiration of the time for which the mandate is given;

7. By other causes of extinction common to obligations.

Revocation and Renunciation

Generally the principal may always cancel a mandate. An agent may always refuse or renounce a mandate. Cancellation may injure one of the parties and may give rise to an action in damages, especially if cancellation was unforeseen and unwarranted.

> *Jones Imports is the exclusive agent for Jacques Haute Couture, a French high fashion dress manufacturing company. Without warning or justification just before the spring season delivery, Jones notifies Jacques that he refuses to act as agent. Jacques is unable to find another satisfactory outlet to carry this year's dress line and he suffers severe financial loss. Jacques can successfully claim damages from Jones.*

Death and Interdiction

Since mandate is one of personal representation, it is only natural that death of either principal or agent, terminates the contract. Likewise, the same observations apply in the event of interdiction and change of civil capacity.

Accomplishment of the Business

If a mandate is for a specific time period or a certain job, the mandate will end either at the end of that period or when the work is accomplished. For example, Jones is hired to act as salesman until December 31. The contract ends on that date.

Contracts in General

The contract of mandate may be terminated by other causes of extinction common to obligations and contracts in general (see chapters 7 and 9 on obligations and contracts).

Legal Terminology

mandate

agency

employee

mandator

mandatary

principal

agent

special agent

general agent

power of attorney

independent contractor

gratuitous mandate

commission

reimbursement

remuneration

stockbrokers

exclusive agent

prudent administrator

account

undisclosed principal

ostensible authority

Questions

1. What is meant by representation?
2. Who are the various parties involved in mandate and describe their relationship to each other.
3. What is the difference between an agent, an independent contractor and an employee?
4. Name several types of agents.
5. What are the duties of an agent who is a principal?
6. What are the duties of the principal to third parties?
7. What is meant by ostensible authority?
8. What is meant by the undisclosed principal?
9. When may an agent be held liable to third parties?
10. When an agent deals with third parties, what must he do in order not to be personally liable?

SALE

Chapter 11

SALE

The contract of sale is one you make frequently—every time you buy something. Consider how many sales contracts you have made during this past week. What are the special rules governing the contract of sale?

Sale is a contract by which one party, (*vendor* or *seller*) transfers the ownership of a thing to another party (*purchaser* or *buyer*) for a price in money, which the latter obliges himself to pay. This contract is perfected (made effective, entered into) by the consent of the parties, even if the thing sold is not delivered immediately by the seller to the buyer.

RULES GOVERNING SALE

Sale has its own special rules but it is also governed by the general rules of contracts (see chapter 9 on "Contracts in General").

> Art. 1473   The contract of sale is subject to the general rules relating to contracts and to the effects and extinction of obligations declared in the title of obligations, unless it is otherwise specifically provided in this code.

TRANSFER OF OWNERSHIP AND RISK

Unless it is otherwise stipulated in the contract, the ownership of a certain specific thing, such as a machine or an automobile, is transferred by the consent of the parties alone, even before the object is delivered or even before payment.

On May 3, John visits White's TV Store and White sells him a specific Wabash TV set, serial No. 13760. White agrees to deliver the TV to John's house on May 5th and John is to pay the price of $125 on delivery. On the evening of May 4th, two armed robbers break into the closed store, overpower the two guards and steal this TV set. Who was the owner of the TV set when it was stolen? John. Who bears the loss? John. Can White claim the $125 from John? Yes.

The answers to these questions are all based on the fundamental principle: Once there is agreement to sell and to buy, *ownership* passes to the buyer. Once the buyer is owner, he is responsible for the risk of loss or damage to the article he purchased. The only obligation of the seller before making delivery is to act as a "prudent administrator" in safeguarding it. As White was a prudent administrator by having guards and locking the store, he is relieved from the obligation of delivering. John is nevertheless obliged to pay the price.

Goods Not Identified

If the TV set were not specifically identified at the making of the contract, but rather only any TV of a certain model, then ownership would not be transferred until a specific TV had been selected and identified as being John's, and John had been legally notified of this fact.

Things Sold by Weight

Art. 1474 When things moveable are sold by weight, number or measure, and not in the lump, the sale is not perfect until they have been weighed, counted or measured; but the buyer may demand the delivery of them or damages according to circumstances.

At the market, Jones says to the farmer's daughter, "I'll buy ten pounds of those apples." She says nothing and begins to place apples onto the scale. The sale is perfected only after she has weighed out ten pounds of apples, and not before.

OTHER TYPES OF
SALES AGREEMENTS

Clause Reserving Ownership
(Conditional Sale)

Frequently it is stipulated in a contract that although the seller gives possession of the goods to the buyer, the seller retains ownership of the goods until full and final payment for them has been made by the buyer. Such a sale is often made through a conditional sales contract or an instalment sales contract.

Black operates a machine shop and purchases a metal working lathe from Brown Machine Tool Co. By the contract of sale, Brown Machine Tool Co. retains ownership until final payment of the purchase price is made. Black pays $200 cash and agrees to pay the balance in twelve equal monthly instalments including interest. Ownership does not pass from Brown Machine Tool Co. to Black until Black has paid in full and if Black fails to pay, Brown Machine Tool Co. can repossess the lathe, as owner.

What about the money Black paid on account? Brown Machine Tool Co. keeps this money as an indemnity or as rent, pursuant to the terms of the contract.

Is Brown Machine Tool Co. obliged to take back the lathe if Black does not pay? No. Instead, Brown Machine Tool Co. can sue for the balance Black owes the company.

This is the general situation that applies to the sale of moveables such as automobiles, snowmobiles, motor boats,

TV's, stereo sets and furniture sold on credit, on time, at so much a week or a month or on the instalment plan.

Consignment

Businessmen often sell goods to other businessmen on *consignment*. The parties are called *consignor* and *consignee*.

> *Smith has the exclusive Canadian distribution rights for a new type of expensive foreign camera. In order to get Rex Camera shop interested in selling this item, he agrees to deliver ten cameras "on consignment." Smith delivers the goods to Rex Camera on the understanding that the goods will remain the property of Smith until Rex Camera is about to sell the goods, at which time ownership of the goods will transfer to Rex who then, as owner, is able to sell them to his customer. It is a normal requirement in such an agreement that Rex Camera will hold in trust for Smith the price to be paid by Rex out of the proceeds of his sale to his customer. Upon selling each camera, Rex remits to Smith the price fixed in the consignment contract and keeps the "mark up" as his profit. Any cameras that remain unsold are returned to Smith.*

This arrangement is also used when the consignor is concerned about the consignee's solvency. If the latter gets into financial difficulty the consignor can always take back the goods left on consignment since he remains owner until they are sold to a third party.

Sale on Trial, Sale on Approval

In a *sale on trial*, or as it is often called, *sale on approval*, ownership does not pass until either notice of acceptance is given by the buyer to the seller, or unless the buyer retains the goods beyond a fixed or reasonable time.

> *George agrees to buy a set of valuable postage stamps from Jones for $100, on the condition that he be allowed to examine them at his house for seven days. Jones remains owner during this seven-day period. If George keeps the stamps longer than this period, and depending upon the wording of the contract, he may be considered to have accepted them and title passes to him.*
>
> *If the stamps are stolen from George's house, the loss falls on Jones if the theft occurred during the seven-day period; on George if after that period.*

F.O.B.

F.O.B. is a term often seen in sales contracts. It means literally "free on board." Unless otherwise specified by use of this term, the seller pays all the charges and expenses to put the goods on board the named carrier, e.g., C.N.R. railway station at the shipping point. The goods are then transported at the buyer's risk and the buyer pays the freight. Delivery by the seller to the buyer's carrier is delivery to the buyer, the carrier being the agent of the buyer. The buyer should make certain that the goods are insured against loss once they have arrived at the named carrier.

> *In a contract of sale between Rogers Knitting Mills and Smith Textiles Company, yarn goods are to be shipped to Vancouver "F.O.B. Windsor Station, Montreal." The obligation of the seller is to deliver the goods to the carrier, namely, CP Rail, Montreal. However, after they are put on board the train, the transportation costs and risk of loss or damage are borne by the purchaser.*

C.I.F.

This term means "cost, insurance, freight"; the seller is

obliged to deliver the goods to the named destination and the sale price includes the cost of transport and insurance.

THE OBLIGATIONS OF THE SELLER

Art. 1491 The principal obligations of the seller are: (1) The delivery and (2) the warranty of the thing sold.

Seller's Obligations to Deliver

What is Delivery?

Art. 1492 Delivery is the transfer of the thing sold into the power and possession of the buyer.

1. Delivery is the transfer of the thing into the physical possession of the buyer.
2. Delivery does not necessarily mean transportation from one point to another point.
3. Delivery is effected when the seller puts the buyer in actual possession by transporting the thing or allowing the buyer to remove it.

Place of Delivery

Unless there is an agreement to the contrary, the place of delivery is generally where the thing sold is at the time of the sale. Therefore, the seller's obligation to deliver is satisfied by him advising the buyer "here is your thing, take it away." Depending on the written terms of the contract, it is usual for either the buyer to take away the goods physically or the seller to make delivery either by transporting to the buyer's premises or if F.O.B., to the carrier.

Expenses of Delivery

The expenses of the delivery are the charge of the seller, and those of removing the things are the charge of the buyer, unless it is otherwise stipulated (Article 1495).

Condition of Goods

Goods must be delivered in the condition in which they were at the time of the sale. However, if delivery becomes impossible through no fault of the seller, more especially as the consequence of an unforeseen event such as a fire or theft, then the seller is not obliged to deliver. But, the buyer of the clearly identified specific thing would be obligated to pay the price.

Time of Delivery

Unless otherwise stipulated, delivery and payment take place simultaneously, and are due at the same time (C.O.D.—cash on delivery). The buyer may refuse to accept late delivery by the seller and this may be a cause for cancellation of contract, if the delivery date is specifically stated therein. If the seller undertakes to deliver "within a reasonable delay" or "during the summer season" wide latitude is given him as to delivery date. But if the seller is to deliver "no later than June 3rd, 1972," the date is clearly fixed.

All sales are presumed to be for cash (C.O.D.). If the buyer does not pay the full price, the seller is not obliged to deliver. On the other hand, if the seller does not deliver, the buyer does not have to pay the price.

> *John goes into a jewellery shop and says, "I want to purchase that diamond ring. How much is it?" The salesman says, "One thousand dollars." "I'll buy it," says John. The salesman says, "Money please." John says, "I cannot pay it now." "No money, no delivery." Sale cancelled.*

Conversely, if the seller refuses or neglects to deliver, the buyer has an action in damages, being the difference between the contract price and the price he now has to pay for similar goods elsewhere.

> *William purchases a new automobile from Jones Auto, to be delivered within seven days for $3,600, payment to be made on delivery. Jones fails to deliver and William has to pay $3,800 to Rogers Auto for a similar model. William has an action in damages for $200 against Jones—that amount being the increase in price he was obliged to pay elsewhere, and based upon the seller's failure to deliver within the time specified.*

Failure to Deliver

The seller is not obliged to deliver if the buyer is unwilling to pay the price then and there unless the seller has granted terms or credit, in which case he is obliged to deliver even though payment is made later.

> *John goes to a jewellery store where he is a regular customer. He agrees to buy a $200 ring, and the store agrees to give him immediate delivery of the ring and grant him a delay of thirty days to pay.*

It is customary business practice to grant thirty days delay for payment after delivery has been made. Invoices often read "net thirty days." Sometimes a discount is given by the seller if payment is made earlier; for example, if payment is made within ten days after delivery, the purchaser may be entitled to a 2 percent discount on the sales price.

However, even if credit has been extended, the seller is not obliged to deliver if he has reasonable grounds to believe that the buyer has become insolvent since the date of the sale.

Smith gives Harry thirty days to pay after delivery is made. Before making delivery, Smith learns that Harry has many debts and one creditor recently made a seizure of his assets. Must Smith deliver to Harry, who, since the sale, has become insolvent and may not be able to pay? No.

In the event that the buyer, without any justification, refuses to accept delivery or attempts to cancel the sale, the seller can:
1. take an action to cancel the contract and claim damages;
2. sue the buyer for the sales price.

Warranty

You purchase a new TV set from Jones Appliances Co. A week later, the set stops functioning. What are your rights against Jones?

The seller not only has to deliver, he is also obliged by law to warrant or guarantee:
1. that the buyer will not be disturbed or evicted from ownership of the thing bought, that is, that the buyer is obtaining clear title and that the goods sold do not belong to a third party;
2. against latent defects in the thing.

Art. 1507   Legal warranty is implied by law in the contract of sale, without stipulation. Nevertheless, the parties may, by special agreement, add to the obligations of legal warranty or diminish its effects, or exclude it altogether.

The law regards the vendor's warranty as an implicit part of any contract of sale, inserted for the protection of buyers and based on the assumption that the seller knows more about the thing he is selling than the buyer. If nothing is mentioned in the contract about warranty, the parties have implied that legal warranty applies.

However, the parties may, by written conditions contained in the contract, change legal warranty by:
1. adding, modifying or replacing it;
2. diminishing it;
3. excluding it.

Conventional Warranties

A written warranty condition contained in a sales contract is called a *conventional warranty*. New automobiles are sold with conventional warranties, e.g., a "five-year power-train" warranty.

Legal Warranty against Eviction

The seller warrants the buyer against eviction or disturbance of his use or enjoyment by third parties claiming to have a right of ownership over the thing that the buyer bought.

By law the seller is obliged to warrant the buyer that the goods sold do not belong to a third party who claims to have a right of ownership over the thing bought. In other words, "clear title" is given by the seller to the buyer and a guarantee that no one will trouble or "evict" him from his ownership and enjoyment.

> *John buys a car from Smith Auto for $1,200 and pays Smith $100 per month; Smith Auto retains ownership until full payment is made. If John were to sell the car to Bill before full payment was made, he would be selling a car he did not own and Smith Auto might recover the car in Bill's hands. What recourses does Bill have against John?*

The answer to this example depends on whether Bill, at the time of the sale, knew or did not know that the car belonged to Smith Auto. If Bill knew, he recovers the price from John; if he did not know, he recovers the price, expenses and damages.

Legal Warranty against
Latent Defects

A seller is legally responsible for *latent* or hidden defects in the thing sold at the time of the sale.

> Art. 1522   The seller is obliged by law to warrant the buyer against such latent defects in the things sold, and its accessories, as render it unfit for the use for which it was intended, or so diminish its usefulness that the buyer would not have bought it, or would not have given so large a price, if he had known them.

> *On May 1, John buys a used car from Bill. There is no clause in the contract covering hidden defects and thus legal warranty applies. On May 2, the following defects appear: the car does not move in reverse, the block cracks, the brakes suddenly fail. Through an expert, John can prove that these latent (hidden) defects existed at the time of the sale, for which the seller is liable.*

The seller is not bound for defects which are *apparent*, or those which an experienced buyer could have discovered. Legal decisions generally hold that an inexperienced buyer, when buying used things, is obliged to have an inspection made by an expert before he buys, and if this expert could not discover the defects, they would be considered as latent and covered by the legal warranty.

What if the defects are apparent?

> Art. 1523   The seller is not bound for defects which are apparent and which the buyer might have known of himself.

John buys a used car which doesn't have sparkplugs, a radiator, a carburetor or a battery, and the car will not start. John has no recourse. The defects are apparent and are not covered by legal warranty.

The obligation of the inexperienced buyer to intelligently inspect the goods is derived from the Roman law maxim, *caveat emptor* (buyer beware).

The seller is responsible for latent defects even though they were not known to him. The law also considers the seller liable when he is "legally presumed to know the defects."

Smith Auto is actually not aware of the hidden defects in the auto it sells to Jones. Nevertheless as a regular dealer in automobiles, it is presumed to have knowledge of these defects and is obliged to repay the sales price plus all expenses and damages.

Art. 1524   The seller is bound for latent defects even when they were not known to him, unless it is stipulated that he shall not be obliged to any warranty.

Art. 1527   If the seller knew the defect of the thing, he is obliged not only to restore the price of it, but to pay all damages suffered by the buyer.

Art. 1528   If the seller did not know the defects, or is not legally presumed to have known them, he is obliged only to restore the price and to reimburse to the buyer the expenses caused by the sale.

BUYERS RECOURSES AGAINST SELLER

What are the rights of a buyer against the seller when there are latent defects?

> Art. 1526 The buyer has the option of returning the thing and recovering the price of it, or of keeping the thing and recovering a part of the price according to an estimation of its value.

Under both legal and conventional warranty, the buyer has two options. He can take either:

1. a *redhibitory action* in which he demands the setting aside of the sale due to latent defects and recovery of the price, expenses and damages; or,

2. a *Quanti Minoris action* in which he alleges the nature of the defect and that, had he known of the defect before he purchased, he would not have paid so high a price. Consequently, he claims the reduction of sales price by the amount of the cost of repair or replacement of the defect. In other words, the buyer wants to remain owner but he claims a reduction in the price.

> Art. 1530 The redhibitory action, resulting from the obligation of warranty against latent defects, must be brought with reasonable diligence, according to the nature of the defect and the usage of the place where the sale is made.

> *On May 1, after expert examination revealed no defects, John buys an old house. On June 1, the roof suddenly collapses and the foundation cracks. Proceedings to cancel the sale are taken on June 8, i.e., with reasonable diligence.*

Reasonable diligence is a question of circumstances and left to the discretion of the court. However, court decisions hold that if the purchaser wishes to succeed in his action, he must institute proceedings almost immediately on discovering the defect.

There was a case where the purchaser of an immoveable property who sued three months after becoming aware of the latent defect was found not to be exercising his rights with reasonable negligence and therefore he did not succeed in his claim.

The delay is even shorter for moveable objects, such as automobiles, where the purchaser should take legal proceedings not later than four weeks to two months, or even sooner, from the time the defect is discovered.

Before you purchase an appliance, machine, automobile or similar item, read the contract warranty clauses very carefully since these establish the principal warranty rights of the buyer and the obligations of the seller (see chapter 21 on "Consumer Protection").

> *Ronald purchases a secondhand car and the sales contract specifies "thirty days unconditional warranty." What does this warranty cover? It covers any latent and apparent defects, which appear within thirty days after delivery.*

When a thing is sold "as is," does this mean that there is no warranty? No. The seller remains liable for latent defects. The courts have held that the expression "as is" is not an exclusion of warranty. It simply means the buyer accepts the goods with their apparent defects.

Some Court Cases on Latent Defects

B = buyer
S = seller
1. B buys a car from S who warrants that the auto is "in good mechanical condition." B soon discovers that the auto requires considerable motor repairs due to defects which are determinable only by dismantling part of the engine.
Held A hidden defect in an automobile is one which cannot be discovered except by an expert making a careful and minute examination or during the regular usage of the vehicle. The seller is liable as the defects were latent.
2. B, a building contractor, buys a large quantity of one hardware item after careful examination and then sells some of them. He later refuses to make payment claiming the items were defective.

Held   B is an expert and the defects were apparent, and even if the defects had been hidden, B actually dealt with the items by selling some; furthermore, B failed to exercise his recourses within a reasonable delay.

3. B buys a suit from a custom tailor. The suit doesn't fit very well. Nevertheless B accepts delivery and pays the price. Later B sues to cancel the contract and recover the price.

Held   Action dismissed. B knew of the faulty fitting. The seller is not responsible for apparent defects.

4. B buys a refrigerator, discovers latent defects in it, but continues to use it for three years, during which time he repairs it and replaces defective parts.

Held   B is deemed to have accepted the refrigerator and to have renounced his right to demand the cancellation of the contract of sale.

5. B buys a used car with 20,000 mileage. Soon after he buys it, the connecting rod breaks. Such a buyer is imprudent and negligent if he does not have the auto inspected by a competent garage mechanic before his purchase.

Held   A defective connecting rod is an apparent defect, easily discovered; the seller is not liable.

THE OBLIGATION OF THE BUYER

The principal obligation of the buyer is to pay the price of the thing sold to the seller and, unless otherwise agreed upon by both parties, at the time and place of delivery. In other words, all sales are considered to be sales for cash (C.O.D.) unless otherwise stipulated by some credit arrangement extending terms for payment.

RIGHTS OF THE UNPAID VENDOR: DISSOLUTION OF SALE

Nonpayment of the purchase price is a breach of the contract by the buyer. What are the rights of the unpaid vendor?

Sale of Immoveables

Art. 1536   The seller of an immoveable cannot demand the dissolution of the sale by reason of the failure of the buyer to pay the price, unless there is a special stipulation to that effect.

John sells his house to Smith. If the deed has no provision about John having the right to demand dissolution of sale for nonpayment, then Smith has no such right, and John's only recourse is to take an action to recover the unpaid balance.

However, such a clause is usually provided in deeds of sale of real estate by which the vendor is entitled to take back the property sold and retain the moneys already paid.

Sale of Moveables

The rights of an unpaid vendor concerning moveable property depend on whether there has been delivery or not.

Before Delivery

We know that:

a. unless otherwise agreed between the parties, delivery and payment are simultaneous;

b. that unless the seller obtains payment he is not obliged to deliver;

c. that if the seller has granted credit (buy now, pay later) he is obliged to deliver even though payment will be at some future time, (except if it becomes apparent before delivery that the buyer has become insolvent, in which case the seller need not then deliver).

In a cash sale, if the price is not paid and delivery not yet made, the seller has the right to cancel the sale. The cancellation takes place automatically and without any legal proceedings.

In the event that the buyer refuses to pay without

any justification, the seller has the option of either (a) suing the buyer for the purchase price on tendering (offering) the goods to him or (b) notifying the buyer to take delivery and pay. If the buyer fails to do so, the seller can then sell the things to another buyer and claim any loss of price from the original buyer.

After Delivery

If the goods have actually been delivered the unpaid vendor has the following rights:[1]

1. Revendication: if in a conditional sales contract the seller has retained ownership until final payment by the buyer, the seller can always revendicate (take back) the property of which he is owner in the event of default.

> *John buys a car from Smith Auto which remains owner until John pays the balance owing. When John fails to pay a monthly instalment, Smith Auto can repossess* (see chapter 21 on "Consumer Protection").

Where the seller has not reserved ownership, and ownership has actually passed to the buyer, the seller can only take back the goods under special circumstances.

> Art. 1999   The right to revendicate is subject to four conditions:
> 1. The sale must not have been made on credit;
> 2. The thing must still be entire and in the same condition;
> 3. The thing must not have passed into the hands of a third party who has paid for it.
> 4. It must be exercised within eight days after the delivery; saving the provision concerning insolvent traders (in which instance it must be exercised within thirty days after delivery).

---

1. Another right the unpaid vendor has is a *preference upon its price* should the object be sold at a bailiff sale.

Therefore, the goods must not have been sold on credit—since in fact most commercial sales are credit sales, this right of the unpaid vendor is rarely used. If the right to take back the goods is exercised when the debtor is insolvent or bankrupt, it must be done within thirty days from the date of delivery.

2. Dissolution of sale: as long as the moveable thing sold remains in the possession of the buyer and he is not insolvent, the seller may at any time take an action for dissolution of the sale for nonpayment of the purchase price. In the case of insolvency or bankruptcy of the buyer this right of dissolution can only be exercised within thirty days after delivery. In this case the seller is entitled to the return of the goods he sold (see chapter 16 on "Bankruptcy").

> *On April 1, John Wood Ltd. sold and delivered to Termite Paper Co. $10,000 paper boxes. On April 15, Termite goes bankrupt. The boxes are still at Termite's place of business. John Wood is entitled to begin legal proceedings to dissolve the sale and have the paper returned. The proceeding, called a* petition *for the return of thirty-day goods, must be taken by April 30, within thirty days from April 1, the date of delivery.*

> *On March 10, John sold and delivered 1,000 lbs. of steel to Dumpy Houses. On April 15, Dumpy goes bankrupt. The steel is still in Dumpy's possession. John cannot recover since more than thirty days have passed since the delivery.*

BULK SALE

The Civil Code provides that in the sale of a business or of all or a large portion of inventories made outside the ordinary course of the seller's business, the buyer must obtain a sworn statement called an affidavit from the seller listing all his creditors and the amounts due each. Before paying any part of the price to the seller, the buyer must first pay the seller's creditors. Where there is insufficient moneys the creditors should be paid according to the nature of the claim.

> *John sells his restaurant to Paul. The price is $20,000. There are creditors totalling $15,000. The creditors get paid first, then John gets $5,000.*

Legal Terminology

vendor	*credit*
seller	*discount*
purchaser	*legal warranty*
buyer	*conventional warranty*
ownership	*eviction*
risk	*latent defects*
conditional sale	*apparent defects*
consignment	caveat emptor
consignor	*legally presumed*
consignee	*redhibitory action*
on trial	Quanti Minoris *action*
on approval	*reasonable diligence*
F.O.B.	*revendication*
C.I.F.	*dissolution*
delivery	*petition for the return of*
reasonable delay	*thirty-day goods*
C.O.D.	*bulk sale*
	affidavit

Questions

1. Define the contract of sale.
2. What rules govern sale?
3. When does ownership and risk pass to the buyer?
4. What is the obligation of the seller before delivery?
5. When does ownership pass for goods not yet identified and when does it pass for goods to be weighed or numbered?
6. What is meant by a conditional sales contract and how does this contract differ from a C.O.D. sale?

7. What is meant by consignment and how is it used?
8. In a sale on trial, when does ownership pass?
9. When does ownership pass in an F.O.B. contract?
10. Explain what is meant by C.I.F.
11. What is meant by delivery? Where does delivery generally take place, who bears the expenses of delivery and what state must the goods be in when delivered?
12. Discuss time of delivery and failure to deliver.
13. What is meant by legal warranty and how may it be changed?
14. What is meant by warranty against eviction and what are the recourses of a buyer who has been evicted, against the seller?
15. Explain what latent defects are. What is meant by legal warranty against latent defects?
16. Does the law protect an inexperienced and imprudent buyer?
17. Discuss conventional warranties.
18. What are the buyer's recourses against a seller when there are latent defects and when must he exercise these recourses?
19. What is the principal obligation of the buyer and what are the recourses of an unpaid vendor in the following instances:
a. before the goods have been delivered?
b. after the goods have been delivered?
20. What is meant by thirty-day goods and when must the proceeding to have them returned be exercised in the case of bankruptcy?
21. What are the legal formalities required in the sale of a business?

LEASES

Chapter 12

LEASES

On January 1, 1974 a new chapter of the Civil Code concerning lease law, covering all Quebec tenants, came into effect. It is designed to modernize that part of the Civil Code which had hardly changed since 1866 and which heavily favoured the lessor. This updating of the Civil Code is particularly significant since a majority of the Quebec population, including most of those in the Montreal region, live in rental housing.

I RULES APPLICABLE TO ALL LEASES

The chapter on leases in the Civil Code is modified into three Sections. The first Section deals with general rules applicable to all types of leases, e.g., residential, commercial, industrial, both of moveables (automobiles, machinery) and immoveables (buildings, apartments, warehouses and offices).

The second Section deals with rules applicable to immoveables, e.g., land and buildings.

The third Section deals with special rules that refer to residential dwellings.

The first Section to be dealt with in this chapter deals with the general rules covering all leases, moveable and immoveable, but it must be pointed out that these rules may be modified by Sections 2 and 3.

THE DEFINITION OF LEASE

The definition of lease is contained in Article 1600.

The lease of things is a contract by which the lessor

binds himself towards the lessee to grant him the enjoyment of a thing during a certain time, for a consideration, the rent.

You will note from Art. 1600 that there are two parties—the *lessor* or when dealing with immoveables, more commonly called the landlord, and the *lessee* or more commonly called the tenant. The principal obligation of the landlord is to furnish enjoyment not ownership. This observation is made for two reasons—first, if his responsibility were to transfer ownership the contract would be one of sale, not lease; and second, the landlord may not necessarily be the owner of the property. Occasionally, trust companies and real estate companies act as rental administrators for building owners and included in their power of administration is the right to act as lessor. The basic obligation of the tenant is to pay the rent. Usually the rent is a sum of money, but it can be in consideration of services rendered, for example, a janitor receives a rent-free apartment in return for his janitorial work.

A lease may have for its object either a moveable, such as a car, or an immoveable, such as an apartment or house. The term is either for a fixed period, e.g., 12 months, or an indeterminate period (with no fixed date).

THE OBLIGATIONS OF THE LESSOR

Article 1604 contains the basic obligations of the Lessor.

The lessor must:
1. deliver the thing in a good state of repair in all respects;
2. maintain the thing in a condition fit for the use for which it has been leased;
3. give peaceable enjoyment of the thing during the term of lease.

a. Delivery
Art. 1604(1)

One of the principal obligations of the landlord is to deliver, that is, to make available to the tenant the occupancy of the leased premises on the date agreed upon, otherwise the landlord is subject to an action in damages. These damages include such items as the tenant's moving expenses and use of temporary accommodation during the time it takes him to find suitable premises elsewhere.

b. Repairs
Art. 1604(1) and (2)

Another of the principal obligations of the landlord is to deliver the thing in a good state of repair in all respects including major and minor repairs, and to make *lessor repairs* during the period of the lease. There are two periods of time at which the landlord is responsible for making certain repairs, namely immediately prior to the tenant's occupancy and during the term of the lease.

Furthermore the landlord must warrant against defects in the leased thing and may be liable in damages suffered by the lessee, Art. 1606.

c. Recourses
of the Tenant
Against the Lessor

(Example) Brown Machinery leases a factory from Sweet Realties. Soon after taking occupancy the furnace and elevators break down. Two months later a leak in the roof causes damages to the tenant's machinery and prevents continued operation of the factory. What are the recourses of the tenant?

Inexecution of an obligation by the lessor entitles the lessee to demand, in addition to the damages:

1. specific performance of the obligation, in cases which admit of it, Art. 1610(1), e.g., that the lessor make the necessary repairs. The code does not define "landlord repairs" or "tenant repairs". However, the tenant's obligation to repair is one to act reasonably and prudently in the maintenance of the leased premises (see text below on "tenant repairs"). The above described repairs were not due to the tenant's fault, but were due to the poor condition of the equipment and roof even before the tenant took occupancy.

2. cancellation of the lease if the inexecution causes him serious prejudice, Art. 1610(2), i.e., cancellation of the lease if the failure to repair causes him serious prejudice.

3. reduction of rent, Art. 1610(3). If the tribunal grants reduction in rent, the lessor who has remedied the defect is entitled to re-establish the rent for the future, Art. 1611.

If the lessor does not make the required repairs and improvements, the lessee may, without prejudice to his other rights and recourses, apply to the tribunal to obtain permission to withhold the rent on order to proceed thereto, Art. 1612. The tribunal in this case fixes the rent to be withheld and the amount the lessee is authorized to disburse for the repairs, Art. 1613. It must be emphasized that a tenant must be authorized by the tribunal in order to withhold the rent.

What about urgent repairs, the effecting of which cannot be delayed?

> *(Example) The furnace at Super Tool factory explodes resulting in urgent repairs. The lessor cannot be reached as he is out of town. Can the tenant make repairs without the tribunal's permission or that of the lessor?*

After having informed or attempted to inform the lessor, and if the lessor does not act with dispatch, the lessee may undertake *urgent* and *necessary* repairs for the prevention or use of the immoveable leased. The lessor may at any time intervene to continue the work. The lessor must reimburse the lessee for reasonable expenses incurred, Art. 1644.

d. Disturbance

Another of the principal obligations of the landlord is "to give peaceable enjoyment of the thing during the term of the lease", Art. 1604(3).

> *(Example) During the term of the lease part or whole of the leased premises is expropriated by the City. What are the recourses of the tenant?*

The lessor is not liable for damages resulting from disturbance, i.e., annoyance, dispossession etc., by the act of a third person. However if the tenant's enjoyment is diminished, the lessee may demand reduction on his rent or cancellation of the contract but not damages, Art. 1608. (The expropriating party may be obliged to idemnify the Lessee.)

THE OBLIGATIONS
OF THE LESSEE

The principal obligations of the tenants are set out in Art. 1617.

The lessee must:
1. use the thing as a prudent administrator;
2. pay the rent;
3. return the thing on expiry of the lease.

a. Prudent Administrator

The tenant must act prudently and make minor repairs to the leased premises. He is responsible for damages and losses which happen to the thing, unless he proves that they occurred without his fault or that of persons he allowed to have access thereto or use thereof, Art. 1621. Consequently a tenent is responsible for the damages caused by members of his family, guests, sublessees and other persons he permitted to enter the leased premises or use the leased object.

b. Subletting

To sublet means that the tenant leases the premises as a lessor to another person who is called a subtenant.

> The lessee cannot sublet all or part of the thing or assign his lease without the consent of the lessor, who cannot refuse it without reasonable cause. If the lessor does not answer within fifteen days he is deemed to have consented. The lessor who consents to the subletting or assignment of the lease can only exact the refund of the expenses reasonably incurred, Art. 1619.

It can be seen that the lessor's permission is required but the lessor must have a valid and justifiable reason to refuse, the usual one being that the prospective subtenant is insolvent. Therefore the tenant's right to sublet is conditional upon the landlord's permission which cannot be unreasonably withheld. If the landlord remains silent for 15 days his acceptance is presumed.

c. Landlord's Inspection and Posting of Signs

The lessee must permit the lessor to ascertain the condition of the thing. The lessor must exercise this right in a reasonable manner, Art. 1622. Although the lessor is allowed to verify that the lessee is acting prudently in respect to the preservation of the leased object, he must not abuse his visiting rights. Depending on the term of the lease, in leases of houses or buildings the lessor is also allowed to affix "to let" signs, Art. 1645.

d. Tenant Repairs

Since the lessor is obliged to deliver the premises in a good state of repair (Art. 1604) there is a presumption that the tenant received it in good condition. However the tenant may prove that it was delivered in a damaged condition. At the end of the lease the lessee must return the thing in the condition in which he received it, with the exception of changes resulting from normal aging, wear and tear or irresistible force, Art. 1623.

It is advisable for both parties to state in writing the condition and description of the premises at the beginning of the lease.

Article 1624 covers the situation where the lessee has made improvements or additions to the leased premises, e.g., built a new storefront, erected new wall partitions, installed an air conditioning system.

> The lessee may, on the expiry of the lease, remove improvements and additions which he made to the thing.
>
> If they cannot be removed without deteriorating the thing, the lessor is entitled to retain them, on paying their value, or to compel the lessee to remove them. If it is not possible to restore the thing to its original condition, the lessor keeps them without indemnity.

This article follows the principle stated above that the tenant return the premises in a proper condition at the end of the lease.

Since the lessor is obliged to make necessary repairs during the lease, the tenant must suffer such urgent repairs to be made. The tenant is entitled to a reduction of rent according to the circumstances. If the repairs cause the tenant serious prejudice, the tenant may demand cancellation of the lease. In order to make said necessary repairs the lessor may obtain temporary vacating by depossession of the tenant. If the parties cannot agree on the conditions of vacating, the tribunal will provide protection for the rights of the lessee, Arts. 1625 and 1626.

The general obligation of the tenant is to act as a prudent administrator. Although the Code does not enumerate "tenant repairs" the general principle is that the tenant repairs are *lesser* or *minor* repairs for maintenance. Article 1627 states:

> The lessee is obliged to make certain lesser repairs for maintenance.
>
> He is not however obliged to make such lessee's repairs if they result from normal aging of the thing, fortuitous event or irresistible force.

What are "lesser repairs for maintenance" will largely depend either on the nature of the object and/or its usage.

> *(Example) The Manager of Super Tool Machinery Ltd. notices that there is a leaky plumbing joint leading from the washroom sink. He neither makes the repair nor notifies the lessor to do so. Subsequently a flood occurs as a result of the bursting of said joint.*

In the above example, did the tenant act prudently? Does the tenant have a valid defence when sued by the lessor to make tenant repairs? The tenant might argue that this bursting of the pipe was due to a defect in the leased premises for which the lessor is responsible, Art. 1606, or that it was due to normal aging of the premises or irresistible force for which the tenant cannot be held responsible, Art. 1627, 2nd Paragraph. It is more likely however that the tribunal would hold that the tenant did not act prudently in not making this lesser repair and would hold the tenant liable in damages.

e. Recourses of the Landlord Against the Tenant— General Rules

Article 1628 states "Inexecution of an obligation by the lessee" entitles the lessor to demand, in addition to damages:

1. specific performance of the obligation, in cases which admit of it;

2. cancellation of the contract, if the inexecution causes him serious prejudice.

Thus the landlord may demand (a) that the tenant perform his obligations under the lease, e.g., pay the rent, make repairs; (b) cancellation of the contract in case of serious prejudice, e.g., non payment of rent (see Art. 1633 below) or substantial damaging of the premises.

EXPIRY OF THE LEASE[1]

A lease for a fixed term terminates of right at the expiry of the term. For example, a lease for a factory from Apr. 1, 1975 to Apr. 1, 1977 ends on Apr. 1, 1977. No previous notice is required. It ends on the date agreed upon.

However a lease for an indeterminate period of time requires notice by either party as follows:

The delay for the notice is:

1. one month or one week, according to whether the rent is payable by the month or by the week. If the rent is payable according to another term, the notice must be given with a delay equal to such term or, if it exceeds three months, with a delay of three months;

2. three days for moveables. The notice cannot be otherwise than in writing in case of a lease of a dwelling, Art. 1631.

A lease is not cancelled by the death of either party, Art. 1632. Concerning residential dwellings this is tempered by Art. 1664(b) which reads:

"The heir or legatee of a deceased lessee may cancel the current lease. He must send notice thereof to the lessor at

---

1. The reader is reminded that these are the general rules applying to all leases. There are however special rules referring to immoveable property and more particularly to residential dwellings that modify these general rules so as to give the tenant greater protection.

least three months before cancellation. Such notice must be given within six months after the death."

In an action for cancellation for failure to pay rent, the lessee may avoid the cancellation by paying, before judgement, the rent due with interest and court costs, Art. 1633.

II RULES PARTICULAR TO THE LEASE OF AN IMMOVEABLE

This Section contains particular rules on leases of immoveables, including dwellings. In some respects these rules make more specific, or modify or make exceptions to the general rules. The rules contained herein override the general rules of Section I.

A. DISTURBANCE BY CO-TENANTS IN AN IMMOVEABLE

Certain rules are enacted to cover the relationship of co-tenants living in high rise apartment buildings. Tenants are obliged not to disturb the right of enjoyment of other tenants in the same building.

Art. 1635   The lessee must so act as not to disturb the normal enjoyment of other lessees of the same immoveable.

He is answerable to the lessor and the other lessees for damages which may result from a violation of this obligation, either on his own part or on that of persons he allows to have access to the immoveable. Such violation also entitles the lessor to ask for cancellation of the lease.

Art. 1636   In the cases provided for in Article 1635, after putting the lessor in common in default, the lessee disturbed in his enjoyment may obtain, if the disturbance persists, a reduction of rent or the cancellation of the lease, according to the circumstances.

He may also recover damages from the lessor in common, unless the latter proves that he acted as a prudent administrator, saving the recourse of the lessor for repayment against the lessee at fault.

As can be seen an aggrieved tenant may sue not only the disturbing tenant but also the lessor in common if the lessor has been negligent in his choice of tenants or if the lessor neglects to evict a troublesome tenant. The lessor, in turn, may sue the tenant at fault in cancellation of the lease and damages.

B.   THE LANDLORD'S PRIVILEGE

(Example) Jones Machinery has failed to pay the rent for two months. What recourse does the landlord have?

A principal obligation of the tenant is to pay the rent. If the tenant fails to do so, thereby not fulfilling his obligations under the lease, the landlord has the following recourses:

1. He may sue for the arrears of rent only. In this case two months' rent is due.

2. He may sue for the arrears of rent and for cancellation of the lease plus damages. The damages are calculated on the loss of rental that he reasonably expects to suffer until he finds another tenant. Generally the Court will award a sum equal to three months' rent for residential leases but sometimes more for long-term commercial leases.

When the landlord sues the tenant for nonpayment, he may instruct the lawyer to make a *seizure* of the furniture and moveable effects within the leased premises, in virtue of the right given to the landlord called the *landlord's privilege*. By exercising this right the landlord can have the bailiff immediately seize and remove certain household effects belonging to the tenant. When the landlord obtains judgment against the tenant, the court will authorise the moveables seized to be sold at a bailiff sale and the landlord will be paid out of the proceeds of this sale.

The right of seizure extends to property belonging to third parties in the premises as follows:

a. Subtenants: with certain limitations the landlord is allowed to seize the moveable effects belonging to a subtenant.

Article. 1638 states that the right of the lessor to seize includes also the effects of the subtenant insofar as the latter is indebted to the tenant.

b. Third parties: if a third party has moveables belonging to him in the premises of the tenant at the time of the seizure, they are subject to seizure. However, if, before the seizure, the third party has notified the landlord that certain of his assets are in the tenant's apartment, the landlord is not allowed to make a seizure of these moveables. Consequently, finance companies and leasing companies which retain ownership of things they sell until they are fully paid, notify the landlord that these goods are located at the tenant's premises and belong to them. The landlord who has been so notified cannot seize those moveables for rent accruing subsequent to the notice. If the owner notifies the landlord before delivery, the things cannot be seized for rent owing prior to delivery.

If the tenant moves or "skips out" during the term of the lease, the landlord's privileged right to seize can be exercised, but it must be done within fifteen days from the time the tenant removed his effects. The landlord may seize the goods at the tenant's new residence. If the landlord cannot find his tenant within the fifteen days, he has lost his right to seize, but he has a valid action for arrears of rent, cancellation of the lease and damages.

The Tenant's Exemption

There is, however, a limit to what the landlord can seize. The tenant has a personal exemption of $1000 on household effects and food and fuel required by him and his family, which cannot be seized by the landlord even if the rent is owing. In addition, necessary clothing and bedding belonging to the tenant and his family, books, instruments and tools necessary to carry on his profession, his automobile, if it is required for earning a livelihood, family papers and portraits, are also exempt from seizure.

C.   RENEWAL OF LEASES[2]

(Example) Smith Candy's lease is for two years terminating in September. At the end of the lease the tenant remains in occupation, without a new lease being signed. In December the lessor demands that the tenant leave.

A lease is tacitly renewed for one year (or for the same terms if it was originally less than one year) where after the expiry of a lease with a fixed term (e.g., two years) the lessee continues to occupy the premises for more than eight days without opposition by the lessor. It is noted that even if the original lease was for two years the renewal is for one year and is subject to the same rules as the original lease. The renewal also is subject to renewal, Article 1641, that is, upon its expiry if the tenant stays on for eight days unopposed by the lessor, the lease renews again for another year. A lessor may evict a tenant who continues to occupy the premises after the expiry of the lease, Article 1648.

D.   FIRE

(Example) A fire of unknown origin destroys the factory leased by Smith Candy. The lessor sues the tenant for property damages.

2. This does not apply to residential buildings.

In the event of fire in the leased premises, the lessee is not liable for damages unless his fault, or that of persons whom he has allowed to havè access thereto (guests, employees) is established. The burden of proof is upon the lessor to prove the tenant's liability.

E. TERMINATION OF THE LEASE BY THE SALE OF THE BUILDING

(Example) During the term of the lease which is for five years the lessor sells the building to Mr. Smith. Smith wants to occupy the building himself and orders the tenant out.

A lease is not terminated due to the sale or transfer of the building to a third person. However if the lease is not registered[3] and there remain more than 12 months of the lease still to run from the date of the said sale, the purchaser (Smith) may terminate it at the expiry of such term by giving six months written notice to the lessee if the premises are used for industrial, commercial, professional or handicraft purposes, or a 3 month notice in other cases. The tenant with a registered lease is protected up to the termination date. However in both cases the tenant cannot leave the premises just because the building is sold and must respect the contract until expiry of the term.

III PROVISIONS PARTICULAR TO RESIDENTIAL BUILDINGS

The new law radically changes the old law in order to ensure effective protection to the tenant. Gone are the leases prepared by landlords which took unfair advantage of tenants. Every residential lease must set out specific provisions that

3. Registration is effected by depositing the lease or extract thereof in proper form at the Registrate office in the District where the immoveable is situated.

are obligatory, binding and imperative and the parties cannot change, delete or modify them.

Furthermore the following articles of general provisions (which have already been discussed in this chapter) are of public orders for residential leases and consequently are an essential part of residential lease law, namely:

1.	Art.	1610	Recourses by the lessee against lessor in default
2.	Art.	1612-1616	Withholding rent
3.	Art.	1619	Subletting
4.	Art.	1622	Landlord inspection
5.	Art.	1625	Right of cancellation or reduction of rent in cases of urgent repairs
6.	Art.	1628	Recourses of lessor against lessee
7.	Art.	1635-36	Relations between co-tenant—co-lessor
8.	Art.	1643	Fire liability
9.	Art.	1646-47	Effect of sale of building

Note: See the form lease in the Appendix.

Since the form lease contains most of the important provisions and sets forth actual articles of the Code, this text will highlight the most significant differences from the general rules of leases.

COMMENTARY ON THE RESIDENTIAL FORM LEASE

The form lease is not compulsory in its entirety. Only Section II must be set forth. Sections I and III are intended as a guide. As of Jan. 1, 1974 the Act applies to every lease made, renewed or extended before that date. However, Articles 1654, 1664b, 1664d, 1664e, 1664m and 1664n to 1664u apply only to leases made, renewed, or extended after Jan. 1, 1974 and to leases made before such date the terms of which begin after Dec. 31. 1973.

However any contravention of any of the imperative conditions does not result in nullity of the lease, Art. 1653.

SECTION I
DESCRIPTION OF PREMISES,
TERM OF THE LEASE AND RENT

This section of the Code (Art. 1650-1665) applies to housing and residential buildings with its services, accessories and dependencies even if part of the premises is used for commercial or professional use, provided that such part does not exceed one third of the total surface area. However, it does not apply to:

1. the lease of a room;
2. the lease of a dwelling in which at least three rooms are regularly leased by the tenant;
3. the lease of a dwelling used as a vacation resort.

SECTION II
OBLIGATORY PROVISIONS

The residential lease must set forth 43 obligatory clauses. The significant modifications to the general rules are:

Obligations of the Lessor

Clause 2   The landlord is obliged to deliver the premises not only in a good state of repair but also to make all repairs imposed by municipal by-laws respecting hygiene and safety, Art. 1655.

Clause 7   Other than cases of emergency or visit by prospective tenants, ordinary inspection visits by a prospective purchaser must be preceded by a 24 hour notice to the lessee.

Obligations of the Lessee

Clause 9   The tenant must act as a prudent administrator. Consequently he must keep the dwelling clean.

Clause 13   Although a tenant may keep products generally allowed in dwellings, including matches and cleaning fluid, it is forbidden without the landlord's permission to use or keep in the dwelling any substance which constitutes a risk of fire or which may affect increase of insurance premiums, i.e., fire insurance coverage.

Automatic Extension of the Lease

Clause 16
17
18

Article 1659 contains an important protection for the tenant in that the lease for a fixed term of twelve or more months is extended of right for another term of twelve months. Therefore a lease of twelve months or more is automatically extended for a period not exceeding one year. If the lease is for a shorter period it is extended for a like period, e.g., a lease of six months is extended for another six months.

In virtue of an Act to Promote Conciliation Between Lessees and Property Owners, the Rental Board has jurisdiction generally to prolong and cancel leases and to fix the amount of rent. It has jurisdiction over dwellings throughout Quebec, except for buildings constructed since December 31, 1973.

If the term of the lease is twelve months or more the lease is extended *of right* for another term—it is automatically renewed under the same conditions and rent until June 30, 1976.[4] The expression "of right" means that the lessee does not require the lessor's permission for the extension of the lease—it is granted by law. If neither party sends the required notice (see below) ending the lease or changing the rent or any conditions, the lease is automatically renewed. However, the parties may agree between themselves to a different extension of the lease. The provisions of automatic renewal do not apply to:

4. After June 30, 1975 renewal can be effected every year for a period of twelve months in accordance with Article 1659. If the lease is for less than twelve months there are other rules for notification and extension.

1. the lease of a room;

2. the lease of a dwelling in which at least three rooms are regularly leased by the Lessee;

3. the lease of a dwelling used as a vacation resort;

4. the lease granted by an employer to his employee accessory to a contract of work.

To avoid automatic renewal of a lease of one year or more:

a. the tenant must notify the lessor not later than three months before the expiration of the lease (i.e., by March 31 if the lease ends on June 30) of his intention to vacate the premises at the end of the present lease;

b. the lessor must send a written eviction notice prior to three months before the expiry of the lease, or the lessor sends within the same delay, a written notice of increase of rent or changes in the conditions in the lease.

Upon receipt of one of the above notices from the lessor the tenant can within thirty days of the notice:

a. advise the landlord of his intent to leave the premises;

b. file an application with the Rental Board to obtain an extension of the lease and/or to fix the amount of the rent.[5] A copy of this request must be sent to the lessor within thirty days.

If the tenant does not answer the landlord's notice of cancellation or the tenant does not apply to the Rental Board within thirty days he is held to have accepted the notice of eviction or rental increase and changes in the conditions of the lease. Upon application to the tribunal, if for reasonable cause one of the parties is late in sending the notice, a delay to send a late notice may be obtained provided it causes no serious prejudice.

The Rental Board and its administrator also have jurisdiction to cancel leases or to adjust the rent for various other causes, including:

---

5. The law does not bring about a rental freeze—but is subject to the Rental Board Control unless the parties amicably agree to a higher rent. For the purposes of fixing the rental, the cost of parking space is deemed to be accessory to the principal lease even if it is subject to a distinct contract. This avoids excessive rental for parking space.

1. When an owner wants the premise for his own use (or for close relatives). The owner must send a notice to the tenant three months before expiration of the lease. The tenant has the right to a hearing as to the good faith of the owner's intent. If the owner obtains the premises under false pretenses, he may be subject to penalties and damages.

2. If the lessee is in arrears of rent for over three weeks, the rental administrator may cancel the lease.

3. If the lessee or members of his family causes a serious disturbance or annoyance to neighbours or to the owner, the lease may be cancelled.

4. If the lessee neglects or voluntarily deteriorates the premises, the lease may be cancelled.

5. If the lessor has reduced the space, services or conveniences, the lessee may ask for cancellation or reduction of rent.

6. A new tenant may request a hearing before the rental administrator (within 60 days of occupancy) if he is paying a higher rent than the former tenant, so that his rent may be reduced accordingly.

From a decision of the Rental administrator, a party may go to appeal before the Rental Commission.

Clause 22   Art. 1664a permits a prospective lessee of a low rental housing or to a reception centre or old people's home to cancel his contract upon due notification.

Prohibitions

Articles 1664d to 1664m prohibit certain agreements which would take unfair advantage of the lessee.

Clause 23   The lessor may exact only one month's rent in advance but no other form of deposit, e.g., against damage or non-payment of rent. However the lessor may request that a third person guarantee payment of the rent.

Clause 24   The lessor cannot demand a series of post-dated cheques for payment of the rent, except for the last month's rent. *However the parties may agree to do so.*

Clause 25   Clauses that stipulate that the entire balance of rent becomes due upon the non-payment by the tenant are illegal.

         Likewise in a lease for one year or less the rent cannot be varied. However in a lease for more than twelve months, it is possible to stipulate a higher rent for the second year.[6]

Clause 26   Clauses that state that the lessor is not liable for any damages resulting from non repairs are forbidden. Likewise any clause making the tenant liable for damages without the tenant's fault are forbidden.

Clause 27   A penal clause sets the amount of damages in advance—consequently if the amount is excessive, it may be annulled or reduced. Likewise any clause that the tribunal considers unreasonable or excessive is forbidden, e.g., in the case of any legal dispute, the lessor has the right to choose the lawyer for the tenant.

Clause 28   Anti-discrimination law now applies to leases. This rule is long over-due.

Clause 29 37   A clause stating that the lease will be cancelled if the tenant has any more children is void, unless the space of the dwelling justifies such a restriction.

Clause 30   Buying furniture on credit or finance does not prevent a person from leasing a residence.

---

6. In a lease for more than twelve months, the parties may agree that the rent will be readjusted in relation with any variation of the municipal or school taxes affecting the immoveable, of the unit cost of fuel or electricity in the case of a dwelling heated or lighted at the cost of the lessor and of premiums for fire insurance and liability insurance. Such readjustment cannot be made during the first twelve months of the lease and cannot occur more than once during each additional period of twelve months, Art. 1664(f).

Clause 31	The lessor or lessee may change the locks only with both parties' consents.
Clause 32	The clause "the tenant has examined the premises and declares that they are to his entire satisfaction" is without effect.
Clause 33 34	Written leases are not obligatory and verbal leases are permitted. However if the parties agree to a written lease it must contain the obligatory clauses and a copy of the lease must be given to the tenant. If it is a verbal lease the lessor must give the tenant the form lease within three days after the verbal agreement.
Clause 35	The language of the lease is at the choice of the tenant; the same type of provision is made with Consumer Sales.
Clause 36	This clause contains regulations for the minimum size of type set.
Clause 37 38	Everyone is entitled to rented premises including children and members of minority groups.
Clause 39 ↓ 43	These clauses refer to a system of fines for contravention of specific violations, e.g., changing of locks, not using the form lease, language of the lease, discrimination, restrictions on children, exacting deposits. Clause 41 states that contravention of any of the articles does not entail nullity of the lease—otherwise one of the parties might invoke an offence in order to break the lease.

SECTION III
ADDITIONAL CLAUSES

The parties may agree to special clauses not inconsistent with the law, e.g., removal of ice and snow, keeping of pets, use of swimming pool, garbage disposal, noise after certain hours, posting of signs, awnings and use of garage and storage space.

Legal Terminology

lease
lessor
lessee
moveables
immoveables
peaceable enjoyment
term
delivery
repairs
inexecution
specific performance
cancellation
serious prejudice
disturbance
prudent administrator
sub-let
inspection
maintenance
fortuitous event
fixed term
reduction

indeterminate term
notification
delay
co-tenants
landlord's privileges
tenant exemption
tacit renewal
termination of lease
register lease
residential dwelling
description of premises
obligatory provisions
automatic extension of lease
rental board
application
rental administrator
rental commission
prohibitions
penal clause
deposit
anti-discrimination

Questions

1. In the chapter on leases, the civil code is divided into three sections. What are they?
2. Describe the basic difference between the contract of lease and the contract of sale.
3. What are the basic obligations of the lessor?
4. What is meant by the obligation of the landlord to deliver?
5. What are landlord repairs?
6. What are the recourses of the tenant against the lessor for inexecution of an obligation by the lessor?
7. What are the recourses of a tenant in the event of the need for urgent repairs?

8. What are the recourses of the lessee in the event of disturbances?

9. What are the principle obligations of the lessee?

10. To what extent is the lessee responsible for damage to the premises?

11. What right does the tenant have to sub-let?

12. What is the lessor's right to inspection?

13. What are tenant repairs to an immoveable?

14. What is meant by a prudent administrator?

15. What are the recourses of the landlord against the tenant who is in default of his obligations?

16. In a non-residential lease of an immoveable, when does the lease expire?

17. What are the recourses of a co-tenant in an immoveable who is disturbed?

18. What is meant by the landlord's privilege?

19. What is the "tenants exemption"?

20. When is a lease tacitly renewed?

21. Under what circumstances will a tenant be held responsible for damages caused by fire?

22. Does a lease terminate due to the sale of a building?

23. List at least five clauses in the residential lease which are obligatory.

24. What is meant by automatic extension of a residential lease?

25. How does a lessor or lessee avoid automatic renewal of a residential lease?

26. On what grounds can the rental board cancel a residential lease?

27. List five agreements which are prohibited in residential leases?

28. List three agreements which may be included under section three of a residential lease?

LOAN AND INTEREST

Chapter 13

LOAN AND INTEREST

Art. 1762   Loans are of two kinds:
1. The loan of things which may be used without being destroyed, called loan for use;
2. The loan of things which are consumed by the use made of them, called loan for consumption.

LOAN FOR USE

A loan for use is gratuitous and the thing lent is to be returned by the borrower to the lender who continues to own it. If the borrower pays rent for it, it is not a contract of loan but of lease.

Al lends Bob an electric drill for the weekend. He expects that Bob will use the drill without destroying it.

Art. 1763   Loan for use is a contract by which one party, called the lender, gives to another, called the borrower, a thing to be used by the latter gratuitously for a time, and then to be returned by him to the former.

Art. 1764   The lender continues to be the owner of the thing lent.

Obligation of the Borrower

The borrower must act as a prudent administrator in safekeeping and preserving the thing lent. He must not use it for a longer time than agreed upon, nor for any other purpose than that for which it is intended by its nature or by agreement, otherwise he is liable for the loss of it arising even from an unforeseen event.

> *Al lends Bob a car to go skiing at St. Sauveur in Quebec. Instead of going skiing, Bob goes to Toronto where the car is stolen. Bob is liable.*

The borrower is not liable for deterioration by normal use occurring without fault on his part. The borrower pays the expenses arising from the use of the thing.

Obligation of the Lender

Art. 1773   The lender cannot take back the thing, or disturb the borrower in the proper use of it, until after the expiration of the term agreed upon, or if there be no agreement, until after the thing has been used for the purpose for which it was borrowed; subject nevertheless to the exception declared in the next following article.

Art. 1774   If before the expiration of the term, or, if no term has been agreed upon, before the borrower has completed his use of the thing, there occurs to the lender a pressing unforeseen need of it, the court may according to the circumstances, oblige the borrower to restore it to him.

In essence, the above Articles state that the lender cannot recover the thing lent before the time agreed upon or before the borrower has used it for the purpose for which it was borrowed, unless the lender has a pressing and urgent need for it.

Art. 1776   When the thing lent has defects which cause injury to the person using it, the lender is responsible if he knew the defects and did not make them known to the borrower.

Al knows that the car which he lends to Bob has faulty brakes, but does not tell Bob. Bob gets into a serious automobile accident as a result of the malfunctioning of the brakes. Al is liable for damages and injuries.

LOAN FOR CONSUMPTION

Art. 1777   Loan for consumption is a contract by which the lender gives the borrower a certain quantity of things which are consumed by the use made of them, under the obligation by the latter to return a like quantity and of things of the same kind and quality.

Art. 1778   By loan for consumption the borrower becomes owner of the thing lent, and the loss of it falls upon him.

The lender must be owner of the thing lent and capable of transferring title. The borrower becomes owner of the thing lent and he has the right to use it up or dispose of it. His obligation is to return to the borrower a like quantity of the same quality and kind, at the time agreed upon.

Al lends Bob a barrel of oil for consumption. A fire destroys the oil. Bob bears the loss and must return another similar barrel of oil to Al.

Lending Money

Art. 1779   The obligation which results from a loan in money is for the numerical sum received.

If there be an increase or diminution in the value of the currency before the time of the payment, the borrower is obliged to return the numerical sum lent, and only that sum, in money current at the time of the payment.

> *Al lends Bill $500 U.S. payable in one year. Several months later the U.S. money is devalued, lessening in value. Bill returns only the numerical value—$500 U.S.*

If Bill had borrowed the money in bullion, he would be obliged to return the same quantity and quality as received.

A contract of loan of money may be in the form of an acknowledgement of a debt, such as an I.O.U. or a promissory note. However, a cheque presumes payment to the payee and is not a loan.

Loans may be secured or unsecured. In the following chapter, "Secured Transactions," we discuss examples of how loans may be secured by hypothecs, trust deeds, assignments and other forms of collateral.

INTEREST ON LOANS

Under the B.N.A. Act, interest is in the jurisdiction of the federal government. The basic interest law is the Interest Act; moneylenders are governed by the Small Loans Act (see infra) and banks are governed by the Bank Act.

What Is Interest?

Interest is the compensation for the use of money borrowed for a period of time, and is payable only if the parties have specifically agreed to or if it is presumed as a result of previous dealings between the parties.

If no interest rate is agreed to, the legal rate is fixed at 5 percent per annum.

> *Al lends Bob $100 "with interest," for one year. Bob is obliged to repay $105.*

Any rate of interest may be stipulated, but if the court finds the rate to be usurious, harsh or excessive, it may be reduced or annulled (Article 1040c) (see chapter 21 on "Consumer Protection").

If interest is payable at a rate or percentage per day, week or month, or for any period less than a year, the yearly rate must be indicated, otherwise only 5 percent per annum is chargeable. For example, interest charged at the rate of "1 percent per month" is considered at 5 percent per annum. But interest charged at the rate of "1 percent per month, 12 percent per annum" is considered at 12 percent per annum. (The foregoing does not apply to hypothecs.)

Interest on Hypothecary Loans

In the next chapter on "Secured Transactions" we discuss the usage of hypothecs. A borrower often obtains a loan because he is prepared to grant a charge on his immoveable property in favour of the lender to secure repayment of the loan. The loan is in fixed monthly or quarterly payments including interest. The hypothec must state the amount of the principal and interest.

Moneylenders

The federal Small Loans Act governs professional moneylenders and loan companies making loans of $1,500 or less. The amount of interest chargeable is:

a. 2 percent per month on any part of the unpaid balance not exceeding $300;

b. 1 percent per month on any part of the unpaid principal balance exceeding $300 but not exceeding $1,000;

c. ½ of 1 percent per month on any remainder of the unpaid principal balance exceeding $1,000.

If the loan is less than $500 and is repayable over at least 20 months, or if a loan of over $500 is made for over 30 months, the interest is 1 percent per month on the unpaid balance.

Credit Unions

A credit union or caisse populaire (e.g., Caisse Desjardins,

Savings Union) is a nonprofit organization constituted by the Quebec Savings and Credit Union Act. Credit unions generally offer to their members attractive interest rates, both on deposits and loans. Generally, the maximum interest rate on loans is 1 percent per month, based on the outstanding balance; the member who makes a loan may get a rebate based on the annual surplus earnings of the union.

Loans to Business

Both the federal and provincial governments have enacted legislation to afford financial assistance to business. Under the Quebec Industrial Credit Bureau Act, loans may be granted by the government to promote the development of the manufacturing industry in the province. The federal Small Business Loans Act enables banks, trust companies, credit unions and insurance loan companies to lend money to a small business enterprise for the improvement, modernization, expansion and renovation of its premises and equipment. The Industrial Development Bank is a governmental body assisting businesses that require financing which they are unable to obtain from other sources on suitable terms.

Legal Terminology

loan	*Small Loans Act*
loan for use	*Bank Act*
interest	*usury*
lender	*hypothecary loans*
borrower	*moneylenders*
prudent administrator	*credit unions*
loan for consumption	*Industrial Credit Bureau Act*
Interest Act	*Small Business Loans Act*
	Industrial Development Bank

Questions

1. Define the contract of loan for use. What are the principal obligations of each party?

2. In a loan for use what are the obligations of the lender for defects in the thing lent?

3. Define the contract of loan for consumption. What is the obligation of the borrower?

4. What is the obligation of the borrower in a loan of money?

5. What is the basic law dealing with interest?

6. What is interest?

7. What is the legal rate of interest?

8. How must the yearly rate of interest be indicated?

9. Give one instance where payment of interest is secured.

10. What type of loans are covered by the Small Loans Act?

11. What is a credit union?

12. Under what Acts do the federal and provincial governments offer financial assistance to businesses?

SECURED TRANSACTIONS
[Mortgage in Default]

Chapter 14

SECURED TRANSACTIONS

John purchases a new colour TV set from Brown TV Sales for a total sales price of $500. He pays $100 on signing, the balance to be paid by monthly instalments of $50 each. Under the terms the store remains owner until the price is fully paid. Brown sells its rights under the contract to Easy Finance Co., and John makes the payments to Easy Finance Co.

The above example is a typical illustration of buying on credit. The majority of us buy goods now and pay later, at least to some degree, so that we can have immediate possession and use of goods but pay for them out of future income. Credit buying is often made with credit cards for use at department stores, gasoline stations, airlines, restaurants, etc.

The retail outlet, whether it sells televisions, household appliances, machinery or automobiles, is willing to grant terms of payments by monthly instalments. How can a retail store afford to sell much of its inventory by credit sales in which only small initial down payments are made and the remainder of the sales price paid over a period of possibly two years?

The retailer can do this because he usually has the backing of a finance company which has the necessary funds to buy these contracts. In other words, the retailer sells to the consumer, then he sells his rights, including ownership and title in the sales contract, to the finance company which pays the retailer a price for the contract. Everyone is satisfied. In the above example, John has possession of the TV, Brown TV Sales sold the TV at a profit having received the balance of the purchase price from the Easy Finance Co. and the finance company can look forward to payments from John, including interest.

What protection is afforded to the seller or finance company if Brown fails to pay? This chapter reviews several methods of giving the finance company or retailer-creditor additional protection in the event the buyer does not pay. This protection is called collateral or security.

INSTALMENT OR CONDITIONAL SALES CONTRACT

Why would a finance company accept a transfer of a retailer's sales contract? First, it has verified the solvency and ability of the consumer to pay. Second, the finance company receives repayment of capital plus its interest charges. Third, it has the right to sue the consumer for nonpayment. Fourth, it is afforded security for repayment by retaining ownership in the object sold until full payment. In the event of nonpayment it has the right to recover possession and forego claiming the balance unpaid and to retain the moneys paid on account by the purchaser. This type of contract is often called an instalment sales contract (see chapters 11 and 21 on "Sale" and "Consumer Protection").

CONTRACT OF PAWN OR PLEDGE

John asks Bill to lend him twenty-five dollars. Bill agrees, but to guarantee payment he asks John to give him his watch. "If you repay me within one week you get the watch back, otherwise I retain it as security," says Bill.

Bill has made a contract of pledge or pawning with John because a thing is deposited or placed in the hands of the creditor (Bill) as security for his debt. With the exception of licensed pawnbrokers, if the debtor does not pay, the creditor cannot sell or keep the article. He must first obtain a judgment and then may have it sold by bailiff's sale, and get paid out of the proceeds. The advantage to the creditor is that he has in *his possession* property belonging to the debtor which will eventually satisfy the judgment debt and he will have a priority over the proceeds as compared to the other creditors.

Commercial Pledge

In the preceding discussion of pledge or pawning it can be seen that possession of the thing must be transferred to the creditor. Pledge therefore would be very impractical for a manufacturer who requires his machinery for production. Consequently, in 1962, a special form of pledge was added to the Civil Code called commercial pledge, by which a person carrying on business may pledge his machinery and equipment to secure a loan, and still retain possession. The pledge is made by special deed and registered at the local registry office.

TRUST DEED

Under the Quebec Special Corporate Powers Act, a limited company (corporation) may give security by notarial trust deed whereby the company may hypothecate (mortgage) in favour of creditors its property, moveable and immoveable, while retaining possession of it.

ASSIGNMENT OF BOOK DEBTS

John, a businessman, requires a loan from a finance company which requests as security the transfer of all John's accounts receivable, that is, John's claims and accounts against his own customers.

Smith Printer is printing a book for John's Publishing Company for $15,000. Smith Printer orders $10,000 worth of paper from Brown Paper. Brown Paper *receives an assignment (transfer) of the contract that Smith has with John up to $10,000.*

In the first example, all of John's accounts, claims and contracts are transferred to the finance company. This is called a general assignment. In the newspaper you may read notices in which a finance company notifies John's customers that his accounts have been transferred to it and that they are to pay the finance company and not John.

The second example illustrates a specific assignment of one contract. In this case, John has been notified by Brown Paper of the assignment and John is required to pay the $10,000 directly to Brown.

SECTIONS 86 AND 88 OF THE BANK ACT

Under the federal Bank Act, Sections 86 and 88, a bank has wide powers to lend money and obtain as security not only accounts receivable, but also inventory and machinery. This security is commonly used between a bank and its commercial clients.

SURETYSHIP (GUARANTEE)

John wants to borrow money from a finance company but has no security to give. The finance company may ask for the name of a third person as guarantor who will be liable in the event John fails to pay.

In this example, the lender wants a third person who is financially sound to guarantee John's indebtedness. This is called suretyship and is defined as the act by which a person, called the surety, undertakes to fulfil the obligation of another (John) in case of his nonfulfilment. This guarantee or suretyship may be in a separate contract or as is often the case, the surety cosigns with the principal debtor.

PRIVILEGES

A *privilege* (sometimes called a *lien*) is a right under the Civil Code given to certain specific types of creditors by which they have a preferred payment position as compared to other creditors who do not have privileged rights. These privileges or liens are generally created by the labour and/or material supplied, that the creditor has furnished to his debtor in relation to a specific property.

> *John takes his car to a garage for repairs. John refuses to pay for the repairs. The garage is entitled to retain possession of the vehicle as security until payment is made.*

This is an example of a repairman's privilege upon a moveable in his possession.

In practice, the most important privileges are those of the workman, supplier of materials, builder and architect. They are entitled to a privilege upon the additional value given to the immoveable by their work and/or materials furnished. The purpose of this privilege is to ensure that if they (as creditors) do not get paid, they may bring the land and building to sale and get paid by preference over other creditors.

> *John is owner of some vacant land and Smith, as general contractor, undertakes to build him a house on this land. Smith makes contracts with various subcontractors such as the electrician, plumber, bricklayer, suppliers of building materials. Each subcontractor wants to be certain he is going to be paid.*

In order to be entitled to a privilege, the subcontractor and supplier of work and/or materials must:
1. Prior to furnishing work or materials, notify the owner of the land of the existence of the contract, its nature and price.
2. Within thirty days of the completion of the building,

register at court a privilege which is an affidavit stating the amount of his claim.

3. Sue the owner and contractor within three months after registration.

Privileged claims also lie in such diverse matters as:

a. Privilege of the landlord over the moveable effects on leased premises (see chapter 12 on "Leases").

b. Municipal tax claim for land for unpaid taxes.

c. Unpaid vendor who has a privilege upon things he sold and for which the debtor has not paid (see chapters 11 and 16 on "Sale" and "Bankruptcy").

d. Rights of the Crown.

HYPOTHECS (MORTGAGES)

We often use either word to refer to this area of law, however, the Quebec legal term is hypothec.

> *John is interested in purchasing a house in Montreal which is owned by Smith Realty Company. The price is $24,000, with $6,000 down payment and a balance of $18,000. The Jones Insurance Company is prepared to lend John the $18,000 at 9 percent repayable to it at the rate of $150 a month, payable over the next twenty-five years.*

In granting John this loan, the Jones Insurance Company will pay the $18,000 directly to Smith Realty Company. As security for repayment of the loan, John will grant the insurance company a hypothec in its favour upon his new house.

> Art. 2016   Hypothec is a real right upon immoveables made liable for fulfilment of an obligation, in virtue of which the creditor may cause them to be sold in the hands of whomsoever they may be, and have a preference upon the proceeds of the sale in order of date as fixed by this code.

This means that Jones Insurance has a charge upon the immoveable property belonging to John to secure the repayment of the loan. A hypothec has several characteristics:

1. It ceases to exist once the debt to the hypothecary creditor has been paid. Once John pays off the debt he can demand that the hypothec be radiated (cancelled).

2. It exists on the whole and every portion of the immoveable property, even if a part of it is sold. Thus, if John later sells a portion of his lot of land to Charles, the hypothec in favour of the insurance company continues to exist on both John's and Charles's lots as security for the repayment of the debt.

3. It extends to all improvements, additions or buildings which the owner (John) may make later on his land. The additional buildings or improvements being immoveable form part of the security.

> *John builds a garage next to his house after granting the hypothec: the garage forms part of the immoveable property and is therefore part of the security.*

4. It can only be granted on immoveable property, that is, on land and/or buildings.

What Are the Formalities Required to Create a Deed of Hypothec?

1. A hypothec must be granted by a deed made and signed before a notary.

2. The immoveable property hypothecated must be fully described in the deed. Generally, the civic street is specified, (it may be vacant land or a new street with no civic numbers yet given), but also and more importantly, an approved land description called the *official cadastral description* must be given. In Montreal, and in most of the urban areas in Quebec, property is described by lot numbers (or if subdivided, by subdivision number) within a specific area or within a parish.

Consequently, a particular property might be described as subdivision 4, of lot number 23, Parish of Hochelaga, Montreal. Its dimensions and location are usually described in full including details of lots and subdivisions bordering it.

3. A description of the obligation and of the hypothec must be given. In our example it secures the repayment of John's $18,000 loan at $150 per month at 9 percent interest.

4. Descriptions of the hypothecary creditor and debtor are given.

5. Hypothecs must be registered. A notary deposits the deed at the registry office of the court where the property is situated and it is entered in the registry books. A first hypothec is one which is registered before a subsequently registered hypothec, (called a second hypothec).

> *Suppose John has by now repaid $8,000 of his $18,000 and he needs another $2,000 to buy a car. John gets a second loan secured by hypothec for $2,000 and because it is registered second, it is a second hypothec and it ranks for payment after the first hypothec.*

Types of Hypothecs

There are three types of hypothecs: legal, judicial and conventional. For the purposes of this course, only the judicial and conventional will be discussed.

Judicial Hypothecs

A judicial hypothec results from a court judgment. When a creditor obtains a judgment he may register it against immoveable property owned by his debtor, and he may bring the property to sale at any time, even if the property is later transferred or sold to a third party. However, before buying the property the third party has a title search of the registry books made by his lawyer or notary, and this will reveal that a judgment has been registered against the property, and the third party will probably insist that the property be sold to him free and clear of such charges, that is, he wants "clear title."

Conventional Hypothecs

A conventional hypothec results from an agreement in notarial form between the property owner who is granting the hypothec and the party in whose favour it is being granted. Conventional hypothecs usually are made:
1. to secure a loan from a lender to borrower (see example on page 202);
2. to secure the repayment of the balance of sale.

> *John buys a house for $20,000 and makes a down payment of $3,000. By agreement the balance of sale of $17,000 will be secured by a hypothec in favour of the seller, repayable at $150 per month at 9 percent interest.*

**The Effect of Hypothecs on
Debtor, Owner and Other
Holder**

Art. 2053   Hypothecs do not divest the debtor or other holder, either of whom continues to enjoy the property and may alienate it, subject however to the privilege of the hypothec charged upon it.

The meaning of Article 2053 is that the owner of a piece of property which is subject to a hypothec may sell the property to a third person. However, the third person takes the property subject to the hypothec and obliges himself to assume the payments outlined in the mortgage deed as part of the purchase price.

> *In the example on page 202, John bought a house from Smith Realty for $24,000 with a $18,000 mortgage in favour of Jones Insurance Co. John has been*

paying his monthly instalments regularly and he now agrees to sell the house to Wilson. John is able to sell it for $25,000, but it is subject to a balance of hypothec of $14,400. Wilson undertakes in the deed of sale to continue to pay directly to the insurance company the monthly instalments and agrees to pay John cash for the balance of sale.

PRICE	*$25,000*
BALANCE OF MORTGAGE ($150 PER MONTH TO JONES INSURANCE COMPANY) —	*$14,400*
CASH TO JOHN	*$10,600*

In theory, John still remains personally liable for the balance of the loan (since he borrowed the money). In practice, however, the insurance company looks to the present owner, Wilson, for repayment.

Recourses of the Unpaid Hypothecary Creditor

Art. 2058   The hypothecary action is given to creditors whose claims are liquidated and exigible, against all persons holding as proprietors the whole or any portion of the immoveable hypothecated for their claim.

Art. 2061   The object of the hypothecary action is to have the holder of the immoveable condemned to surrender it in order that it may be judicially sold, unless he prefers to pay the debt in principal, interest as secured by registration and costs.

If the owner of a piece of property subject to hypothec does not pay the instalments according to the deed, what can the hypothecary creditor do? Most hypothecs give the hypothecary creditor two rights, either of which he may exercise at his option.

Exigibility Clause

In the event of default (usually nonpayment of the instalments due) under the hypothec, the hypothecary creditor may institute legal proceedings against the present owner of the land, obtain judgment, and have the property sold, and out of the proceeds of the sale, obtain the balance outstanding due under the hypothec.

One can see from Article 2061 that the holder of the immoveable property (John, or later Wilson) is ordered to surrender the property to the mortgagee in order that it may be judicially sold, unless the holder of the property wishes to pay the whole debt.

Dation en Paiement Clause

Usually in the hypothecary deed there is a clause to the following effect, "If you do not pay the instalments and are in default to pay arrears for thirty days, then automatically we will take legal proceedings to become owner of the property as payment of the balance of the mortgage and what you have paid to date is forfeited to us, the creditor." This is a dation en paiement (giving in payment) clause and means that instead of asking that the property be sold, the creditor is asking for the property itself, so that he may become owner.

After the thirty-day (sometimes longer) default period mentioned in the deed, the creditor must by law give a further notice of sixty days (called "sixty-day notice") demanding the debtor to pay the arrears. If the debtor does not pay the arrears within sixty days, then the creditor may take an action to be declared owner and retain the moneys already paid.

Resolutory Clause

If the seller sells an immoveable property with a balance of sale outstanding, then the effect of the dation en paiement clause is achieved by what is called a resolutory clause, namely, the creditor-seller becomes owner, and the property reverts back to the seller.

> *Bob buys a country cottage from Jones Real Estate for $14,000 and pays $3,000 down; the balance is $11,000. Jones obtains a hypothec in its favour for $11,000 to secure the balance of sale. In this case, the hypothecary creditor is the seller. In case of default the seller can reclaim ownership under the resolutory clause.*

> *The Position of the*
> *Second Hypothecary Creditor*

> *When Bob sells his cottage to Ross, if Ross cannot pay the entire $6,400, Bob may take part in cash and the balance secured by a mortgage. As there is already a first mortgage on the property, in favour of Jones Insurance, Bob would have a second mortgage at $50 per month at 12 percent interest.*

> | | |
> |---|---:|
> | *PRICE* | *$15,000* |
> | *FIRST HYPOTHEC BALANCE* | |
> | *PAYABLE TO JONES* | |
> | *INSURANCE COMPANY* | *— 8,600* |
> | *BALANCE OF SALE* | *6,400* |
> | *CASH* | *— 3,000* |
> | *SECOND HYPOTHEC PAYABLE* | |
> | *TO BOB* | *$ 3,400* |

The first hypothec is first because it is registered before Bob's, which is second. If Bob is not being paid on his hypothec, then he may bring the property to sale but the first hypothec would be paid first out of the proceeds of the sale, the balance going to Bob.

Ross does not pay Bob. Bob sues, gets a judgment and a buyer at the sheriff's sale pays $13,000 for the cottage. The first hypothecary creditor gets the balance of the first mortgage of $8,600, Jones then gets $3,400 and Ross gets the balance.

Likewise, if Bob, as vendor, exercises the resolutory clause rights and again becomes owner—his ownership will be subject to the existing first hypothec—upon retaking ownership he must continue payments to the first hypothecary creditor.

Legal Terminology

credit
credit cards
instalments
collateral
conditional sales contract
instalment sales
pawn and pledge
commercial pledge
trust deed
assignment of book debts
general assignment
specific assignment
bulk sale
affidavit
suretyship

surety
privilege
lien
municipal tax
unpaid vendor
hypothec
mortgage
cadastral description
registration
judicial hypothecs
conventional hypothecs
exigibility clause
dation en paiement
resolutory clause
first mortgage
second mortgage

Questions

1. Discuss what is meant by buying on credit.
2. In a credit sale, what is the relationship between the retailer and the finance company, and between the finance company and the consumer?

3. What is a conditional sales contract and what protection does it give to a retailer or finance company?

4. Describe the contract of pledge.

5. What is a commercial pledge?

6. What is a trust deed?

7. Describe the two types of assignment.

8. What is a bulk sale? What must the buyer obtain from the seller?

9. What is meant by security under Sections 86 and 88 of the Bank Act?

10. What is a privilege? What must the supplier of materials or labour do in order to have a privilege?

11. Describe suretyship.

12. How would you use a hypothec if you were purchasing a house?

13. What are the characteristics of a hypothec and what are the formalities for making a hypothec? Describe two types of hypothecs.

14. What is the effect of a hypothec with regard to the debtor, owner and the possessor of the land?

15. Describe what is meant by exigibility, dation en paiement and resolutory clauses.

16. What is a second hypothec?

BUSINESS ORGANIZATIONS

Chapter 15

BUSINESS ORGANIZATIONS

Whenever you buy something from a store, whether from a corner grocery store, bakery or automobile dealership, you are transacting with a business organization. There are three forms of business organizations, each with its own set of rules. The three forms are:
1. the sole proprietorship;
2. the partnership;
3. the corporation.

BUSINESS NAME

The word company is often used loosely by laymen to refer to all three, for example, "I work for Jones Company," when in fact Jones Company is a partnership or a sole proprietorship. Strictly speaking, the word company should be used only when referring to a corporation. The law governing corporations is often called company law. Notwithstanding this observation, the business names of sole proprietorships and partnerships often include the words "Company," "Co.," "Cie.," "Corp." Business names also often include the words "and Sons," "Reg'd.," "Registered." Companies are free to choose any business name, but the name chosen must not be identical or similar to that of an already existing business name, especially, if it is in the same line of business.

Sole proprietors and partners are required to register their business ownership and any changes therein, at the Superior Court business registration office where information concerning corporations is also available. It is through this source that lawyers, acting on behalf of clients, including creditors, can determine the ownership of a particular business organization and consequently, who is responsible for business debts.

> *Jones & Co. owes Roger Sales $5,000. The claim is given to Johnsen, a lawyer, who verifies at the business registration office that the debtor organization was originally a sole proprietorship owned by Jones, who, ten months ago dissolved his sole proprietorship and immediately registered a partnership with Williams under the same name. If the invoices owing are spread over a one-year period, only Jones will be liable for those prior to ten months ago and both Jones and Williams will be liable for the subsequent invoices.*

Art. 1834b 1. Whenever any person or persons make use in business of the name of another person, the contracts, agreements, notices, advertisements, signs, bills of exchange, promissory notes, endorsements, cheques, orders for money or goods, bills of parcels, receipts and letters, which they make, publish, sign or issue under such name in the course of business, shall bear after such name: the word "registered" or an abbreviation thereof.

The above rule is often ignored by the business community.

THE SOLE PROPRIETORSHIP

For the past five years you, along with three employees, have been operating a small retail shoe store in downtown Montreal under the firm name of XYZ Shoe Co. This is a sole proprietorship. The main advantages of a sole proprietorship are:

a. The sole owner keeps all the profits for himself and owns all the assets.

b. He makes all the business decisions and is "his own boss."

The main disadvantages are:

a. He is solely responsible for all the business debts and almost all his assets, including his business, home, car and bank account, are liable to seizure and sale for business debts.

b. Investment and expansion are limited to his own personal resources and borrowing power.

PARTNERSHIP

In order to expand a business, more investment and effort is required. Should the sole proprietor seek one or more partners?

> *You learn that Jones and Smith, whom you know, and both of whom have many years of experience in the shoe industry, want to become partners in an operating shoe store.*

Advantages of entering into a partnership as compared with a sole proprietorship are:

a. Banks, lending companies and suppliers may be more likely to increase loans and credit since the liabilities are fully borne by all the partners.

b. Hopefully, two can manage more and better than one; the partners can divide the management responsibilities.

c. Each partner makes an investment which may result in expansion.

Disadvantages are:

a. The acts of one partner bind the other partners.

b. Profits are divided as each partner must participate in the profits.

c. If the partners disagree, the business may deteriorate.

d. Generally, any partner can end the partnership at any time and if one of them dies the partnership terminates. In both cases, the assets of the partnership may have to be sold and divided. It is important to cover these situations in the partnership agreement so that the partners who want to continue the business can do so by paying off, in a reasonable and equitable manner, either the partner who wants to leave or the heirs of the deceased partner.

After many meetings with Jones and Smith, you decide to go into partnership with them. Your shoe store inventory and "goodwill" of the clientele are evaluated at $30,000. They agree to each invest $30,000 over a two-year period; all of you are to work full time and to divide the profits and losses equally. XYZ Shoe Co. will remain the business name.

You should then visit a lawyer to prepare a partnership agreement and to be advised as to your partnership rights and obligations.

Essential Elements of Partnership

Partnership has been defined as "a contract by which two or more persons put, or oblige themselves to put, something in common, to make, in common, an honest profit." Its purpose is the making of profit by joint common action between two or more persons, called partners.

Common Contribution

Art. 1830   It is essential to the contract of partnership that it should be for the common profit of the partners, each of whom must contribute to its property, credit, skill, or industry.

Participation in Profits and Losses

Art. 1831   Participation in the profits of a partnership carries with it an obligation to contribute to the losses.

Any agreement by which one of the partners is excluded from participation in the profits is null.

An agreement by which one partner is exempt from liability for the losses of the partnership is null only as to third persons.

Article 1831 provides that all the partners must share to some degree in the profits and the partners decide upon its division. It is legal for the partners in their agreement to decide as to how the losses are to be divided between them, and even to exclude one of the partners from bearing the losses. However, such an agreement has no effect upon a creditor who can claim against all the partners who are jointly and severally liable (each is fully responsible) for all the debts. If a partner pays out more than his share, he can claim its repayment from the other partners in accordance with the terms of the agreement.

Art. 1848   When there is no agreement concerning the shares of the partners in the profits and losses of the partnership, they share equally.

Salary

Partners are not entitled to remuneration or salary. However, in practice, they often do draw salaries, which may be considered as partners' drawings against anticipated sharing of profits.

Commencement of Partnership

Art. 1832   If no time for the commencement of the partnership be designated, it takes effect from the date of the contract.

Duration

Art. 1833   If the term of the partnership be not designated, it is considered to be for the life of the partners; subject to the provisions contained in the fifth chapter of this title. (See the discussion on the dissolution of a partnership.)

Rights of a Partner
against the Partnership

Art. 1847   A partner has a right against the partnership not only to recover money disbursed by him for it but also to be indemnified for obligations contracted by him in good faith in the business of the partnership, and for the risks inseparable from his management.

A partner acts as agent for the partnership and as such he binds not only himself as a partner but also the other partners. He is entitled to recover expenses incurred while carrying out his functions.

Management of
Partnership Affairs

Where a manager is appointed either in the original partnership agreement itself or in a subsequent agreement, the following rules apply:

Art. 1849   A partner charged with the management of the business of the partnership by a special clause in the contract, may perform all acts connected with his management, notwithstanding the opposition of the other partners, provided he acts without fraud.

Such power of management cannot be revoked without sufficient cause while the partnership continues; but if the power be given by an instrument posterior to the contract of partnership it is revokable in the same manner as a simple mandate.

Art. 1850   When several of the partners are charged with the management of the business of the partnership generally, and without a provision that one of them shall not act without the others, each of them may act separately; but if there be such a provision, one of them cannot act in the absence of the others, although it be impossible for the latter to join in the act.

If a partner is named manager in the original partnership contract, such appointment is considered as a condition of the original partnership contract and this explains why in the second paragraph of Article 1849 the manager's powers are so difficult to terminate; he may perform administrative acts and his powers cannot be revoked "without sufficient cause," e.g., gross negligence or dishonesty.

However, if the manager is appointed from among the partners by an agreement made subsequent to the original partnership contract, his manager's powers may be revoked by agreement of the other partners. If no partner has been specifically appointed as manager, each partner has equal power to act in the management of the business. Any partner has the power to stop a transaction being entered into by another partner before it is concluded.

> Art. 1851   The partners are presumed to have mutually given to each other a mandate for the management, and whatever is done by one of them binds the others; saving the right of the latter, together or separately, to object to any act before it is concluded.

It is, of course, possible for the partnership to hire a person who is not a partner to act as manager. If such a person is appointed, he binds the partnership so long as he acts within the bounds of his powers as the agent of the partnership (see chapter 10 on "Mandate").

Can a partner associate himself with an outsider as to his own share in the partnership?

> Art. 1853   Each partner may, without the consent of his co-partners associate with himself a third person in the share he has in the partnership. He cannot without such consent associate him in the partnership.

Each partner has the right to dispose of his share but he can sell or otherwise transfer only his right to profits to an outsider. However, this does not mean that a partner has a right to force upon his other partners a new partner to take his place.

What is the power of one partner to bind the partnership?

Each partner is, as regards outside third parties, an agent of the partnership, possessing the authority consistent with the type of partnership business, unless in actual fact the partner so acting clearly has no such authority to act for the partnership.

> *If Jones orders grocery merchandise allegedly for the business of the partnership and it is really for Jones's own family use, the partnership business is not bound and Jones himself is personally responsible and liable.*

Are members of a partnership liable for the wrongful acts of a partner?

> *Jones, a partner in a garage takes the tow truck to pull out a client's (Smith's) automobile caught in a snow bank. On the way back to the garage, Jones goes through a red light and damages Brown's parked car. Since Jones was in the performance of partnership work, the partnership is liable to the same extent as Jones himself. This liability of the firm for Jones's wrongful act means that the partners in the firm are liable jointly and severally for the damage caused to Brown's automobile.*

What is the effect of bringing a new partner into the partnership?

The old partnership is dissolved and a new partnership is formed. The new partner is not liable to the creditors of the partnership for the debts incurred before he becomes a partner. However, the partner who retires from a partnership business remains liable for the debts of the partnership incurred before he left the partnership.

It is important, whenever dissolving a partnership and starting a new one, to immediately register the dissolution of the old partnership and the new registration to give notice to third parties as to who now owns the business.

Partnership Books

The books and ledgers of the partnership are usually kept at the business office of the partnership and if there is more than one place of business, for example, if there are several stores in the operation, then they are kept at the principal place of business. Every partner has the right to inspect these books and records and the manager must render account and give full particulars of all his management to the partners.

Dissolution of Partnership

Art. 1892   Partnership is dissolved:
1. By the efflux of time;
2. By the extinction or loss of the partnership property;
3. By the accomplishment of the business for which it was contracted;
4. By bankruptcy;
5. By the death of one of the partners;
6. By the interdiction or bankruptcy of one of the partners;
7. By the will of one or more of the partners not to continue the partnership, according to Articles 1895 and 1896;
8. By the business of the partnership becoming impossible or unlawful.

By the Efflux of Time

If the partners are agreed to carry on the partnership for a period of three years only, at the end of three years, the partnership is dissolved.

Extinction or Loss of the Partnership Company

Art. 1893 When one of the partners has promised to put in common the property in a thing, the loss of such thing before the contribution of it has been made, dissolves the partnership with respect to all the partners.

The partnership is equally dissolved by the loss of the thing when only the enjoyment of it is put in common, and the property of the thing remains with the partner.

But the partnership is not dissolved by the loss of the thing of which the property has already been brought into the partnership; unless such thing constitutes the whole capital stock of the partnership, or is so important a part of it that the business of the partnership cannot be carried on without it.

There must be a loss of something so important to the partnership business that without it the partnership business cannot be carried on, e.g., if all the machinery in a factory business is destroyed by fire.

By the Death of One of the Partners

Generally, the partnership is dissolved by the death of one of the partners. However, Article 1894 states:

Art. 1894 It may be stipulated that in case of the death of one of the partners, the partnership shall continue with his legal representatives, or only between the surviving partners. In the latter case, the representative of the deceased partner is entitled to a division of the partnership property, only as it exists at the time of the partner's death. He cannot claim the benefit of any transaction subsequent thereto, unless such transaction is a necessary consequence of something done before the death occurred.

By the Will of One or More of the Partners

This refers to partnerships entered into without a period of time stipulated and in which case a partner can dissolve the partnership at any time. A partner must not be held for all of his life to the obligations of the partnership, this being contrary to the principal of personal liberty. However, such a partner must act in good faith and must not demand dissolution at a time which is unfavourable for the partnership.

> Art. 1895 Those partnerships only which are *not* limited as to duration can be dissolved at the will of any one of the partners, by a notice to all the others of his renunciation. Such renunciation must be in good faith, and not made at a time unfavourable for the partnership.

> Art. 1896 The dissolution of a partnership limited as to duration, may be demanded by one of the partners before the expiration of the stipulated term, upon just cause shewn, or when another partner fails to fulfill his engagement, or is guilty of gross misconduct or from habitual informity or physical impossibility is unable to attend to the business of the partnership, or when his condition and status are essentially changed, and in other cases of a like nature.

COMPANY LAW

Your partnership with Jones and Smith is now successfully operating a chain of five retail shoe stores selling medium- and low-price shoe lines. There are plans for further expansion; some friends would like to invest. But the partners are concerned about personal responsibility for business debts.

What if business were to fail because of a serious economic recession? The business would soon be unable to meet its obligations. Each partner's personal property including his house, boat, automobile and bank account could be seized and sold by the business' creditors. The three of you consult with your lawyer and he advises you to incorporate, that is, to form a corporation—XYZ Shoe Co. Limited. What are the reasons for incorporating and what are the main characteristics of a corporation?

Limited Liability

In a sole proprietorship, the individual owner is fully liable for all the business debts; in a partnership, the owners are each fully liable for the business debts. In both cases, virtually all their assets are seizable by the creditors. There is thus individual unlimited liability for business debts.

A corporation, which is created by either the federal or provincial government on application is a legal person with rights and obligations and is separate and distinct from its owners who are called shareholders. The liability of the shareholder is limited to payment of the price of the shares purchased. The investment of you and your associates in a corporation might be largely through the purchase of shares, although you could also lend money to the corporation. As long as you paid for these shares you would not be personally liable as shareholders for company debts. The creditors only have recourse against the company's assets and not the personal assets of the individual shareholders. The risk is limited to the amount of investment. This is why corporations and businessmen are prepared to invest in new business ventures through the setting up of new corporations.

Some major creditors, such as a bank or a landlord, before extending credit to a new corporation, will insist upon a personal guarantee of the principal shareholders. Generally speaking, however, suppliers of goods are anxious to get new customers and will extend some credit without personal guarantees. The advantage of the liability being limited to the company is obvious. One can carry on business and be assured that should the venture be unsuccessful, what has been put in the form of share investment may be lost, but no more.

Why invest? Profit making is the investment motive; the investors hope that the company will succeed, that profits will be realised and that these profits will, at least in part, be distributed to the shareholders as *dividends*. If the operation is successful, the value of the shares goes up and if they wish, such shares can be sold at a profit to other persons.

Companies are not established to avoid business responsibilities, but rather as an act of prudence. You would be well advised to incorporate, consequently separating your obligations from those of the company. Often when an established company decides to start an entirely new business venture, it will do so by setting up and investing in a new and separate corporation and it does this at least partly in order to limit the risk to its investment. If the new venture is unsuccessful only the share investment is lost.

Distinct Personality
of the Corporation

To form a corporation in Quebec, you and at least two associates (a minimum of three incorporators is required) sign an application for incorporation and submit it to the appropriate federal or provincial government authority, which, after due consideration, may grant a corporate charter. XYZ Shoe Co. Limited will then become a distinct legal personality with its own name and specific objects. Its existence is separate from that of its shareholders, directors, officers and employees. Thus, if all of these persons were to suddenly die, the corporation would continue to exist, and its assets would not form part of the deceaseds' estates. The shareholders have certain rights which are primarily to vote at shareholders' meetings, to receive dividends when they are declared, and to share in the capital assets, if any, when the company ceases operations and is "wound up."

This is unlike a partnership where, upon the death of

one of the partners, the partnership is dissolved and the assets divided. Also, remember that any partner can, at any time, dissolve the partnership and that to bring in a new partner requires the unanimous consent of all the partners.

In a corporation, a person can become a part owner by the purchase of shares, and this in no way affects the corporate existence. Similarly, a shareholder can leave the corporation by disposing of his shares. There are exceptions to this rule of distinct separation between share owners and the corporation where the courts will "lift the corporate veil."

> *Where shareholders use a company for fraudulent purposes the courts have held that the operators themselves are personally liable. It is no valid defence for them to claim that since the transactions were carried on in the company name, it is only the company that is responsible. They cannot hide their acts behind this "corporate veil."*

Depending upon the nature and size of the business, there may be distinct tax advantages in operating as a corporation. It is a truism that, in North America, for a business to expand beyond a certain point, it must incorporate: efficient business management requires it.

Disadvantages of Incorporating

1. Operating under a partnership can be informal; its termination is accomplished at the will of any one partner. On the other hand, a corporation is surrounded by formalities, records, reports to government authorities, annual meetings, auditors, etc.
2. If a company share owner wants to get his money back he cannot force the company to buy back his shares, nor can he force the company to "wind up" except in unusual circumstances, in which event the assets would be eventually divided

among the shareholders, and if the share owner cannot find a buyer he is locked into an unsatisfactory position.

3. When the application for incorporation is sent to the government it is accompanied by a cheque to cover the incorporation fee. This cost, which may vary depending upon whether it is a federal or provincial application, is based upon how much authorised capital you request in your application. If you ask that the company be authorised to issue $50,000 worth of shares, the filing fee is approximately $150.

A Federal or Quebec Charter

The federal government, through the Canada Corporations Act, and Quebec, through the Quebec Companies Act, both exercise their authority to issue corporation charters, incorporating commercial and industrial organizations as well as nonprofit organizations (religious, philanthropic, professional) without share capital.

In theory, provincial companies can exercise their power only for provincial purposes. To operate in another province the company may first have to obtain the right to do so by registering as an extraprovincial company. By agreement, however, Quebec and Ontario incorporated companies are exempt from such registration in the other province.

Difference between a Private and a Public Company

If a corporation is to be owned by only a few interested persons, then it may be dependent for its success upon how well these few persons work together. If requested, the company may be structured so as to limit the number of shareholders to fifty and to restrict shareholders transferring their shares to outsiders. This is referred to as a *private company*. These shares are not traded through a public stock exchange, and any invitation by the company to the public to buy these shares is prohibited. Many "one man" or "family held" businesses operate as private companies. So long as the share owners are able to obtain sufficient money and other required resources, there is no need to look elsewhere. However, if in order to operate or expand substantial further capital is required, then this private company may, by following specific formalities convert to a *public company* and offer shares for sale to the public.

In order to sell shares to the public a great number of laws and regulations must be complied with to ensure that the public is fully protected as to the nature of the company, its operations and the value of the shares.

Most provinces have a Provincial Securities Commission which regulates the sale of such shares. Immediately before any share offering is made to the public, a complete outline called a *prospectus* must be filed and receive the approval of the Securities Commissions in each province in which the shares are to be offered. This prospectus should set out in a clear manner, among other things, the nature of the company operations, its history, financial position and immediate prospects.

After giving consideration to the above facts and law and more particularly since you intend to do business both across Canada and in foreign countries, you and your two associates decide to incorporate a private company under the federal Canada Corporations Act. It should be noted that both the federal Act and the Quebec Companies Act have their origins in English company law and are, broadly speaking, quite similar.

What information is required in the application for federal incorporation which you and your associates will sign?

1. Names, addresses and occupations of the applicants, each of whom must agree to purchase at least one share.

2. The company name: you cannot choose a name which is the same name or similar to the name of another business carrying on its operations in Canada. However, if you are incorporating a company to carry on the business previously carried on by the partnership, you probably can obtain the partnership name: XYZ Shoes Co. becomes XYZ Shoes Co.

Limited because it is now a company. The name may be both in English and French or in either language, and if it's in both languages, the company may use either name from time to time. Generally, no name indicating royalty or government will be granted to a new company, e.g., "Royal," "Empire," "Queen's." One of the aims of these restrictions is to avoid confusion in the mind of the public as to who is carrying on business. The last word under the federal Act must be "Limited" or "Ltd." This is to indicate to third persons that they are dealing with a corporation and consequently, with the limited liability of shareholders. Under the Quebec Companies Act, a wider latitude is permitted in choosing the last word of the corporate name, such as "Company," "Cie.," "Corp.," "Corporation," "Incorporated," "Inc."

3. The *objects clause* describes the business operation to be carried on. The company will be taking over the partnership's five retail shoe stores which presently buy shoes, leather goods and accessories direct from Canadian and foreign manufacturers. However, you might at some future date consider manufacturing these items. The following might be suitable as an objects clause:

To engage in the manufacture, import, export, sale and distribution, both wholesale and retail, of shoes, leather goods and accessories.

It is always possible later, if necessary, to change the objects clause by amending the charter. The various Companies Acts give the company additional incidental powers which do not need to be applied for.

4. Head office: your main business office is on Ste. Catherine Street in Montreal where you keep your books and records, where you have your executive offices and where the administrative functions are carried on. A company must have a head office and this is generally where it will be; it can be changed with only minor formalities.

CAPITALISATION

How does a newly-formed company acquire capital assets? It may acquire them through purchase, lease (e.g., machines, building) or borrowing (e.g., money) and in so doing, the company incurs liabilities and creditors. Often when the company borrows on a large scale, it issues a bond or debenture in favour of the lender which gives the lender security upon corporate assets so that in the event of nonpayment these assets may be sold and the proceeds paid to the lender.

If the company sells its shares to investors, the latter are not company creditors, rather they are share owners (shareholders) who have bought shares in the expectation that the company will be successful, thus paying dividends and probably increasing the value of their shares. If the company is unsuccessful, the shareholders cannot claim the return of their investment. They are not creditors; they are investors who have risked their capital hoping to make a profit.

A wide choice of type and amount of share capital is available to the applicants. *Total authorised capital* means the total number and value of shares which the company is authorised to issue, that is, the maximum permitted. *Issued capital* refers to the shares that have been sold to shareholders. The money paid for shares is called *paid-up capital.*

There are two main classes of shares, namely, preferred shares and common shares.

Preferred Shares

These are shares which have special rights and limitations attached to them. Usually these rights entitle the holders to be preferred in the receipt of a dividend in a specified amount or percentage over the holders of common shares.

> *An 8 percent $100 preferred share entitles its holder to receive dividends of up to $8 for each share before the holder of the common shares receives any dividend.*

Preferred shares have other features; they are either cumulative or noncumulative, participating or nonparticipating. *Cumulative* means that the dividend right accumulates year by year.

When dividends are not paid out for two years on an 8 percent $100 share, but are paid in the third year, the holder is entitled to 3 X 8 percent = 24 percent for each share, or $24, before dividends are paid to the holders of common shares.

Noncumulative means that if dividends are not paid one year no accumulation occurs; the preferred dividend is available only for those years in which a dividend is declared and paid, and if it is omitted in any year there is no right to a dividend in other years.

If preferred shares are *participating,* their owners, after receiving their preferred dividend, then participate further by additional dividends. If the preferred shares are not specifically described as participating, they are deemed *nonparticipating.*

Voting Rights

Preferred shareholders often have no right to attend or to vote at shareholders' meetings except under certain company acts which provide such right if dividends have not been declared for a certain period, usually two years.

Preferred shares often carry the *right of redemption;* the company may, at its option and out of funds specially set aside for that purpose, buy back the preferred shares and repay the original purchase price with a premium in some instances. For example, a company may buy back fifteen $100 preferred shares and pay the $100 plus a premium of $20 (total $120) for each share. The preferred shares usually have the right to be repaid their value out of the proceeds upon the company ceasing its operations and being wound up, before common shareholders receive anything but only after all creditors have been paid.

Common Shares

Common shares are nonpreference, ordinary shares with no peculiar rights attached. However, common shares do have certain very important rights. The holders of these shares have voting rights at shareholders' meetings where such matters as the election of directors, appointment of auditors and changes in the company's charter have to be approved. Although the preferred shareholders may have priority as to dividends, the dividends of common shareholders may be larger.

Par Value Shares, No Par Value Shares

Both common and preferred shares are either *par value* or *no par value*. Par value shares are shares whose individual minimum price is fixed in the charter.

> *A company may be authorised to issue 1,000 par value common shares, each at the par value of $10. The company cannot sell such shares for less than $10 each. It can, however, sell the shares for more.*

The weakness of having only par value shares is that the face, or par, value of $10 each may not reflect the actual worth of the shares and they may be difficult to sell.

> *A company is experiencing financial difficulties and tries to raise money by selling its $10 par value shares. Investors are only prepared to pay $6 per share, which reflects the actual worth of the shares. Since the company cannot sell the shares for less than par value, these shares cannot be sold. However, holders of such shares, unlike the company, can sell them below par, that is, at less than $10.*

Preferred shares with their preferred dividend rights are often par value. In small, private companies where there may be no need to raise money, shares are often par value only or divided into both par value and no par value.

No par value shares do not have a stipulated value and can be sold by the company at any price.

The charter of Jones Manufacturing Co. Ltd. authorises the issuance of 1,000 no par value shares for a maximum total aggregate price of $100,000. This means that the company can issue up to 1,000 shares but can sell them for no more than a total price of $100,000. On April 1, 100 shares are sold at $50 per share—$5,000 worth. This leaves another 900 shares which can be sold at a total maximum price of $95,000. On September 15, the company's financial position and prospects have greatly improved and buyers are prepared to pay $100 per share. Another 500 shares are sold for $100 each—for a total of $50,000. This leaves 400 shares which can later be sold by the company for a total remaining price of $45,000. The price at which no par value shares are sold is usually a good reflection of their actual worth.

After considering the types of shares available you and your associates might decide to apply for authorised capital of $50,000 divided as follows:

a. 1,000 no par value common with a maximum total aggregate value of $40,000;

b. 100 8 percent noncumulative preferred with a par value of $100 each.

A company is not required to sell most or all its authorised capital. The minimum requirement is that each applicant for incorporation purchase a share and that each member of the board of directors own a share and be an officer or director of a corporate shareholder. Often, only a small portion of the authorised capital is issued, and this is especially true for the private company that is able to arrange its financing other than through the sale of its shares.

The danger of selling shares is that newcomers will be able to vote at shareholders' meetings including the election of directors. If, however, all the authorised capital is issued, the company can apply for further authorised capital by making an application for supplementary letters patent.

There are a number of general rules of company law found in most jurisdictions whose purpose is to protect creditors and shareholders from unwarranted depletion of company funds. These rules include the following:

1. No dividends can be issued if the company is insolvent or if by issuing dividends its financial position will be impaired.
2. Usually no loans are permitted to directors.
3. Annual audited financial statements must be submitted to the shareholders at the annual meeting of shareholders.

How do you become a shareholder?

a. by being an applicant for incorporation;
b. by agreeing to purchase shares from the company after incorporation;
c. by acquiring shares from another shareholder, generally by purchase but sometimes by inheritance.

In public companies, shares are bought and sold freely, but in private companies there are usually restrictions on share transfers set out in the charter itself, or in the by-laws of the company (see the discussion of by-laws in this chapter). This means that before a shareholder can transfer his shares to another person he must comply with certain formalities.

The usual share transfer restriction clause provides that no shares may be transferred without the consent of the board of directors. It may also provide that in the absence of such consent no shares may be transferred without first offering them for sale to the already existing shareholders.

The purpose of restricting transfer of shares is to protect the private nature of the company and make it difficult for "outsiders" to become shareholders.

The application for the incorporation of XYZ Shoes Co. Limited, along with the filing fee, is forwarded by your lawyer to the Corporation Branch, Department of Consumer and Corporate Affairs, Ottawa. If the application is under the Quebec Companies Act, the documents are forwarded to the Department of Financial Institutions, Companies and Co-operatives, Quebec City. If there are no objections to the application, notice will be received that the application has been approved and a short time later the charter itself will be forwarded.

The company is now ready to begin operations.

WHO RUNS THE COMPANY?

The Board of Directors

A company exists in virtue of its charter as a legal person with rights and obligations. However, only through people can it make decisions and function.

The top decision-making body in the corporation is the board of directors. Its principal features are as follows:

a. It is composed of at least three directors, each of whom is elected at the annual meeting of shareholders. To qualify for election, one must be a shareholder or an officer or director of a corporate shareholder.

b. The directors act collectively rather than individually. They sit together "as a board" and make decisions on behalf of the company.

c. The board makes the major management decisions, forms company policy and controls the overall company operation. It alone decides whether or not profits are to be retained or distributed in the form of dividends to the shareholders.

d. In small, private, "closely held" companies such as XYZ Shoe Co. Limited, where there are few shareholders, all or most of whom are involved in the operation of the business, it is usual for these shareholders to be the directors.

e. In large, private firms, both the major shareholders or their representatives plus professional experts, with nominal shares are usually elected to the board.

f. In public companies, especially those operating internationally, shareholders may number in the thousands and a relatively small portion usually exercise their voting rights at shareholders' meetings. The board of directors is composed for the most part of professional management experts, drawn from law, management, finance, engineering, marketing and production, whose shareholdings are often nominal and who are often re-elected from year to year as long as the company performs reasonably well. The board of directors, controlling relatively small blocks of shares, can by strategic voting, ensure their re-election.

Officers

The board of directors elects from among its members the president and also appoints senior company employees as "officers." These officers usually have delegated to them important individual powers and duties. The officers include in addition to the president, the vice-presidents, the secretary, the treasurer, etc.; their responsibilities are often set forth in the general by-laws. A company often has senior officers who are not directors. Thus, a number of vice-presidents may be appointed to be in charge of marketing, sales, production, etc., none of whom has to be a director. These various officers usually have authority to hire and fire certain personnel in their own departments and to enter into contracts with third persons. For example, a sales manager can approve orders made by salesmen under his jurisdiction up to a certain value. He, in turn, reports to the vice-president of sales for approval of larger orders.

It is through this chain of command that the corporation functions. It is a bureaucracy shaped like a pyramid. The board is at the top, the senior officers are next in line, then comes middle management officers such as the assistant treasurer and the assistant controller, followed by personnel with limited authority, white collar and blue collar employees performing routine work.[1]

The top officers are responsible to the board which can at any time relieve any or all of these officers of their positions, from the president down, and can elect other persons to fill these offices.

1. For more information in this area, an interesting and challenging book is highly recommended: J.K. Galbraith's *The New Industrial State,* 2nd ed. (Boston: Houghton Mifflin Co., 1967). Read also Charles A. Reich's *The Greening of America* (New York: Random House, Inc., 1970). Excellent journals include *Fortune* and *Harvard Business Review;* for example, see the article by M. L. Mace, "The President and the Board of Directors," in *Harvard Business Review,* 50, no. 2 (March–April 1972): 37.

Responsibility of Directors

Fiduciary (Trust) Position

The position of a director in relation to the company is similar to that of an agent; he owes it loyalty and honesty and must not benefit secretly at the expense of the company (see chapter 10 on "Mandate"). When they vote at directors' meetings, directors must do so solely in the best interests of the company.

> Ross is a director of company A. Unknown to the other directors, he has major shareholdings in company B. Company A is about to enter into a contract with company B, to the greater benefit of company B. Ross votes for acceptance of the contract. Ross should have advised the board of directors of company A of his conflict of interest, and should have declared his interest and abstained from voting. Company A may take steps to have the contract cancelled or have Ross reimburse profits realised.

Degree of Care and Skill

A director is required to act reasonably and with the diligence and skill which an average and reasonable businessman would exercise. There is a growing trend which requires a director to act diligently, although if he has been misled by company personnel he will probably not be liable. He certainly must not be wilfully or deliberately dishonest, nor must he shut his eyes to others acting dishonestly or negligently.

Legal Liability of Directors

There are certain company debts which, if the company is

unable to pay, may become the joint and several responsibility of the directors. These debts include:

a. six months' unpaid wages of employees;
b. certain taxes;
c. loans to shareholders;
d. excessive dividends.

RIGHTS OF THE SHAREHOLDERS

The principal features of the annual shareholders' meeting are:

a. The shareholders vote for directors in accordance with their own personal preferences and interests. These may not necessarily be in the best interest of the company. In voting they keep in mind the board's past performance including the corporation's financial health, prospects and dividends record.

b. Only shareholders can qualify for directorship.

c. Each shareholder has one vote for each of his voting shares; the more shares, the more votes. Thus ownership of 51 percent of the voting shares means voting control of the election to the board.

However, once the directors are elected, the shareholders do not as a general rule (except to ratify by-laws) participate or engage in policy-making decisions. The shareholder's recourse, if he is dissatisfied, is to sell his shareholdings wherever possible or to vote for different directors at the next annual shareholders' meeting.

In XYZ Shoes Co. Limited, you and your associates wear "two hats," one as majority shareholders voting in yourselves to sit on the board and the other one as directors.

Before the annual shareholders' meeting, the company forwards to the shareholders an up-to-date financial statement of the company audited by the company's auditors. This information assists the shareholders in determining the value and the performance of the company.

The shareholders are entitled to examine certain documents at the company's head office, including the company charter, by-laws, minutes of shareholders' meetings, share transfers, and names and addresses of all shareholders, details which may be useful in the event that a group of shareholders want to organise the shareholders to depose the current board.

WHAT RULES GOVERN THE BUSINESS OPERATIONS OF THE COMPANY?

1. The charter is the corporate constitution which sets out only the broad guidelines—company name, authorised capital, head office, objects, etc. This is the framework.

2. The law: the government statute under which the charter is issued is a document containing many important provisions. There are also an increasing number of other government regulations (federal, provincial and municipal) covering such matters as workmen's compensation, income tax, excise tax, antipollution, securities, zoning, health and fire.

3. By-laws: these are rules created from time to time by the board of directors and approved by the shareholders. They are sometimes changed and replaced by new by-laws whenever the situation requires it. These rules govern the day-to-day operation of the business. There are basically three types of by-laws.

a. General by-laws: these are the first by-laws passed by the board and approved at the first meeting of shareholders. They are very detailed and extensive, and cover such matters as directors' meetings, including requirements as to chairman, quorum, remuneration, officers and their powers, shareholders' meetings, including voting procedures, banking and borrowing, and dividends.

b. By-laws concerning changes in the charter: if the board decides to change, for example, the authorised capital, the company name, or the location of head office, it passes a by-law to that effect and calls a special meeting of the shareholders to approve of these changes.

c. By-laws concerning certain special transactions or ones not covered by the general by-laws: e.g., sale of a major part of the company's assets.

Legal Terminology

sole proprietorship
partnership
corporation
company
Co., Cie., Corp.
Registered (Reg'd.)
partners
liabilities
credit
investment
profits
debts
assets
inventory
goodwill
partnership agreement
common contribution
participation
losses
joint and several liability
drawings
commencement
duration
indemnification
manager
administration
sufficient cause
agent
partnership books
dissolution

renunciation
limited liability
shareholders
shares
investment
dividends
distinct personality
application
incorporators
charter
assets
private company
public company
securities commission
prospectus
objects clause
head office
capitalisation
authorised capital
issued capital
paid-up capital
preferred shares
cumulative
noncumulative
participating
nonparticipating
voting rights
right of redemption
common shares
par value

no par value　　　　　　vice-president
stock exchange　　　　　secretary
transfer　　　　　　　　treasurer
board of directors　　　　annual shareholders' meeting
officers　　　　　　　　financial statement
president　　　　　　　by-laws

Questions

1. What are the main forms of business organizations?
2. List the various names to designate a business.
3. Where are sole proprietors and partners required to register their business name?
4. Describe the main advantages and disadvantages of being a sole proprietor of a business.
5. Describe the main advantages and disadvantages of a partnership.
6. Define partnership.
7. Explain the partners' participation in profits and losses.
8. When does a partnership commence and what is its duration?
9. What are the rights of a partner against the partnership?
10. Discuss management of the partnership.
11. Can a partner associate himself with an outsider?
12. What is the effect of bringing a new partner into the partnership?
13. What are partnership books, where are they kept and who has a right to inspect them?
14. How is a partnership dissolved?
15. What is meant by limited liability of a corporation?
16. How is a corporation created?
17. What is the liability of the shareholder?
18. What is meant by the distinct personality of the corporation?
19. Discuss the differences between a limited company and a partnership.
20. What is meant by the "corporate veil"?
21. What are the disadvantages of incorporating?
22. Name the two principal company Acts.

23. Describe the difference between a private and public company.

24. What is a prospectus?

25. What is the role of the Provincial Securities Commission?

26. What information is required in the application for incorporation?

27. What restrictions are there in choosing the company name?

28. What is meant by the objects clause?

29. What is meant by the head office?

30. How does a newly formed company acquire capital assets?

31. What rights do shareholders have against the company that is unsuccessful?

32. Describe the following:

a. total authorised capital;

b. issued capital.

33. Describe the general characteristics of preferred shares and include in your answer the right to dividends, participation and voting rights.

34. Describe the general characteristics of common shares, and include in your answer the meaning of par value shares and no par value shares.

35. What is the requirement to be a member of the board of directors?

36. What rules protect creditors and shareholders from unwarranted depletion of company funds?

37. How may a person become a shareholder?

38. How may the transfer of shares be restricted?

39. Who constitutes the board of directors?

40. What is the role of the board of directors?

41. What is meant by officers of a company?

42. What are the responsibilities of a director?

43. What are the liabilities of a director?

44. What are the rights of shareholders at the annual shareholders' meeting?

45. What rules and laws govern the business operation of a company?

46. Describe the various types of by-laws.

BANKRUPTCY

Chapter 16

BANKRUPTCY

John Smith operates a garage. Unfortunately, another garage opens nearby and he loses a substantial part of his business causing him to be unable to make prompt payment of his business debts. Creditors begin pressing him for payment. One sues and the others are threatening to do the same. He borrows some money to stem the tide but this does not really help. His accountant advises him he is hopelessly insolvent.

What should John do? He can:

a. voluntarily go into bankruptcy; or

b. continue to operate the garage and wait for a creditor to "force him" into bankruptcy; or

c. make an offer of settlement to his creditors (a proposal).

The law governing bankruptcy is found in the Bankruptcy Act, a federal statute, bankruptcy being one of the matters falling within federal jurisdiction under the terms of the B.N.A. Act. (Our references throughout this chapter will be to various sections of the Bankruptcy Act). Thus, bankruptcy law and procedure is uniform across Canada. The law has gradually evolved to the point where today there is no presumption of fraud on the part of the bankrupt. He is presumed to be and usually is a perfectly honest individual who for any of a multitude of reasons is in a bad financial condition and is unable to meet his obligations as they become due. In our highly flexible economy it is not uncommon for a business enterprise to suffer serious financial loss within a very short period of time and to be reduced to an insolvent position. Some bankruptcies are, on the other hand, fraudulent, and if proven so, persons involved are subject to punitive measures under the Bankruptcy Act and the Criminal Code.

The purposes of the Bankruptcy Act are:

a. to distribute the bankrupt's assets among the various categories of creditors;

b. to release the honest bankrupt debtor from his debts so that he can have a chance to start afresh.

To be eligible for bankruptcy, one must be insolvent.

Who Is Considered an Insolvent Person?

An insolvent person is one who is not bankrupt and who resides or carries on business in Canada, whose liabilities to creditors, provable as claims under the Bankruptcy Act, amount to $1,000, and

1. who is for any reason unable to meet his obligations as they generally become due; or

2. who has ceased paying his current obligations in the ordinary course of business as they generally become due; or

3. the aggregate of whose property is not, at a fair valuation, sufficient, or, if disposed of at a fairly conducted sale under legal process, would not be sufficient to enable payment of all of his obligations, due and accruing due.[1]

Who May Be Declared Bankrupt?

An individual, a partnership, a corporation, an unincorporated association, a cooperative society are all entitled to go into bankruptcy.

You do not have to be in business to "go bankrupt." A labourer, housewife, artist—all qualify.

ADMINISTRATION OF THE BANKRUPTCY ACT

The top official is the *Superintendent of Bankruptcy* in

---

1. The property of a bankrupt estate is everything which the bankrupt person owns except for that which is exempt from seizure under the provincial law (see chapter 3).

Ottawa. He provides overall supervision of the administration of bankrupt estates. His duties include issuing annual licences to trustees and examining their reports. The Superintendent also orders investigations and inspections of certain bankruptcies. *Trustees* attend to the administrative details and arrange for the collecting and liquidation of the assets and the distribution of the proceeds, after expenses, among the creditors. Each bankrupt estate is administered by a licensed trustee.

Canada is divided into ten bankruptcy districts, each province constituting one district. Each district is divided into two or more bankruptcy divisions. In each division there is one or more bankruptcy court officers called *official receivers* who make reports to the Superintendent concerning each bankruptcy case occurring in that judicial division. There are twenty bankruptcy divisions in Quebec.

Qualifications for Declaring Bankruptcy

In order for an insolvent person to qualify for bankruptcy he must have committed "an act of bankruptcy." The most common act of bankruptcy is that the debtor "ceases to meet his liabilities generally as they become due." This means that the debtor doesn't pay his debts to his creditors when due. Other acts of bankruptcy include leaving Canada permanently in order to avoid creditors, the fraudulent transfer of property to a third person to avoid payment to creditors, notifying creditors that there is no money available to pay claims.

How to Declare Bankruptcy

There are two ways to become bankrupt:
1. The debtor may voluntarily decide to go bankrupt.
2. A creditor or creditors may force the debtor into bankruptcy.

Voluntary Assignment

The insolvent debtor owing more than $1,000, whether an individual, a partnership or a limited company, with creditors pressing for payment, goes to a licensed trustee to transfer (assign) to him all his assets and liabilities. He is saying in effect, "Here are my assets as well as all my liabilities.[2] Pay off my creditors as best you can."

When a debtor makes a voluntary assignment, the debtor's property transfers immediately into the hands of the trustee. Thus the trustee has the right to claim the debtor's assets.

The trustee obtains from the debtor a list of the creditors and the amount owing to each and files in court the debtor's voluntary assignment. From that moment the debtor is in bankruptcy.

The trustee sends to the creditors by registered mail:
a. notification that the debtor is bankrupt and of the date and time of the *first meeting of creditors* which is to be held at the bankruptcy office at court;
b. a list of the names of the creditors and the amounts owing to each;
c. a claim form (called proof of claim) which the creditor fills in with the details of his claim. For example, John Wilson, a creditor, makes a claim in the amount of $375 for merchandise sold and delivered and attaches proof of his claim, usually the statement of account and invoices. This proof must be filed with the trustee before the meeting of the creditors if the creditor wants to vote there. The larger the claim the more votes the creditor can cast.

Petition in Bankruptcy
or Receiving Order

By this procedure the debtor is forced into bankruptcy by a creditor. The creditor with a current claim of not less than

---

2. See footnote on page 244 describing the property of a bankrupt estate.

$1,000 (or two or more creditors with claims totalling at least $1,000) can, through his lawyer, file a petition in bankruptcy requesting that the Bankruptcy Court declare the debtor bankrupt and that a receiving order be made against the debtor.

The creditor's petition generally alleges the amount owing to him, the nature of the claim and that the debtor has ceased to meet his liabilities generally as they came due, and suggests the name of a trustee to act upon the debtor being declared bankrupt. Attached to the petition is the sworn statement (affidavit) of the creditor. This petition is served upon the debtor who is given at least eight days from the date of service upon him to contest the petition. If the debtor does not contest, or if his contestation is not maintained by the judge, then a receiving order is made against the bankrupt, and the trustee takes over the estate of the debtor. From this point on, the procedure is the very same as that followed in the case where the debtor has made a voluntary assignment and the trustee mails the notices of the first meeting of creditors.

The Interim Receiver

A creditor has filed a petition in bankruptcy today against a debtor. The date of hearing before the court is, let us say, ten days from now. However, during this ten-day period the debtor is not in bankruptcy and, if he is dishonest, may take the opportunity to secrete and otherwise illegally dispose of his assets. Therefore, immediately after filing the petition in bankruptcy the creditor can apply to the court for appointment of a trustee to act as interim receiver, to look after the debtor's assets until the petition has been later decided upon by the court.

Section 28 (1)   The court may, if it is shown to be necessary for the protection of the estate, at any time after the filing of a petition and before a receiving order is made, appoint a licensed trustee as interim receiver of the property of the debtor or of any part thereof and direct him to take immediate possession thereof upon such undertaking being given by the petitioner as the court may impose as to interference with the debtor's legal rights and as to damages in the event of the petition being dismissed.

(2) The interim receiver may, under the direction of the court, take conservatory measures and summarily dispose of property that is perishable or likely to depreciate rapidly in value and exercise such control over the business of the debtor as the court deems advisable, but the interim receiver shall not unduly interfere with the debtor in the carrying on of his business except as may be necessary for such conservatory purposes or to comply with the order of the court.

The First Meeting of the Creditors

The creditors attend the Bankruptcy Court on the date fixed by the trustee in the notice sent out to them, and can vote either personally or by proxy (appointing someone to vote on their behalf).

The chairman of this meeting is the *official receiver* who is a court official. The trustee actively participates in the meeting. The creditors' powers are rather limited at this stage. The creditors can vote only if they have filed their proof of claims with the trustee before this meeting. The proceedings at the meeting are quite brief and informal with three purposes:

1. to determine the state of affairs of the debtor;
2. to confirm the appointment of the trustee or to substitute another trustee in his place (rarely done);
3. to appoint the inspectors.

Section 93 Subject to this Act, all questions at meetings of creditors shall be decided by resolution carried by the majority of votes, and for such purpose the votes of creditors shall be calculated as follows:

(a) for every claim of or over twenty-five dollars and not exceeding two hundred dollars—one vote;

(b) for every claim of over two hundred dollars and not exceeding five hundred dollars—two votes;

(c) for every claim of over five hundred dollars and not exceeding one thousand dollars—three votes;

(d) for every claim of one thousand dollars—three votes and one additional vote for each additional one thousand dollars or fraction thereof.

Inspectors

At the meeting the creditors elect from among themselves one to five representatives called *inspectors*. These inspectors will attend meetings to be called later by the trustee or at the request of the majority of inspectors. The inspectors, in theory, direct the trustee as to the administering and winding up of the estate, but in practice it is usually the trustee who runs the show.

The First Meeting of Inspectors

This meeting is held usually quite soon after the first meeting of the creditors. In fact, it may take place in the court house after the first meeting of the creditors has ended, for the purpose of effecting important measures such as the immediate sale of perishable goods, appointment of an auditor to bring the books up to date, naming of a lawyer to collect accounts receivable and to investigate certain questionable transactions, and determining the best method of selling the assets of the bankrupt estate in order to realise the most money. The lawyer may play a very important part in the bankruptcy process, especially if investigations and legal proceedings are required.

THE ADMINISTRATION
OF THE BANKRUPT
ESTATE

The Trustee's Role

The trustee administers the entire property of the bankrupt. This includes taking possession of books, records, all other property, making an inventory of assets and liabilities, taking such conservatory measures as insuring the debtor's property.

Before taking important steps such as deciding how the assets will be sold, whether court actions against the estate will be contested, whether to institute legal proceedings, the trustee seeks the directions of the inspectors. He calls the inspectors to meetings to discuss and approve these important matters and relies upon their opinions.

The Inspector's Role

This is one of the few occasions when businessmen and other creditors have an opportunity to be involved, in a limited but important way, in the process of the administration of justice. There are three methods of selling the assets of the bankrupt:[3]
1. private sale without soliciting tenders;
2. sale by tenders using newspaper advertisements;
3. sale by public auction.

What method of sale is best? The answer to this question depends upon the nature of the assets and the likelihood of there being interested buyers.

Private Sale

When the assets for sale have no competitive market value and possibly only one or two persons have an interest in buying, private sale is the best method of disposing of them. For example, if the items for sale are very specialised

3. In the case of a bankruptcy in Quebec, there are certain formalities for the sale of immoveables with an existing hypothec or privilege.

machines, only a handful of people in the trade might be interested in buying them. The trustee will contact these people and try to get offers to purchase which he will then submit to the inspectors.

Sale by Tender

The most usual method of disposing of assets is sale by tender. In the back pages of the daily newspapers trustees advertise the sale of job lots by tender; the assets can be examined at a fixed date, and the bids must be filed before a specific date. When the inspectors meet to open the tenders, the highest bid is usually accepted. But not necessarily. This applies most especially in the case where the debtor, through members of his family or if the debtor is a limited company, through the principal shareholders, bids to repurchase the assets for the purpose of starting up business again under another name. The inspectors who represent the creditors might not be anxious to do the debtor a good turn and thus a lower bid might be accepted.

Public Auction

Sometimes a licensed auctioneer is appointed to auction off the assets on behalf of the trustee. This auctioneer is an expert at selling large quantities of stock. Auctioneers usually work on a commission basis. You will see their advertisements as to dates and place of auction in your local daily newspaper.

Settlements and Preferences[4]

One week before going bankrupt, John transfers his house to his wife, makes a $5,000 gift to his brother and pays a friendly creditor in full.

---

4. The area of preferences is very technical, particularly in regard to amendments passed in 1966. Instead of giving all the rules as to length of time a contract is reviewable, the meaning of "related persons" and the burden of proof, general observations will suffice for this introductory text.

These transfers and payments made on the eve of John's bankruptcy are illegal and can be recovered by the trustee. Generally speaking, if a transaction is made in the normal course of business and is in good faith, the transaction is valid. If the transaction were made so as to give a third party a preference, it is subject to review by the courts. The purpose of examining receivable transactions is to possibly order the beneficiary to return to the trustee what he has received, and therefore increase the assets available for distribution.

Distribution of Assets

After the assets have been sold and the trustee has money in his hands, he will, in due course, distribute the money to the creditors. There are three classes of creditors.

The Secured Creditor

Secured creditors have top priority, e.g., hypothecary creditors or creditors who have sold goods to the debtor under a conditional sales contract or who have placed merchandise on the debtor's premises on consignment and, in the two latter cases, remain owners of the items sold. Each of these creditors is secure in that he can, if necessary, proceed to "realise" or take back his security.

However, the trustee usually has the option of either allowing the secured creditor to take the asset or paying the secured creditor the amount of his claim and retaining the asset.

> *Creditor Smith sold certain restaurant fixtures to debtor Brown under a conditional sales contract. Smith remains owner of the fixtures because Brown owes moneys under the contract and unless full payment has been made, title remains with the vendor. If the account owing to the vendor is not too large, the trustee may, if the fixtures could bring a substantial price, pay the balance owing out of available cash to*

the vendor and then the fixtures become assets of the bankrupt estate.

The trustee would only do this if there were some equity to be gained for the bankrupt estate.

"Thirty-Day Goods"
Claim

A creditor who has sold and delivered merchandise to a bankrupt may make "a petition for the return of thirty-day goods" requesting the cancellation of sale and return of goods delivered by the vendor. This petition is subject to two conditions:

1. The goods must be in the bankrupt's possession.
2. The petition must be made within thirty days of delivery.

Jack sells Bill 10,000 lbs. of steel on April 1st. On April 15th, Bill goes bankrupt. The steel is still in Bill's possession. Today is April 25th. Jack has five days to make the petition.

The Preferred Creditor

There are certain creditors who are preferred in payment as compared with the mass of ordinary creditors. Subject to the rights of secured creditors, the proceeds realised from the property of the bankrupt are paid to the following preferred creditors (partial list). Each preferred creditor gets paid *in full,* before the next ranking preferred creditor:

1. funeral and testamentary expenses;
2. costs of administration of the bankrupt estate, e.g., trustee and legal fees;
3. wages, salaries and commissions owing during three months preceding the bankruptcy up to $500, e.g., each unpaid employee has a claim;
4. municipal taxes;
5. rent—landlord's privilege (see chapter 12);
6. claims of the federal and provincial governments.

The Ordinary (Unsecured) Creditor

After the secured and the preferred creditors have been paid in full, if any money still remains undistributed, the ordinary (unsecured) creditors will receive a dividend on a pro rata basis. An example of an ordinary creditor is a merchant claiming for goods sold and delivered under a normal contract of sale.

A wife who is a creditor in her husband's bankruptcy (e.g., a gift in a marriage contract) is not entitled to receive any payment until all claims of the other creditors are satisfied. She is called a *deferred* creditor.

Summary Administration

Where the bankrupt is not a corporation and in the opinion of the official receiver the realisable assets of the bankrupt, after deducting the claims of secured creditors, will not exceed $500, the provisions of the Bankruptcy Act relating to summary administration of estates will apply. These provisions reduce the formalities and expenses of administration.

DISCHARGE

When the trustee has concluded the administration and distribution of the estate, he applies to the court to be "discharged" from his duties. The bankrupt also applies to the court for his release or discharge.

Once the debtor is discharged, all debts at the time of the bankruptcy are cancelled except for the following which the debtor still must pay:
a. fines;
b. alimentary debts;
c. debts incurred fraudulently;
d. debts for goods supplied as necessities of life, e.g., clothing, food, prescription drugs.

PROPOSALS

Let's examine the example of John and his unsuccessful garage business again. John owes fifteen creditors a total of $7,000. He wants to continue business and believes that all he needs is some additional time to pay his creditors. He is prepared, over a one-year period, to pay his creditors 60 percent of their claims (60 cents on the dollar). He has considered paying 100 percent of the claim but knows that this is impossible. The creditors are aware that if John goes bankrupt, they may realise much less than 60 percent, since the real value of the garage lies in its being operated.

There are three types of proposals.

Proposal outside the Bankruptcy Act

John, perhaps through an accountant or lawyer, makes direct contact with his creditors, explains that he is unable to pay their claims in full, but that he can pay 60 percent over a one-year period in settlement. The creditors may, or may not accept this offer. If they do accept and he carries out his undertaking, i.e., 1/12 of the 60 percent each month until in the twelfth month the 60 percent of the creditors' claims have been paid, then the creditors who have accepted the settlement cannot demand more than the agreed amount. This is an *informal proposal.*

Proposal before Bankruptcy but under Provisions of Bankruptcy Act

John goes to a licensed trustee and explains to him that he is prepared to pay 60 percent of all his debts over twelve months, in equal monthly instalments while continuing to operate his garage. The trustee files this proposal in court. The debtor is not a bankrupt but rather is availing himself of the provisions of the Bankruptcy Act. The trustee sends notices by registered mail to the creditors, e.g., "Take notice that John Smith has lodged a proposal with me." The notice sets out the date of the meeting of the creditors at court and includes a copy of the proposal, with a financial statement of the business affairs and a proof of claim form which the creditor fills out and attaches to his account. The creditor then returns the form to the trustee, (sometimes along with his vote—either for or against the acceptance of the proposal).

In order to vote at the creditors' meeting, a creditor must file the proof of claim with the trustee prior to the meeting. The creditors have three alternatives:

1. They can vote against the proposal and thus defeat it.
2. They can vote that the meeting be adjourned and the debtor's affairs be further investigated.
3. They can accept the debtor's proposal. The debtor, realising that he may have a difficult time having his proposal accepted, may amend his proposal from 60 percent to, let us say, 65 percent.

To obtain acceptance of a proposal, there must be at least 75 percent in value, plus 51 percent in number of the creditors in favour, either present at the meeting or voting through proxy.

Therefore, it is possible to have a proposal rejected by the negative vote of creditors in excess of 25 percent in value or 51 percent in number of those present and voting.

If the offer is accepted, the trustee sends to the creditors notice of the date of presentation at court for ratification of the proposal. On that date creditors can appear in court and if they wish, state why the proposal should not be ratified. It is not usual for the court to refuse ratification but the court has this discretion if the proposal is unreasonable or unfair.

If the proposal is refused at the creditors' meeting, John is automatically in a state of bankruptcy. If the proposal is ratified, John continues to operate his garage and carry on business. His obligation is to meet the terms of the proposal.

The danger for creditors of a proposal made before bankruptcy is that the debtor is not as yet a bankrupt and if he is dishonest he can dispose of his assets, if there are any.

However, the creditors may, with John's consent, have some degree of supervision over his operations.

> Section 37   At a meeting to consider a proposal the creditors, with the consent of the debtor, may include such provisions or terms in the proposal with respect to the supervision of the affairs of the debtor as they may deem advisable.

> Section 38   The creditors may appoint one or more, but not exceeding five, inspectors of the estate of the debtor, who shall have the powers of an inspector under this Act but subject to any extension or restriction of those powers by the terms of the proposal.

Proposal after Bankruptcy

John Smith is a bankrupt having made an assignment or against whom a receiving order has been made. He is now entitled to make a proposal. His actual assets are negligible, the garage equipment and premises being owned by an oil company, and the only value of the premises is in its continuation as a business. Smith submits to a proposal explaining that it would be far better to allow him to carry on with the garage business and pay off 60 percent on the dollar (for if this proposal is not granted, the creditors will probably realise nothing whatsoever). The trustee will give the inspectors a statement of assets and liabilities to examine and the inspectors will most probably decide that such a proposal is fair and reasonable.

> Section 41 (9)   The approval by the court of a proposal made after bankruptcy operates to annul the bankruptcy and to revest in the debtor, or in such other person as the court may approve, all the right, title and interest of the trustee in the property of the debtor, unless the terms of the proposal otherwise provide.

ALTERNATE DEBTOR-
CREDITOR
ARRANGEMENTS

Federal legislation concerning insolvency also includes: the Farmers' Creditors Arrangement Act, the Companies' Creditors Arrangement Act and the Winding-up Act.

Provincial legislation includes the "Lacombe Law" by which a worker or salaried employee may voluntarily deposit the seizable portion of his salary (see chapter 3) into a court office within five days following payment. The court notifies the creditors that he is depositing, the creditors file their claims and periodically the court distributes the moneys deposited to the creditors.

When a person deposits regularly under the Lacombe Law, unless the debts are overwhelming, his creditors will be paid ultimately in full. As long as he continues to deposit, his creditors cannot seize his salary or household furniture.

Legal Terminology

bankruptcy
insolvency
obligations
Superintendent of
  Bankruptcy
trustees
districts
divisions
act of bankruptcy
voluntary assignment
first meeting of creditors
proof of claim
official receiver
petition in bankruptcy
receiving order
interim receiver
proxy

inspectors
private sale
sale by tender
public auction
settlements
preferences
distribution of assets
secured creditor
realise security
thirty-day goods
preferred creditor
unsecured creditor
deferred creditor
summary administration
discharge
proposals
Lacombe Law

Questions

1. What is the purpose of the Bankruptcy Act?
2. Who is considered an insolvent person?
3. Who can become bankrupt?
4. What persons administer bankrupt estates?
5. What are the qualifications for declaring bankruptcy and what are the methods of becoming bankrupt?
6. What is an interim receiver?
7. What occurs at the first meeting of the creditors?
8. How are inspectors appointed and what is their role?
9. Discuss the administration of the bankrupt estate by the trustee.
10. How are assets sold?
11. What is meant by a preferential settlement?
12. How are the assets distributed and what are the various classifications of creditors?
13. What is summary administration?
14. What is meant by discharge?
15. What is meant by proposals? Describe the three types of proposals and include in your discussion how a proposal is accepted by the creditors.
16. What is meant by Lacombe Law?

LABOUR LAW

Chapter 17

LABOUR LAW

The purpose of labour legislation generally is to regulate the relations between employer and employee. Both the federal and provincial governments have jurisdiction in labour matters under the British North America Act, and both have enacted legislation in this area. Provincial legislation applies to those industries and businesses over which the province has exclusive jurisdiction, and federal legislation applies to industries and businesses under federal jurisdiction.

PROVINCIAL LEGISLATION

In Quebec the Department of Labour and Manpower regulates and administers provincial labour legislation. Employees in the province are generally considered in two categories—unionized and nonunionized.

Unions

The principal legislation concerning unions is contained in the Quebec Labour Code, which authorises the setting up of a Labour Court and allows the Department of Labour and Manpower to appoint officers, such as a Chief Investigating Commissioner, investigating commissioners and investigators, to perform the duties assigned by the Code.

Every employee has the right to belong to and participate in the activities and management of an employees' union without hindrance from the employer. No employer may dominate, hinder or finance the formation or activities of any association of employees, nor refuse to employ a union member or prevent an employee from joining a union, nor dismiss or transfer an employee for belonging to a union or because of union activities. Any employee who believes he has been dismissed or transferred for such activities may complain to the Chief Investigating Commissioner who will then order an investigation. If it is found that the employee was dismissed or transferred for union activities, then the employer may be ordered to reinstate the employee and pay an indemnity.

Similarly, employers have the right to belong to an organization of employers, to which employees may not belong, free from hindrance, domination or finance from any association of employees.

The Labour Code sets out when and how employees' unions may apply for certification, that is, acceptance by the investigating officer as an appropriate and representative group to negotiate a *collective agreement* with the employer.

When there is no absolute majority of employees or agreement between the employer and applying employees as to the group, the investigating commissioner decides. He may order a secret vote of any group of employees, especially if he believes that constraint has been used to either prevent or force employees to join or not to join an association of employees.

Once the association is certified, the employer must negotiate to make a collective agreement—a written agreement as to wages, hours, overtime, vacations and general working conditions, etc. Once the collective agreement has been successfully negotiated by the parties, in order to be effective it must be filed with the Chief Investigating Commissioner. If no agreement is reached in thirty days, notice is sent to the Minister who appoints a conciliation officer. If conciliation is unsuccessful, the employees have the right to strike and the employer to lock out after sixty days, or ninety days if it is a first agreement, unless the parties submit to arbitration.

A collective agreement must be in writing and can be for a period of between one to three years. It is binding on all present or future employees in the group. In some cases, employees who in fact are not union members are bound by the terms of the collective agreement and are presumed to be union members. This is often referred to as the *Rand Formula,* named after The Honourable Justice Ivan Rand of the Supreme Court of Canada. Similarly, an agreement made by an association of employers binds all employers who are members and who become members of the association.

The Code provides for the settlement of disputes and grievances by a council of arbitration. Strikes and lock-outs are regulated by chapter 5 of the Code. It is forbidden to strike during the period of a collective agreement.

There are various other provincial labour Acts covering particular industries, such as the Construction Industry Labour Relations Act, the Civil Service Act and the Professional Syndicates Act.

A collective agreement may be extended by decree of the Minister of Labour to a whole industry in the Province of Quebec, or to a specific zone of the province in virtue of the Collective Decrees Act. Terms such as wages, hours, apprenticeship, vacations with pay and social security benefits are then obligatory and bind all the employees and employers in the industry in the province or in an area of the province. The extension may be requested by a party to a collective agreement. If a decree is passed it is administered by a joint committee of the parties called a *parity committee,* which protects the interests of both employees and employers and sees that the terms of the agreement are followed. The parity committee can act on behalf of a worker, e.g., if the worker is not paid the rate set in the agreement, the committee can claim from the employer. It also administers such things as issuing certificates of competence to employees and apprentices.

Nonunions

An employee working in a nonunion business or office and who is not covered by a collective decree is protected by the general law of the province, such as the Minimum Wage Act which sets the minimum hourly rate of pay, hours of work and vacations with pay for workers in the province.

The Civil Code governs the contract of hire of personal service and its termination. The Code makes specific provision for notice of termination to be given to certain classes of workers, such as domestics, servants, journeymen or labourers, but is silent as to other employees.

No notice of termination is required when an employee is hired on trial, or for a definite period of time or a specific job or season. When the contract of hire is for an indefinite period, although generally notice is required, the law is not certain as to the length of notice required in any given case, except for the classes of workers already mentioned—domestics, servants, journeymen or labourers—who, if hired by the week are entitled to one week's notice, by the month to two weeks' notice, and by the year to one month's notice. Cases have held that the length of notice should correspond with the pay period, i.e., if a worker is paid daily, then one day's notice should be given, if paid weekly then one week's notice, if paid every two weeks then two weeks' notice and if paid monthly then one month's notice. However, there is another series of cases holding that the appropriate length of notice is that which is reasonable in view of all the circumstances, taking into consideration the status and importance of the employee, his length of service, the difficulty he might have in finding another job, his level of salary.

As an alternative to giving notice the employer may pay the amount that would be normally earned or risk an action in damages before the courts. Notice is not required when an employee is dismissed for cause, such as dishonesty.

FEDERAL LEGISLATION

The principal legislation enacted by the federal government in this field is the Labour Code. This applies to employers and employees engaged in federal work, undertakings or business. The Act covers ground similar to that of the Quebec Labour Code; it states that all federal employees may join a union and employers may join an association of employers and provides for certification, collective bargaining, negotiation, conciliation, strikes and lock-outs. The Act sets up a Labour Relations Board to decide such matters as whether a person is an employee within the meaning of the Act, whether a collective agreement has been entered into, etc.

The federal Code also contains regulations forbidding discrimination because of race, national origin, colour or religion by employers or trade unions; it stipulates equal pay for equal work by female employees; it regulates hours of work, minimum wages, vacation pay; and provides for the safety of employees.

LABOUR WELFARE LEGISLATION

The field of labour welfare legislation is also divided between the federal and provincial governments. The legislation of the Quebec provincial government includes the following Acts.

The Minimum Wage Commission is established under the *Minimum Wage Act* with power to make ordinances as to minimum wages, hours of work, terms of payment, working conditions, overtime pay and vacations with pay. This Act applies virtually to everyone, except farm workers, household servants and workers covered by a collective decree.

The *Weekly Day of Rest Act* provides that the government may order that an hotel, restaurant or club owner will be bound to give his employees one day of rest in each week.

The *Industrial and Commercial Establishments Act* concerns safety and sanitary conditions in factories, workshops, workyards and mills (but not mines, which are covered by the Mining Act). If the establishment is classified as dangerous, unwholesome or incommodious, boys under sixteen and girls under eighteen may not be employed there and if an establishment is deemed dangerous or harmful to their health, the employment there of women and girls, and of boys under eighteen may be prohibited. In any event, no one may employ boys or girls under sixteen, except for the summer vacation when a permit may be issued for the employment of fifteen-year-olds. The Act also regulates the number of working hours of girls and boys, and women over eighteen and forbids night work, except for women over eighteen with a permit.

The *Employment Discrimination Act* prohibits employers employing more than five persons from discriminating as to race, colour, sex, religion, national extraction of social origin, in the hiring, promoting, laying off or dismissing of an employee. Anyone discriminated against may make a written complaint to the Minimum Wage Commission and the Commission investigates and makes a settlement, or if necessary it may take legal proceedings.

As of October 1, 1972, the *Workmen's Compensation Act* covers all salaried persons in the Province of Quebec, except domestics and farm employees. An employee who is injured in the course of his work may claim compensation or if he is killed in an accident, his family may make the claim. The employee may not claim against the employer, but if the accident was caused by someone other than the employer then he may claim compensation and also take legal proceedings under the Civil Code for the difference between the amount of compensation and the loss actually sustained.

Compensation in the case of death takes the form of funeral expenses and widows', orphans' or other dependents' pension; in the case of disability the compensation allowed is a percentage of the average weekly earnings of the year preceding the accident, based on the degree of disability. The injured employee may also receive medical aid and rehabilitation assistance.

Federal legislation in this field is of two kinds—that which applies to federal employees and that which applies generally to all employees, whether employed by the federal government or not.

The *Unemployment Insurance Act* applies to almost all employees, whoever the employer. Both the employer and the employee contribute according to the employee's salary to a fund, from which the worker may claim if he is unemployed, provided he had made a certain number of contributions to the fund. The amount he receives from the fund is based on his salary. He may be disqualified if he knows of suitable employment and refuses to apply for or accept it without good cause.

Legislation which applies to workers employed by the federal government includes the *Fair Wages and Hours of Labour Act,* which stipulates that persons employed by contractors on construction or demolition sites under contract with the federal government shall be paid fair wages and be paid overtime if they work more than eight hours a day or forty hours a week; the *Adult Occupational Training Act* provides for the training of people wishing to gain or increase their skill in an occupation.

Legal Terminology

British North America Act
Department of Labour and
    Manpower
unions
labour court
Chief Investigating
    Commissioner
employees' union
certification
collective agreement
conciliation
arbitration
strikes
lock-outs
decree

parity committee
notice of termination
Labour Relations Board
Minimum Wage Act
Weekly Day of Rest Act
Industrial and Commercial
    Establishments Act
Employment Discrimination
    Act
Workmen's Compensation Act
Unemployment Insurance Act
Fair Wages and Hours of
    Labour Act
Adult Occupational
    Training Act

Questions

1. What is the purpose of labour legislation?

2. Under the British North America Act, which governments are entitled to legislate labour law?

3. What is the principal legislation in the province of Quebec concerning unions?

4. What are the rights of an employee to join an association and what are the restrictions on the employer?

5. Can an employer organise a union of employers?

6. What is meant by certification?

7. What is the role of the investigating commissioner?

8. What is a collective agreement and what is the procedure if such an agreement is not reached amicably?

9. What is the binding effect of a collective agreement?

10. How may a collective agreement be extended to a whole industry and how is such an extension administered?

11. What laws regulate nonunion workers?

12. Discuss notice of termination of a nonunion employee who is paid by the week.

13. What is the principal legislation enacted by the federal government in labour law and what are its general provisions? What board enforces the Act?

14. What antidiscrimination provisions are contained in the federal Labour Code?

15. Outline briefly labour welfare legislation in the Province of Quebec under the following headings:

a. Minimum Wage Act

b. Weekly Day of Rest Act

c. Industrial and Commercial Establishments Act

d. Employment Discrimination Act

e. Workmen's Compensation Act

f. Unemployment Insurance Act

BILLS OF EXCHANGE

Chapter 18

BILLS OF EXCHANGE

John, who is employed by a large company, buys some groceries totalling twenty-six dollars from the local grocery store owned by Ben. John has no money with him, except for his salary cheque for eighty dollars. John asks Ben if he will cash his cheque. Ben says, "Of course. I know you and certainly the cheque is good." John endorses the cheque, that is, he writes his signature on the back of the cheque and gives it to Ben, who gives John the difference in cash. [1]

Instead of depositing a cheque payable to themselves, people will often transfer it to a third person. This also occurs in transactions involving a finance company.

Lucky Auto Sales sells a used car to John for $1,000. John pays $200 now, and the balance by postdated monthly cheques. Lucky Auto then endorses John's cheques to a finance company which buys them from Lucky. Lucky therefore does not have to wait for the cheques to become due; they get paid immediately (less a discount).

Why are the grocer and the finance company willing to accept the cheques signed by John? What rights do the grocer and finance company have if these cheques are returned by the bank marked "N.S.F." (nonsufficient funds)? What right does the finance company have to cash the cheques, if John's automobile breaks down?

---

1. Endorsement is the act whereby the person to whom the cheque is payable, or made payable, signs his name, usually on the back of the cheque.

Cheques, promissory notes and drafts[2] are forms of commercial instruments or paper and are regulated by the Bills of Exchange Act, a federal law applicable throughout Canada. The Sections referred to here are from this Act.

PROMISSORY NOTES

Smith is the maker; Ross is the payee.

> S. 176 A promissory note is an unconditional promise in writing made by one person to another, signed by the maker, engaging to pay, on demand or at a fixed or determinable future time, a sum certain in money to, or to the order of, a specified person or to bearer.

There are two parties: the person who promises to pay—the maker (Smith)—and the person to whom the promise is made—the payee (Ross). When a note reads "I promise to pay" and is signed by two or more persons, it is deemed to be their joint and several note, and therefore each maker is liable for the full amount.

2. A bill is commonly called a draft. A draft is an order from one person to another demanding payment of money payable at a certain date, generally for goods or services rendered.

July 1 1972 $

ON DEMAND AFTER DATE FOR VALUE RECEIVED *I* PROMISE TO

PAY TO *R. B. Ross* OR ORDER

AT THE ROYAL BANK OF CANADA , *Dorchester & Union* THE SUM OF

One Hundred DOLLARS

WITH INTEREST ON $ *100 —* PAYABLE MONTHLY AT THE RATE OF *9* PER CENTUM
PER ANNUM AS WELL AFTER AS BEFORE MATURITY. *S. H. Smith*

C. D. Brown

Both Smith and Wilson sign a note reading "I promise to pay Jones $200." Before payment is due, Wilson disappears. Smith is obliged to pay the payee (Jones) the complete amount.

If the note reads "We promise" and is signed by two persons, it is usually a *joint* note and each maker is only liable for his half. However, if the promissory note was given in connection with a commercial transaction, the makers will be presumed to be obligated jointly and severally (Article 1105).

DRAFTS

One of the principal problems in commerce is obtaining payment for merchandise sold and delivered. This is particularly difficult if the transaction is made with a foreign customer.

A Montreal cutter producer, Smith, sells some of his cutters to White in London, England. The terms of the contract are for payment to be made thirty days after delivery in England. Smith gives a full set of commercial documents to his bank, including a draft, which is a written order to White to pay Smith's bank.[3] *Smith's bank sends these documents and the draft to their London branch (or to White's bank) which presents the draft and other documents to White. If White is satisfied with the documentation and the terms of the draft, he signs the draft "accepted." The bank retains the accepted draft and gives White the documents so he can get the goods at the port. On the due date, i.e., after thirty days, the bank will present the accepted draft for payment to White who has to pay the bank which, in turn, forwards payment to Smith's Montreal branch.*

S. 17   A bill of exchange is an unconditional order in writing, addressed by one person to another, signed by the person giving it, requiring the person to whom

3. A full set of commercial documents generally consists of a commercial invoice, packing list, custom invoice, certificate of origin, insurance policy (if C.I.F.) and the bill of lading. A bill of lading has been defined as follows:

"A bill of lading is a receipt for goods shipped on board a ship signed by the person who contracts to carry them, or his agent, and stating the terms on which the goods were delivered to and received by the ship. It is not the contract, for that has been made before the bill of lading was signed and delivered, but it is excellent evidence of the terms of the contract."

it is addressed, to pay, on demand or at a fixed or determinable future time, a sum certain in money to or to the order of a specified person, or to bearer.

In the illustration, Smith is the *drawer* of the draft. White is the *drawee* and if he accepts he is the *acceptor.* The bank is the *payee.*

CHEQUES

No._____

THE ROYAL BANK OF CANADA

DORCHESTER & UNION BRANCH
MONTREAL, P.Q.

July 1 19*72*

PAY TO THE
ORDER OF ___ *R. B. Ross* ___ s *200 —*

___ *Two Hundred* ___ DOLLARS

PERSONAL
CHEQUING ACCOUNT   NO. *517*   *John Wilson*

A cheque is a draft drawn on (addressed to) a bank. Cheques are always payable on demand. A cheque may be:
1. dated today;
2. ante-dated (today is the 15th, you date the cheque the 10th); or
3. postdated:
a. On the 15th, you date a cheque the 20th. It is payable on demand on the 20th.
b. You date the cheque November 15th, 1972, payable November 20th, 1972. This cheque is negotiable only for payment on the 23rd—three days of grace for payment are given on such a postdated cheque.

Negotiation

In the example on page 270, how does John "give" or transfer the cheque to the grocer?[4] In law this transfer is called *negotiation*. Cheques are negotiated by *endorsement*. Endorsing a cheque means that the person to whom the cheque is made out signs his name on the back of the cheque. There are, however, several methods of endorsing, depending on whether the cheque is payable to the bearer or payable to a specific person.

Instruments Payable to Bearer

In effect, "pay to holder" means pay to anyone who has the cheque in his hands. If a cheque is payable to bearer it can be transferred just by handing it over, by delivery. No endorsement is necessary.

Instruments Payable to a Specific Person

The payee, Mr. Jones, has several ways of endorsing a cheque.

Blank Endorsement

---

4. It is possible to make a cheque non-negotiable, that is, not transferable from the payee to another person. This is done by writing "not negotiable" on the face of the cheque of by adding the word "only" with the name of the payee, e.g., payable only to Jack Jones.

If Jones simply signs his name on the back of the cheque, it becomes payable to anyone. That is why it is not advisable to endorse a cheque unless you intend immediately to deposit it in your bank or negotiate it to another person. Once a cheque is endorsed in blank it is negotiated simply by delivery. For example, Jones signs a cheque made payable to him, then delivers it to Callan who can negotiate it to Easton, without endorsing it.

Special Endorsement

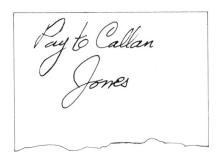

In *special endorsement* Jones specifies on the back of the cheque that it is payable to Callan and then signs his name beneath this statement. Callan then has to sign his name to negotiate the instrument.

Conditional Endorsement

In a conditional endorsement, Jones specifies, "Pay to the order of Callan, provided that the goods delivered by him are in good condition." The bank can ignore this condition and pay the endorsee (Callan). However, in a dispute between Jones and Callan as to the quality of the goods, Jones would show that his payment to Callan was conditional.

Endorsement without
Recourse

An endorsee may add the words "without recourse" after his

signature which means that no party can sue him for the cheque.

> *A friend of yours, John, asks you to cash his salary cheque at your bank. Since your bank does not know John, they will ask you to endorse it. You should write your name and add "without recourse and for identification only."*

Restrictive Endorsement

An endorsement is restrictive which prohibits the further negotiation of the bill, or which only expresses an authority to deal with the bill as directed, and not a transfer of the ownership. For example, a bill may be endorsed "pay to Smith only" or "pay Smith for the account of Ross."

LIABILITY OF PARTIES

In the second example on page 270, the finance company has cheques or notes which John has made payable to Lucky Auto and which, in turn, have been endorsed to them. If, for some reason, the cheques or notes are not honoured (N.S.F., stop payment, no bank account), to whom does the finance company look for payment on the cheques or notes?

If it is a promissory note, the maker is liable; if it is a cheque, the drawer is liable; if it is a draft, the acceptor of the draft is liable. If the finance company is not paid by these persons who are primarily liable, then it can sue the endorsees.

HOLDER IN DUE COURSE

What is the position of the grocer or the finance company on the cheques which have been negotiated to them? If the goods sold are not according to the contract, can the finance company nevertheless sue the maker of the promissory note?

The legal position of the finance company is that of a *holder in due course,* having received the cheque properly negotiated (endorsed) by the payee.

The Bills of Exchange Act defines a holder in due course:

> S. 56 (1)   A holder in due course is a holder who has taken a bill, complete and regular on the face of it, under the following conditions, namely:
>
> (a) that he became the holder of it before it was overdue and without notice that it had been previously dishonoured, if such was the fact;
>
> (b) that he took the bill in good faith and for value, and that at the time the bill was negotiated to him he had no notice of any defect in the title of the person who negotiated it.
>
> (2) In particular the title of a person who negotiates a bill is defective within the meaning of this Act when he obtained the bill, or the acceptance thereof, by fraud, duress or force and fear, or other unlawful means, or for an illegal consideration, or when he negotiated it in breach of faith, or under such circumstances as amount to a fraud.

The most important characteristic of a holder in due course, is that he must be in good faith, honest and not aware of any irregularity whatsoever, either regarding the cheque itself, e.g., forgery or alteration, or the circumstances of its issuance, e.g., fraud or breach of contract.

> *Charles persuaded Al to draw a cheque in his favour by pointing a gun at him. Charles negotiated the cheque to Don, a holder in due course. For Don to be a holder in due course, he must not be aware of the gun incident. If he knows of the gun incident, he is not then in good faith; furthermore, he must not close his eyes to any suspicious circumstances.*

DEFENCES

Generally speaking, when an action is brought by a holder in due course against a person who is primarily liable—for example, the maker of a promissory note—the maker has no defence, he must pay the holder. However, there are some exceptions.

For purposes of clarification, there are two types of parties: (a) immediate parties, those which have direct dealings with one another; and (b) remote parties, where the relationship exists because of the intervention of another party.

> *Sam makes a promissory note in favour of Dick. They are immediate parties. But if Dick endorses the note to Bob, the relationship between Sam and Bob is remote.*

Defences against
Immediate Parties

What are the defences of a maker against a payee of a promissory note or a drawer of a cheque?
1. Compensation: Charles owes Al $100. But Al owes Charles $100. One debt sets off the other.
2. Fraud, misrepresentation, violence.
3. Forgery.
4. Breach of contract: for example, Lucky Auto sues John on a cheque. John refuses to pay because the car has serious latent defects.

Defences against a
Holder in Due Course

A holder in due course may generally successfully sue the maker of a promissory note, the drawer of a cheque or an acceptor of a draft despite the following defences.

1. Violence.

> *Charles forces Al at gun-point to write a cheque payable to him. Charles endorses the cheque and gives it to Don who becomes a holder in due course.*

2. Fraud and breach of contract.

> *Charles persuades Al to make a cheque payable to him for an order of merchandise that Charles doesn't deliver. Charles endorses the cheque to Don, who becomes a holder in due course.*

In the preceding cases, the maker and drawer have no defences against a holder in due course.

In what cases do the maker, drawer or acceptor *have* a valid defence?

1. incapacity
2. forgery
3. material alteration
4. consumer sales

Incapacity

If a person is incapable of entering into contracts, such as an interdict, then he and he only has a defence against the holder in due course. If Louis, who is insane, signs a cheque and finally it falls into the hands of Don, a holder in due course, Don cannot successfully sue Louis.

Forgery

If a drawer can prove that the signature that appears on the cheque was not signed by him or was not authorised by him, then this defence is good, even against the holder in due course. If the drawer's signature was forged and his bank pays out and debits his account, then, of course, the drawer can have his account reimbursed by the bank.

If the payee or endorser's signature is forged, then the

holder in due course cannot collect from the drawer but only against the forger and any endorsers after the forgery.

> *Al makes out a cheque to Charles; Frank, who works in Charles's office forges Charles's name, signs it and negotiates it to Doug, who negotiates it to Evan. Evan can only sue Frank and Doug.*

Material Alteration

If there is any material alteration in the cheque, the holder in due course can only collect the original amount of the cheque.

> *Al makes out a cheque to Sam for $500. Sam alters the amount to $1,500, and negotiates it to Dick. What are Dick's rights?*

Dick can only collect $500, the original amount of the cheque from Al. For the other $1,000 he sues Sam. Al's bank is entitled to debit Al's account for $500 only.

CONSUMER SALES

If the cheque, promissory note or draft, is issued for consumer goods it must be clearly marked with the words, "consumer purchase." The rights of the holder in due course of such a note or cheque are subject to any defence or right of compensation that the purchaser would have had in an action by a seller. In other words, the holder is in no better position than the seller; if the buyer has a valid defence against the seller such as breach of contract, fraud, nondelivery, it will succeed against the holder.

Section 18 of the Quebec Consumer Protection Act states that all bills of exchange signed at the time of a contract to acknowledge deferred payments form part of the whole contract and neither they nor the contract can be assigned (negotiated) separately by the merchant (seller) or by any subsequent assignee, e.g., a finance company.

Section 19 states that the assignee (the finance company) of a debt of a merchant who is a party to a contract shall not have more rights than the merchant and shall be responsible for the performance of the merchant's obligations (within the limits set by the Act).

The meaning of these two Sections is:

1. The contract *and* the promissory notes or cheques of a consumer purchase form a whole and are not to be transferred separately.

2. The person to whom the contract and cheques have been transferred is:

a. in the same legal position as the original seller—no better, no worse;

b. the purchaser has the same defences available against the assignee—holder as against the seller;

c. the purchaser can sue the assignee—holder to perform the seller's obligations under the contract.

> *John buys a car from Lucky Auto for $1,000, $200 down and $800 by deferred payments of $100 each month, by a series of postdated cheques payable to Lucky, who, in turn, endorses them to Happy Finance Co. The car is under a ninety-day warranty and becomes totally inoperative within twenty days. John stops payment of the cheques. Happy Finance Co. cannot collect on the cheques and John can sue Lucky and Happy Finance Co. in virtue of the contract's warranty clause.*

For a full explanation of consumer sales, see chapters 15 and 21 on "Business Organizations" and "Consumer Protection."

Signature by Agent

> *Jones is an accountant and signing officer for Moon Real Estate Ltd. How does Jones sign cheques for the company without personal liability?*

If Jones signs using his personal signature or title—Jones; Jones, Accountant; Jones, Agent—he might be personally liable. Jones should sign specifying his agency, if he is not to be held personally liable—Moon Real Estate Ltd., per Jones.

Legal Terminology

finance company
cheque
promissory note
draft
negotiable instrument
bills of exchange
maker
payee
joint and several liability
joint liability
acceptance
drawer
drawee
acceptor
bearer
negotiation

endorsement
non-negotiable
blank endorsement
special endorsement
conditional endorsement
endorsement without
   recourse
restrictive endorsement
endorsee
holder in due course
good faith
defences
immediate parties
remote parties
material alteration
consumer purchase note
signature by agent

Questions

1. Discuss the role of a finance company in relation to the negotiation of cheques.

2. What is a promissory note and how should a promissory note be worded in order to render the maker jointly and severally liable?

3. What is a draft and how is it used in connection with commercial sales?

4. What is a cheque and what is meant by a postdated cheque?

5. What is the meaning of negotiation and when is a cheque not negotiable?

6. How is a blank endorsement made and how is such a cheque negotiated?

7. What is meant by a special endorsement and how is such a cheque negotiated?

8. What is the meaning of the following endorsements?

a. conditional

b. without recourse

c. restrictive

9. What persons are primarily liable for:

a. a cheque?

b. a promissory note?

c. a draft?

10. What are the characteristics of a holder in due course?

11. What defences are available against immediate parties to a cheque?

12. What defences are not available against a holder in due course?

13. Describe the following defences against a holder in due course:

a. incapacity

b. forgery of the drawer's signature and payee's signature

c. material alteration

14. Discuss federal and provincial legislation regarding consumer purchases.

15. In order for an agent not to be personally liable for a cheque he signs for a limited company, how should he sign his name?

INSURANCE

Chapter 19

INSURANCE*

In Quebec, the sources of insurance law are:

1. The Articles of the Civil Code found in TITLE FIFTH starting with Article 2468 which define the general principles relating to various insurance contracts and outline some particular ones, as well.

2. Highway Victims Indemnity Act (See Chapter 8 on "Civil Responsibility".)

3. Bill No. 7 An Act respecting insurance.

Insurance is defined in the Civil Code as follows:

> Art. 2468 A contract of insurance is that whereby the insurer undertakes, for a premium or assessment, to make a payment to a policyholder or a third person if an event that is the object of a risk occurs.

> Art. 2494 Civil responsibility is not lessened or altered by the effect of insurance contracts and the amount of damage is determined without regard to such contracts.

Article 2468 of the Civil Code defines and outlines all the elements of the insurance contract:

1. the contracting parties, called the *insurer* (e.g., the insurance company) and the *policyholder* (e.g., the owner of an automobile who takes out a general automobile coverage policy);

2. the consideration, that is, the premium or assessment which is the fee that is paid in return for the insurance coverage;

3. indemnification by the insurer to the insured for direct damage to the insured in some cases, or for liabilities incurred

*See the Note at the end of this Chapter.

by an insured as the result of an event defined in the insuring agreement (e.g., auto accident, death, fire) arising out of an insured risk.

The policy either declares the value of the thing insured and is then called a *valued policy,* or it contains no declaration of value and is then called an *open policy.* An open policy puts a limitation on the total amount of a claim, e.g., $10,000 maximum claim for all household effects destroyed by fire. A valued policy is used to insure valuable articles such as jewellery and paintings (which have been appraised by an expert) and this is the amount which should be paid to the insured in the event of a claim.

Article 2583 states "The amount of the insurance does not make proof of the value of the property insured; proof of such value must be established in the usual manner unless the policy contains a valuation of the property insured." Article 2473 provides for Life Insurance to pay the agreed amount.

THE POLICY OF INSURANCE

Article 2476 states that the insurance is formed upon the insurer's acceptance of the policyholder's application. Article 2477 states that the policy is the document evidencing the insurance contract and Article 2478 obliges the insurer to provide the policyholder with the policy and a copy of the application. In case of inconsistency, the application is the prevailing document unless the insurer has in writing indicated the inconsistencies to the policyholder. Articles 2480-2501-2502-2579-2601-2609 stipulate certain information which each class of insurance policy must contain, which includes:

1. the name and address of the insurer;
2. the name and address of the insured;
3. the name of the beneficiary;
4. the amount of the premiums and the dates when due;
5. the object and amount of the coverage of the thing insured;

6. the nature of the risk insured against;
7. the time during which the policy is to be in force;
8. the conditions of the policy—what requirements must be met by the insured, e.g., no driving while intoxicated;
9. exclusions and limitations of coverage;
10. provisions for cancellation and reinstatement.

TYPES OF INSURANCE

There are many different types of insurance, the principal ones are automobile, fire, marine, life and health, liability, property, and boiler and machinery. Bill 7 divides insurance into Marine and Non-Marine (Art. 2469). It subdivides Non-Marine into Insurance of Persons and Damage Insurance (Art. 2471). Insurance of Persons is subdivided into Individual or Group (Art. 2472). Damage Insurance is subdivided into Property Insurance and Liability Insurance (Art. 2475).

Automobile Insurance

The province of Quebec regulates the form of policy used and prescribes for use by insurance companies, a standard form (see Art. 2479) very similar to the form generally in use in the other provinces. The standard policy is divided into three parts:
1. Section A covers third part liability for bodily injury and property damage; the insurance company will pay damages caused to others up to the insured value of the policy.
2. Section B covers medical expenses for the passenger and driver: and whether at fault or not the insurance company will pay medical bills up to the amount of the insurance (e.g., $2000), and also death and disability benefits.
3. Section C is called "own damage coverage" and includes collision insurance: the insurance company will pay the insured for damage to his car (less a stipulated deductible amount) whether or not he is at fault. This type of coverage, of course, costs more than if you have just section A public liability. Section C also covers named perils such as fire and

theft, or comprehensive coverage, which includes all perils except collision.

Sections B and C are basically for the protection of the insured and thus are not compulsory. Section A, however, is both a protection for the insured and for others who might suffer injuries or property damage on account of the insured's fault. (See Chapter 8 on "Civil Responsibility".)

Fire Insurance

Article 2590 stipulates that the insurer is liable for all damage to buildings and their contents against loss by fire or combustion, whatever the cause. The policy includes explosion and lightning coverage; extended coverage can be purchased for sprinkler leakage, smoke damage and storms. You can also be insured against loss of business profits due to fire.

In order for there to be a valid fire insurance policy:
1. Article 2480 must be complied with.
2. The insured must have an insurable interest as defined in Articles 2580 and 2581. The insurable interest in the thing insured exists where one is an owner, a creditor or has a monetary interest; but when it is other than owner, the nature of the interest must be specified. The fire policy usually contains a condition which reads as follows: "The company is not liable for the loss of property owned by any other person than the assured, unless the interest of the assured is stated in or upon the policy."
3. It is important that a proper description of what is to be insured is given so that the insurer may judge it (a) for rating purposes or (b) for acceptability. It should be specified whether it's a house, a factory, a wholesale warehouse, a retail store. If, for example, the insured designates a building which he wants to insure against loss by fire, as a retail furniture store when, in fact, it is being used as an upholstery factory, then there is misrepresentation. Two facts of misrepresentation exist:
a. An upholstery factory is a more hazardous undertaking and would require a much higher premium;

b. It is possible that the insurer might not accept an upholstering occupancy or if it did it is possible that it would wish to insure for a smaller amount than in the case of a furniture store.

4. The amount of insurance must be declared as well as the premium, the date of the commencement and the duration of the risk.

5. Article 2488   In damage insurance, unless the bad faith of the proposer is established, the insurer is liable for the risk in the proportion that the premium collected bears to that which it should have collected, except where it is established that it would not have covered the risk if it had known the true facts.

Ocean Marine Insurance

This insurance is available to cover the ship, freight and cargo against the perils of the sea.

Art. 2609   The policy of marine insurance contains:

The name of the insured or of his agent;

A description of the object insured, of the voyage, of the commencement and termination of the risk, and of the perils insured against;

The name of the ship and master, except when the insurance is on a ship or ships generally;

The premium;

The amount insured;

The subscription of the insurer with its date.

It also contains such other clauses and announcements as the parties may agree upon.

Art. 2610   Insurance may be made on ships, on goods, on freight, on bottomry and respondential loans, on profits and commissions, on premiums of insurance, and on all other things appreciable in money and exposed to the risks of navigation, with the exception of seamen's wages, upon which insurance cannot be legally made, and subject to the general rules relating to unlawful and immoral contracts.

Art. 2612   Insurance may be made for any kind of voyage or transport by sea, river or canal navigation and either for the whole voyage or for a limited time.

Art. 2613   The risk of loss or damage of the thing insured by perils of the sea is essential to the contract of marine insurance.

The risks usually specified in the policy are tempest and shipwreck, stranding, collision, unavoidable change of the ship's course, or of her voyage, or of the ship herself, fire, jettison, plunder, piracy, capture, reprisal and other casualties of war, detention by order of a sovereign power, barratry of the master and mariners, and generally all other perils and chances of navigation by which loss or damage may arise.

The parties may limit or extend the risks by special agreement.

Accident and Sickness Insurance

The Province of Quebec has a compulsory medical insurance programme called Medicare. One may have supplemental medical insurance, such as group accident and sickness insurance or Blue Cross, which cannot, however, be held in lieu of the government programme, but only to supplement the government plan, e.g., to cover the difference between the cost of a public room and a private hospital room. Accident and sickness insurance now falls under Insurance of Persons,

Art. 2472, and is done on an individual or group basis. It also includes loss-of-income insurance.

> Art. 2534   Where the indemnities for income losses under one or more insurance contracts, exceed the average income from the work of the insured during the three best remunerated years comprised in the five years preceding the loss, the indemnities are proportionately adjusted to the amount of the said income but are never less than the minimum fixed for the regulations made for that purpose by the Lieutenant-Governor in Council.

Life Insurance

Basically, a life insurance policy pays a sum of money upon the death of an individual to the policyholder, the participant (in a group policy), a specified beneficiary (Art. 2540) or to an assignee (Art. 2509). There are three major types of policies:
1. whole life,
2. term,
3. endowment.

In a *whole life contract*, proceeds are payable upon death. Premiums are paid every year until death occurs. In a *term contract*, proceeds are paid in the event of death, only while the policy is in force and premiums are being paid. In an *endowment contract*, proceeds are payable at a specified "maturity" date, e.g., ten or twenty years later or at death.

The person receiving the proceeds of the policy at death is the specified *beneficiary* named in the policy. If the policy names the estate of the deceased as the beneficiary, then his heirs receive the proceeds.

The designation of any beneficiary is revocable unless otherwise stipulated; that made in a will is always revocable, Art. 2546. The designation by the policyholder or participant of his consort as beneficiary is irrevocable unless otherwise stipulated (Art. 2547).

OTHER TYPES OF
INSURANCE

1. Fidelity bonds: a three-party contract in which an insurance company guarantees an employer against all losses due to a dishonest employee.

2. Floater: an insurance policy guarantees payment of loss due to all risks (subject to certain specified exclusions) or insures the goods located in a wide geographical area, e.g., a jewellery or fur floater, or does both.

3. Composite Dwelling Policy and Homeowners' Package: covers damage or loss to insured's premises, household effects and also liability for accidents.

WHY DOES THE INSURANCE
COMPANY REFUSE TO PAY?

The causes of refusal to pay fall into five main categories:
1. Policy void,
2. Aggravation of risk,
3. Exclusions,
4. Failure to notify,
5. Fraud.

Policy Void

The policy was null and void from the very beginning, as in the case of misrepresentation or deceitful concealment, Art. 2486, at the time of the making of the contract or lack of insurable interest.

Insurable Interest—
Property Insurance

Art. 2580   A person has an insurable interest in a property whenever he may sustain direct and immediate damage by its loss or deterioration. Future property and incorporeal property may be the subject of a contract of insurance.

Art. 2581   The interest of the insured in the property must exist at the time of the loss.

It is not required that the same interest exist throughout the duration of the contract.

Art. 2582   The insurance of a property in which the insured has no insurable interest is without effect.

Insurable Interest—
Insurance of persons

Art. 2506   In individual insurance, the contract is without effect if at the time of contracting it the policyholder has no insurable interest in the life or health of the insured.

Art. 2507   A person has an insurable interest in his own life and health and in the life and health:

(a) of his consort;

(b) of his descendants and of those of his consort, whatever their affiliation;

(c) of any person upon whom he is dependent for support or education;

(d) of his employees and staff;

(e) of any person in whose life and health the insured has a pecuniary interest.

Art. 2508   The absence of an insurable interest does not prevent the formation of the contract of insurance if the insured gives his written consent.

When the insured is a minor, such consent is given by his father, mother, tutor or curator without consulting the family council or obtaining judicial authorization.

In life insurance, the insurable interest must exist at the conception of the contract, but not at the time of loss. The interest need not be as owner. It could also be as creditor as in the case of a bank from which the insured has borrowed money.

Misrepresentation or Concealment

Art. 2485   The policyholder, and the insured if the insurer requires it, must represent all the facts known to him likely to materially influence a reasonable insurer in the setting of the premium and the appraisal of the risk or the decision to cover it.

Art. 2486   The obligation respecting representations is deemed met if the facts are substantially as represented and there is no material omission.

There is no obligation to represent facts known to the insurer or which from their notoriety he is presumed to know, except in answer to inquiries.

Misrepresentation or deceitful concealment by the insured is in all cases a cause of nullity of the contract that the party acting in good faith may invoke.

Art. 2487   Subject to articles 2510 to 2515, misrepresentation or concealment by either the policyholder or the insured, in regard to the facts contemplated in articles 2485 and 2486, nullifies the contract at the instance of the insurer, even for losses not connected with the risks so misrepresented.

Art. 2488   In damage insurance, unless the bad faith of the proposer is established, the insurer is liable for the risk in the proportion that the premium collected bears to that which it should have collected, except where it is established that it would not have covered the risk if it had known the true facts.

In absence of fraud or deceitful concealment, a misrepresentation must be *material* in order to void the policy. A material fact is one concerning the nature and extent of the risk and which therefore affects the insurer's decision to insure, or the rate of premium. For example, it is important in the case of the application for automobile insurance that the driving record of the applicant be known. The age of the owner or the principal driver could be an important factor in the acceptance or rejection of the risk by the insurer. These facts will also help to determine a higher or lower premium to be charged.

The incorrect description of a building, or of its construction or the use to which it is put are causes of nullity only if the bad faith of the proposer is established (Art. 2488). In all other cases in Non-Marine Insurance, unless the insurer can establish that it would not have covered the risk at all if it had known the true facts, the insurer must meet the loss in the proportion that the premium collected bears to that which it should have collected.

In an Ontario case, an action by the plaintiff to recover damages to his truck was dismissed on the grounds that the plaintiff had failed to declare that he had been in nine motor accidents within the three years preceding the application and also that he had been refused insurance by another company. The policy was held null and void.

In a 1949 Quebec case, a father failed to get the proceeds of a policy on the life of his son. The insurance company contended that the policy was void for nondisclosure of such material facts as that the insured had suffered from rheumatic fever or that he had consulted his physician about his condition. Any statement to diminish the appreciation of the risk is a cause of nullity.

Aggravation of Risk

Art. 2566   The insured must promptly advise the insurer of any aggravation of risk coming to his knowledge which is likely to materially influence a reasonable insurer in the setting of the rate of premium, the appraisal of the risk or the decision to continue to insure it.

The insurer may then cancel the contract in accordance with article 2567 or propose in writing a new rate of premium which the insured must accept and pay within thirty days of its receipt, failing which the policy ceases to be in force.

The insurer is deemed to have acquiesced in the change communicated to him if he continues to accept the premiums or pays an indemnity after a loss.

If the insured fails to discharge his obligation under the first paragraph, article 2488 applies *mutatis mutandis.*

Art. 2482   Subject to provisions peculiar to marine insurance, the insurer cannot invoke conditions or representations not written in the contract.

Every change made by means of an endorsement is part of the contract. However, an endorsement stipulating the reduction of the liability of the insurer is without effect if it is not countersigned by the policyholder.

Art. 2489   A breach of warranty aggravating the risk suspends coverage until the insurer's acceptance.

Art. 2629   It is an implied warranty in every contract of marine insurance that the ship shall be seaworthy at the time of sailing. She is seaworthy when she is in a fit state, as to repairs, equipment, crew, and in all other respects, to undertake the voyage.

In an Ontario case, action was taken by the insured to recover, under policies of fire insurance, a tobacco processing barn and a farm barn. The defendant company alleged in respect of the claim for the processing barn, a breach of the warranty that the tobacco steamer would not be left operating unattended. This warranty was the basis on which the insurance was written and in consequence of which the premium was reduced. It was while it was unattended that the fire broke out and this breach of warranty resulted in the dismissal of the part of the action pertaining to the claim for the loss of the processing barn. (See Art. 2579.)

Change of the risk to the prejudice of the insurer can be a cause of suspension of coverage (Art. 2489) in the case of warranties. Damage insurance is governed by the provisions of Article 2566 which states:

Art. 2566   The insured must promptly advise the insurer of any aggravation of risk coming to his knowledge which is likely to materially influence a reasonable insurer in the setting of the rate of premium, the appraisal of the risk or the decision to continue to insure it.

The insurer may then cancel the contract in accordance with Article 2567 or propose in writing a new rate of premium which the insured must accept and pay within thirty days of its receipt, failing which the policy ceases to be in force.

The insurer is deemed to have acquiesced in the change communicated to him if he continues to accept the premiums or pays an indemnity after a loss.

If the insured fails to discharge his obligation under the first paragraph, Article 2488 applies *mutatis mutandis.*

Exclusions

The insurer may claim simply that the loss is not covered under the policy either by reason of the extent of coverage, or description of the risk or because the loss falls within an exclusion in the policy.

Although certain contracts, such as fire and automobile are statutory forms and must be worded identically, while others such as marine, are usually worded alike by every insurance company, there are a number of policies which differ from one insurance company to the next and these must be carefully scrutinized by the insured so that he knows exactly what coverage he is getting.

Read your insurance policies carefully and be sure you understand the exclusions and limitations.

Failure to Notify

The claim may be contested because of the failure of the insured to comply with the requirements of notification following the loss.

Damage Insurance

Art. 2572   The insured must notify the insurer of any loss of such a nature as to involve coverage, as soon as he becomes aware of it.

Any interested person may give such notification.

Art. 2573   At the request of the insurer, the insured must notify the insurer as soon as possible of all the circumstances surrounding the loss, including its probable cause, the nature and extent of the damage, the site of the property, the rights of third persons affecting it, and any concurrent insurance.

Notwithstanding any forfeiture time limit fixed by the contract, the insured is entitled to a reasonable extension of time if it is not reasonably possible for him to perform such obligation within the time limit specified.

The insured must also, at the insurer's request, furnish him with vouchers in support of such information and attest under oath or by solemn affirmation to the truth of such information.

If the insured fails to comply with the obligations of this article, any interested person may do so in his place.

Insurance of Persons

Art. 2533 Any aggravation of the occupational risk lasting for six months or longer entitles the insurer to reduce the indemnity to that payable for the new risk according to the premium fixed in the contract.

If there is a reduction of the occupational risk, the insurer must, from his receiving notice of it, reduce the rate of the premium accordingly or extend the insurance by applying the rate corresponding to the new risk, at the option of the policyholder.

Marine Insurance

Art. 2661 The insured is bound when he makes claim for any loss, to declare, if thereunto required, all other insurance effected by him on the thing insured and also the loans taken by him on bottomry and respondentia.

He cannot claim payment for the loss until such declaration is made, when so required and if the declaration be false and fraudulent he loses his right to recover.

There are procedures which must be followed where a claim or possible claim arises. In the case of automobile claims or liability contracts, it is important to report these at once even though the insured may believe that:

a. he was in the right;

b. the other party will make no claim; or

c. the loss seemingly suffered by the other party was too trifling to bother with.

These are decisions which must be made by the insurance company. Many a substantial claim appeared to be very minor at the time it was made—this is especially true for automobile accidents. There must be complete cooperation on the part of the insured who agrees in his policy not to admit fault. If he does admit fault and his insurance company has to pay the third party, they could sue him for moneys paid out!

Fraud

The assured cannot be indemnified for his own criminal acts but, of course, if the loss results from the criminal acts of someone else without the connivance of the assured, then he will be compensated.

> Art. 2574   Any deceitful representation invalidates the rights of the person making it to any indemnity related to the risk so misrepresented.

> Art. 2563   The exclusion of the prejudice caused by a fortuitous event or the fault of the insured is not valid unless it is expressly and restrictively set out in a stipulation in the contract.

> However, the insurer is not liable, notwithstanding any agreement to the contrary, for prejudice arising from the insured's intentional fault.

> *In a 1926 Quebec case, it was decided that "a married woman who is in commerce and whose goods are insured against fire has a right to claim from the insurance company for the loss, even when it was the result of a fire caused criminally and intentionally by*

her husband who was her agent, if it is proved that she had not participated in her husband's act and in fact was completely unaware of it."

In a 1930 Quebec case, it was held that the insurer is not to be held to indemnify the assured who set fire to his buildings while drunk.

INDEMNITY

Art. 2583   The amount of the insurance does not make proof of the value of the property insured; proof of such value must be established in the usual manner unless the policy contains a valuation of the property insured.

Art. 2562   Damage insurance obliges the insurer to repair only the actual prejudice at the time of the loss, up to the amount of the insurance.

Most policies are policies of indemnity, that is, to compensate for actual loss, and the insured can be reimbursed only for actual loss. The amount of insurances does not necessarily determine the amount the insured is to be paid in the event of loss.

SUBROGATION

When the insurer recovers in his own name or in the name of the policyholder, from third parties, it is because there has been a transfer of rights or subrogation from the insured to the insurer. If the insured prejudices the right of the insurer to recover from third parties without permission to do so, he may release the insurer from his obligation to the insured.

Art. 2576   To the extent of the indemnities he has paid, the insurer is subrogated in the rights of the insured against third persons who are responsible for the loss except in the case of persons who form part of the household of the insured.

The insurer may be released, in whole or in part, from his obligation towards the insured when, because of the act of the latter, he cannot be so subrogated.

You have an accident and the other driver is at fault. You have collision auto insurance. When your insurance company pays for your damage you will sign a subrogation form so that your insurance company can sue the third party for the amount they paid you.

ARBITRATION

Art. 2587   An arbitration clause is valid if it is contained in a writing and deals with the nature, extent and amount of the damage and the adequacy of the repairs or replacement. In that case, the provisions of the Code of Civil Procedure respecting arbitration apply.

Arbitration interrupts prescription.

TRANSFER OF THE INSURANCE

Art. 2577   Insurance may be transferred on the conditions contained in the policy; it cannot be transferred except in favour of a person who has an insurable interest in the object of the insurance; it may be transferred at the same time as the property insured is alienated.

Art. 2578   The alienation of the property insured terminates the insurance, unless the policy is transferred at the same time or the insurer consents.

The contrary rule prevails for rights transmitted by operation of law or acquired by succession or by a person already interested in the insurance as owner or otherwise.

Legal Terminology

Civil Code
Highway Victims Indemnity
   Act (Bill 48)
contract of insurance
insurer
insured
policyholder
consideration
premium
assessment
indemnification
damage
liabilities
policy
valued policy
open policy
beneficiary
assignee
object
risk
conditions
amount
damage insurance
property insurance
automobile insurance
property damage
bodily injury
medical expenses
disability benefits

collision
deductible
fire insurance
ocean marine insurance
accident and sickness
   insurance
Medicare
life insurance
term
endowment
fidelity bonds
floater
composite dwelling policy
Homeowners' Package
insurable interest
misrepresentation
concealment
material misrepresentation
express warranty
implied warranty
exclusions
notification
fraud
indemnity
reimbursement
subrogation

Questions

1. What are the sources of insurance law in Quebec?
2. Describe briefly the contract of insurance and what elements are contained in each insurance contract.
3. What is meant by a valued policy and an open policy?
4. What must each policy of insurance contain?

5. The automobile insurance policy is subdivided into what parts? Discuss each.

6. What must a property insurance policy contain?

7. What does ocean marine insurance cover?

8. What does private accident and sickness insurance cover?

9. What are some different types of life insurance? Describe each.

10. Give the meaning of each of the following:

a. fidelity bonds,

b. floater,

c. Homeowners' Package.

11. Discuss the circumstances under which an insurance company can refuse to pay.

12. What is meant by indemnity?

13. What is meant by subrogation?

Note: At the time of writing (May 1975) Bill No. 7—An Act respecting insurance—has been passed by the National Assembly of Quebec and assented to. It has not as yet come into force by the necessary proclamation of the Lieutenant-Governor in Council, nor have the required regulations been made public. Commentary on the articles of the civil code are therefore restricted to those articles essentially unchanged, and articles involving new departures are cited without explanation.

WILLS AND SUCCESSIONS

Chapter 20

WILLS AND SUCCESSIONS

John is a moderately successful businessman, married with two young children. He has a home with a mortgage on it, a car, a bank account of $8,000, stocks valued at $10,000 and $100,000 of life insurance. He is concerned about what would happen to his property in the event of his death. He makes an appointment with his lawyer, Mr. Erskine, to discuss the matter.

SUCCESSION

John asks his lawyer, Mr. Erskine, whether it is advisable to have a *Will.* Mr. Erskine first advises John that all the property of a man at his death is called his *estate* or *succession.*

The word succession has two meanings:

a. the transfer by law or by the Last Will and Testament of a man to one or more persons of the property; and

b. the transmissible property rights and obligations of a deceased person.

TRANSMISSION

Mr. Erskine then discusses:

1. how the estate is transmitted, or transferred to one or more persons;
2. whose property can be transmitted;
3. who can inherit;
4. what can be transmitted.

How Is the Estate
Transmitted?

A person may prepare and sign a Last Will and therein direct who will inherit his property; this is called a testamentary succession. In the event the deceased made no Will his property will pass according to law, that is, by abintestate succession.

> Art. 597   Abintestate succession is that which is established by law alone, and testamentary succession that which is derived from the will of man. The former takes place only in default of the latter.
>
> The person to whom either of these successions devolve is called heir.

Whose Property Can Be
Transmitted?

A property is transmitted on death either by law or Will, but only a person of the full age of majority (now eighteen in the Province of Quebec), of sound intellect and capable of alienating his property can make a Will.

Who Can Inherit?

> Art. 608   In order to inherit it is necessary to be civilly in existence at the moment when the succession devolves (opens) thus, the following are incapable of inheriting;
>
> 1. Persons who are not yet conceived;
> 2. Infants who are not viable when born.

> Art. 609   Aliens may inherit in Lower Canada in the same manner as British Subjects.

> Art. 610   The following persons are unworthy of inheriting and, as such, are excluded from successions;

1. He who has been convicted of killing or attempting to kill the deceased;
2. He who has brought against the deceased a capital charge, adjudged to be calumnious;
3. The heir of full age, who, being cognizant of the murder of the deceased has failed to give judicial information of it.

All persons except these are capable of inheriting, that is, receiving property of a deceased person. Even an unborn child can inherit, provided it is conceived at the date of the death and provided also that it is born viable, that is, normally constituted at birth with all the organs necessary for it to live and that it can exist separate from the mother. Adopted children inherit from their adoptive parents in the same way as lawful children; illegitimate children do not inherit by law unless legitimised by the subsequent marriage of the parents; however they can inherit by Will.

Not only human beings may be heirs but also artificial persons (see chapter 4 on "Persons"), such as educational or charitable institutions.

What Can Be Transmitted?

Property of a deceased may include such things as a house, land, furniture, automobile, stocks, bonds, money in a bank account, proceeds in an insurance policy, and also rights such as the right to take legal action in certain cases. The debts and obligations of the deceased are paid out of the estate.

ABINTESTATE SUCCESSION

Mr. Erskine then tells John what happens if he were to die without a Will:

Art. 606 Abintestate successions pass to the lawful heirs in the order established by law; in default of such heirs they fall to the crown.

If he left no Will then the law decides who will inherit among his surviving relatives. First come the wife and children, then relatives such as his mother and father, brothers and sisters, nieces and nephews. If the deceased leaves a wife and child or children they inherit everything, the wife one-third, the child or children two-thirds.

If he has a wife and no children but has parents and brothers and sisters, his wife will take one-third, the parents one-third and the brothers and sisters one-third. If he leaves a wife and parents but no children or brothers, sisters, nieces or nephews, the wife and parents each take one-half.

LAST WILL AND TESTAMENT

It can readily be seen that if John dies without making a Last Will the succession is divided arbitrarily by law and his personal wishes may be ignored; the friendship or enmity of relatives and their financial position is irrelevant. Under this system the wife would be receiving only one-third of the estate, the other two-thirds going to the children.

Clearly, it is highly advisable for John to systematically and logically leave his estate to those he considers as deserving persons and in a manner which would most benefit them. This can only be done in a Last Will.

Forms of Wills

When a person makes a Will he is called a testator. There are three forms of Wills.

Holograph Will

The testator writes out the Will in his own handwriting and signs it; this is a holograph Will.

English Form Will

The Will must be in writing (usually typewritten) and signed by the testator before two witnesses; this is a Will in English form. This Will form is often prepared by lawyers.

Notarial Will

The testator may also go to a notary who will prepare a notarial Will which the testator signs before witnesses, either two notaries or one notary and two witnesses.

For both the Will in English form and the notarial Will the witnesses must be of the age of majority and they must not be beneficiaries under the Will (if they are they will lose the legacy).

A Will which does not observe the requisite formalities may be declared null. However, a Will which does not fulfil the requirements of one type of Will may be valid in another form. For example, the testator signs a Will he has prepared in his own handwriting before one witness. Although invalid as a Will in English form it may be valid as a holograph Will.

The testator may leave his property to whom he chooses, in the proportions he chooses. In the Province of Quebec there is absolute freedom of willing; a person may leave his property to anyone—not necessarily to his wife or children. In effect, the family is not protected and may be disinherited. The testator may later change his Will at any time, either by destroying it or by making a new Will or by making a codicil, which is a document adding to or altering a part of the Will. The Will and codicil bearing the last date will be accepted as the Last Will of the testator being his last wishes.

TYPES OF LEGACIES

The property the testator transfers on death by his Will is called a legacy; if he leaves the whole of his property to one or more persons, this is a universal legacy. Legacies by general title occur when the testator bequeaths part of his property, e.g., one-half or one-third or the whole of his immoveable property. All other legacies are particular legacies, e.g., a car, painting, $5,000 in cash.

EXECUTOR

The estate of the deceased is administered by his executor, who has charge of the property of the deceased. He pays the debts of the estate, and divides the property among the persons entitled to it according to the Will.

CONTENTS OF A WILL

It is inadvisable to use a holograph Will, because of the testator's inexperience in drafting Wills. Very often such a Will is incomplete, confusing or contradictory.

> *"I leave my car to my brother and my entire estate to my sister." Does "entire" mean that the brother is not to get the car? Also the Will does not mention who is to be the executor.*

It is preferable to seek legal advice concerning this important document which is going to substantially affect your spouse and children. This is particularly true for an estate against which Quebec estate taxes might be levied.

A Will should be tailored to meet the specific needs and requirements of the testator. Although stationery stores supply Will forms, and these are better than having no Will at all, certainly they are a poor substitute for a Will prepared by a lawyer or notary to meet your situation and that of your family.

The contents of a Will, of course, vary according to the wishes of the testator: who is to inherit, whether the entire estate is to go to one person, or specific legacies to others, who is to be executor, etc. If we may generalise, in our example, John may consider the following for his Will:

1. to state his identity: name, address and occupation;
2. to state his marital status and whether he has a marriage contract. The death provisions in a marriage contract will take precedence over a Will.

John has a marriage contract leaving $50,000 to his wife upon his death. He makes a Will leaving everything to his brother. His wife would receive $50,000 and his brother the residue.

3. to revoke all previous Wills, if any. This makes it clear that the Will is his Last Will and contains his complete wishes.

4. a direction as to payment of his debts and funeral expenses;

5. nomination of an executor, one who will carry out the provisions of the Will. Also, he appoints a substitute executor in the event that the executor predeceases him, is absent, etc.

6. a full description of the powers of administration to the executor, particularly if there is a trust;

7. nomination of and description of universal, general and particular heirs and their respective legacies. In the event of nomination of particular heirs, the universal heir would be receiving "the balance, residue and remainder" of the estate.

8. possible creation of a trust. In the event that his wife predeceases him, John wishes his estate to go to his minor children, eight and ten years of age, and to be administered for their education and upbringing, etc. He entrusts his estate to a trustee, perhaps a trust company, for the benefit of the children. The children will get the residue of the estate from the trust company at a stated time mentioned in the Will, e.g., at eighteen years of age, or upon marrying.

As can be seen, a Will can be a complex document and because of its importance should be prepared with legal advice.

ACCEPTANCE OF A SUCCESSION

Art. 641   No one is bound to accept a succession which has devolved to him.

Are John's heirs obliged to accept a succession? What if John's estate has more debts than assets? No one is obliged to accept a succession; an heir can renounce his share. He must do this formally by notarial deed or by a judicial declaration; renunciation is never presumed. However, having accepted he cannot later renounce. If he renounces he inherits nothing, neither property nor debts.

A succession can be accepted outright or it can be accepted under benefit of inventory, that is, a notarial inventory is made of the assets and liabilities of the estate and the heir then has forty days in which to either accept or renounce the succession.

Acceptance may be either express or tacit. For example, if you are the only heir of your uncle and included in the estate is a country cottage which you make use of at the weekends immediately following his death, you may have tacitly accepted the succession. Heirs who accept a succession purely and simply are liable to pay the debts, even if the property received from the estate is less than the debts. A sole heir is liable for all the debts. A universal legatee is liable for all the debts; if there are several heirs or several universal legatees they pay the debts in proportion to their share in the succession. A legatee by general title is liable for the debts in proportion to his share in the succession; a particular legatee is not liable unless the other property of the estate is insufficient to pay the debts. In any event, the debts of the testator must be paid before the legacies are transmitted.

Succession Duties

As of January 1, 1972, the federal government no longer imposes succession duties at the present date (Summer, 1972). However, the Quebec government does impose an estate tax, the amount of which is dependent on the monetary value of the estate and the class of beneficiary to whom it is left, e.g., if left to the wife and children, the tax is less than if left to a stranger.

Legal Terminology

Wills	*inherit*
estate	*testamentary succession*
successions	*abintestate succession*
transmission	*holograph Will*

English form Will
notarial Will
testator
codicil
universal legacy
general legacy

executor
trust
acceptance
renunciation
benefit of inventory
succession duties

Questions

1. What is the legal term for a deceased's property?
2. How is the deceased's property transmitted to his heirs?
3. Whose property can be transmitted?
4. Who can inherit and what persons are unworthy of inheriting?
5. What can be transmitted?
6. What is the meaning of an abintestate succession and how is such an estate distributed?
7. What are the advantages of having a Will?
8. What are the various forms of Wills?
9. What is meant by absolute freedom of willing?
10. What are the formalities for making a codicil?
11. What are the different types of legacies?
12. What is the role of the executor?
13. What are the usual conditions of a Will?
14. What is a trust?
15. Discuss acceptance and renunciation of a succession.

Problems

1. Bill is married to Jane; they have three minor children. Bill is accidentally killed and dies without a Will. How is his property divided among his heirs?

2. Jack is married to Jill; they have two infant children. In a Will, Jack leaves his car to his brother, $5,000 to his mother, one-third of his immoveables to his sister and the rest of his property to his wife.

a. Identify the following heirs: universal, general, particular.

b. What should Jack provide in his Will, in the event that Jill predeceases him?

CONSUMER PROTECTION

Chapter 21

CONSUMER PROTECTION

The area of consumer protection legislation is receiving much attention recently, at both the provincial and federal levels. Its purpose is to protect the consumer from deception and misrepresentation by those manufacturers, merchants and others who use fraudulent sales techniques, false advertising, hidden credit charges and high pressure salesmanship, and who deliver low quality goods or services.

PROVINCIAL LEGISLATION

The Civil Code

The Civil Code specifies that if a buyer has entered into a contract through error, fraud, violence or fear, he may take proceedings to cancel the contract (see chapter 9 on "Contracts in General").

Relatively new amendments to the Civil Code (Article 1040c) have empowered the court to reduce or annul excessively high interest charges on a contract of loan of money (see chapter 13 on "Loan and Interest").

> Art. 1149   However, if the debt is made up of interest exceeding the legal rate, and seems to the court to be usurious, or if it includes such interest, whether such interest is called interest or be claimed under the name of discount, reduction in the advance, commission or otherwise, such court may order that such usurious interest, or such portion of usurious interest, be paid by instalments, and fix the amount of such instalments and their term of payment, at its discretion, according to circumstances.

In the area of product liability, a leading Quebec case was decided in 1967 by the Supreme Court. The implication of this decision is that manufacturers may be held liable in damages to consumers.

> *The plaintiff was injured when a bottle of soft drink exploded spontaneously in his hand. The Supreme Court held that the manufacturer was responsible in the sum of $8,500. The company was negligent in not having an inspection system adequate to prevent defective bottles reaching customers. It was the fault of the defendant that the bottle was not strong enough to withstand the pressure of the gas put into it by the company. The company had control or care of the bottle within the meaning of Article 1054 of the Civil Code.*

The Quebec Consumer Protection Act, 1971

The Act is designed to protect the consumer in his contracts with merchants. A consumer is defined as "any physical person who is a party to a contract in a capacity other than that of merchant." In other words, if two merchants deal with each other or if the buyer is a limited company, the Act does not apply.

The contracts with which the Act deals are those:
1. involving credit of over fifty dollars, including loans of money, contracts extending different forms of credit and instalment sales;
2. entered into with itinerant vendors.

Other sections of the Act deal with information agents (credit bureaus), warranty and advertising, the making and execution of the contract, the Consumer Protection Bureau and the Consumer Protection Council, permits for itinerant vendors and used car vendors. Heavy penalties are provided for those found guilty of contravening the provisions of the Act.

The Act defines certain important words:

1. Goods: "any moveable property or service which is the object of a contract."

Therefore the Act does not cover purchase of land or a house. It does cover services, such as personality or educational courses.

2. Contract: not all contracts are covered, only those extending credit over fifty dollars between merchant and consumer and contracts with itinerant vendors.

3. Itinerant vendor: more commonly called a "door-to-door" salesman, he is defined as "any vendor who elsewhere than at his address, solicits the signing of a contract from a specified consumer or makes a similar contract with a consumer."

4. Sale: sale includes simple sales, conditional sales and leases of goods and services.

Making Contracts

The consumer contracts referred to here are only those involving credit and sales with itinerant vendors.

1. These contracts must be in writing and in duplicate.

2. They must be written in French, but the consumer may request them in English.

3. The merchant must sign the contract first and then give it to the consumer and grant him sufficient delay to examine the contract.

4. Both parties must sign the contract and each party retains a copy.

Contracts Involving Credit

There are detailed regulations in the Act governing contracts such as lease, loan and sale whereby the merchant extends credit or terms of payment to the consumer. The following contracts are exempt from the Act:

1. those extending credit under fifty dollars;

2. those dealing with the purchase, construction or improvement of immoveable property secured by a first mortgage or privilege.

The purpose of the regulations is to safeguard the consumer purchasing on credit or borrowing money by requiring the merchant to clearly state the cost of credit. Contracts of loans of money must clearly state:

1. the amount actually received by the consumer;
2. costs of insurance and duties and any other amounts payable;
3. finance or credit charges;
4. a description of any security given by the buyer;
5. terms of payment.

Likewise, with credit cards and charge accounts, the agreement must state:

1. the credit limit or the fact that there is no restriction, if applicable;
2. the credit charge on the unpaid balance and provide that the consumer be furnished with a statement of account periodically.

Merchants are prohibited from issuing unrequested credit cards. Renewal credit cards may be issued.

In all contracts involving credit, any commercial paper (cheques or promissory notes) signed at the time of the contract forms part of the whole contract and cannot be transferred (negotiated) separately. Previous to the Act a merchant would sell the cheques or promissory notes to a finance company which would become a holder in due course (see chapter 18 on "Bills of Exchange") and would be able to enforce the payment of the notes even though the merchant did not deliver the goods.

Under the new legislation, if the contract is assigned to another party, such as a finance company, this third party has no more rights than the merchant and is responsible for the performance of the merchant's obligations within limits set forth in the Act (see chapter 14 on "Secured Transactions").

John buys an automobile from Lucky Auto for $4,000. The contract and note are assigned to Easy Finance Co. Lucky Auto does not deliver the automobile. John is not obliged to the finance company until delivery is made.

Instalment Sales

Section 29 of the Consumer Protection Act states:

> S. 29   An instalment sale is a contract involving credit whereby the transfer of ownership of the goods sold by a merchant to a consumer is deferred until the latter's performance of all or part of his obligation.

Basically, instalment sales are conditional sales made to consumers (see chapter 11 on "Sale"). The law provides numerous regulations requiring the merchant to set out clearly the details of the total cost of the goods.

If a consumer fails to pay on time, the merchant may repossess the goods only after having given the consumer a thirty-day notice in writing calling upon him to pay. If the consumer has paid at least two-thirds of the total sales price the merchant must obtain court permission to repossess.

Itinerant Vendors[1]

As explained earlier, an itinerant vendor or door-to-door salesman is one who sells from other than his business address. However, certain door-to-door contracts are exempt from the Act and these include the following:

1. the sale of a service to repair, increase or improve a thing in the ownership, enjoyment or possession of the consumer and goods furnished to that effect, e.g., household repairs. However, the Act does not exempt the sale of doors, windows or outside wall coverings, e.g., aluminum sidings.
2. sales made in a public market;
3. sales of unfrozen food and fruit.

If your contract with the itinerant vendor exceeds twenty-five dollars you may cancel the contract with or without reason within five days after signing it and after having

---

1. Every itinerant vendor and every vendor of used cars must hold a permit.

received from the vendor a duplicate copy (seven days, if the period includes a Saturday or Sunday). This is called the "cooling-off" period. Its purpose is to protect the householder from high pressure salesmanship by giving him some time to reconsider the contract.

As a consumer, you may cancel the contract by:
1. returning the goods within the above period of time;
2. notifying the vendor, in which event you have seven days following cancellation to return the goods and within which the seller must return any money received. Saturday, Sunday and holidays do not count in computing these delays.

April 1

Contract made

April 5

Consumer decides to cancel;
notifies vendor or returns goods

April 12

Goods and money returned

Prohibited Sales

Pyramid, chain or reference sales are prohibited and are null and void. This is a type of sale scheme where the buyer gives the seller the names of potential purchasers and receives a rebate on the sales price.

> *John enrols in a personality improvement course for $500. The salesman says that for every person John can recruit to sign similar contracts, he will get $50 or a reduction of his own course cost.*

Warranty and Advertising

Any goods (including services) furnished by a merchant must comply with the description of them given on the contract order catalogue, circulars or other means of advertising. Every warranty in a merchant's advertising respecting goods shall be deemed to form part of the contract. Therefore, if goods are advertised in the newspaper, the printed advertisement is considered part of the contract.

> *John reads in the newspaper that a department store is advertising "unbreakable" kitchen dishes. John buys a set and after a couple of months of use accidentally breaks one. John is entitled to a replacement.*

If you buy goods for a specific purpose, the merchant must indicate this in the contract. The goods are then warranted as being suitable for this purpose.

> *John, a farmer, buys a tractor for the purpose of hauling heavy farm equipment. The merchant warrants that it could normally be used for that purpose.*

Credit Reports

Credit bureaus or information agents are obliged to show you their credit reports concerning your personal reputation and solvency. You are entitled to make comments in writing which will be recorded in their records.

Enforcement of the Act

There are penalties up to $25,000 and imprisonment for a year for infringement of the Act. Any person, officer, salesman, etc., who participated in the infringement may be prosecuted. However, an error or omission made in good faith is not an offence.

The Act is supervised by the Consumer Protection Bureau, which is established in the Department of Financial Institutions, Companies and Cooperatives. The Bureau's duties also include dealing with complaints concerning infringements, protecting the public, as well as educating and informing them about consumer protection.

FEDERAL LEGISLATION

There are numerous federal statutes that encourage free and fair competition among industries and which discourage monopolistic control by one or more large companies. Their purpose is to protect the consumer by safeguarding the competitive nature of the free enterprise system. Through price and product competition, business is induced to produce good quality products at competitive prices. This legislation is administered by the Department of Consumer and Corporate Affairs.

The Combines Investigation Act

This Act deals with illegal restraints of trade, competition and unfair trade practices, including combines, mergers and monopolies, which unduly affect the free market system. There are prohibitions against certain pricing practices; for example, Section 33C prohibits false advertising as to the price of goods—"Regular price $1.95, special $1.29"—when in fact $1.29 is the usual price. Section 34 makes it an offence for a manufacturer or distributor to require a retailer to resell its product at a specified set price. This is called resale price maintenance.

Unfair Trade Practices

There are numerous statutes which safeguard standards of quality, weight, grading and control the inspection of food and drugs: the Weights and Measures Act, the Food and Drug Act, the Opium and Narcotic Act, the Meat and Canned Food Act, the Dairy Products Act, etc.

Trade Marks, Copyright and Design

The Trade Marks Act provides for regulation of trade marks at the Trade Marks Office in Ottawa. Once the mark is registered, its owner is entitled to exclusive use and no person may use a mark that is similar enough to confuse the public as to which product is being purchased.

Other similar legislation includes the Industrial Design and Union Label Act, the Patent Act, the Copyright Act.

Bills of Exchange Act

Under the federal Bills of Exchange Act all cheques, promissory notes and drafts arising out of a consumer purchase must be marked consumer purchase on the face of the note.

Remember that under the Quebec Consumer Protection Act:

1. All cheques and promissory notes signed at the time of the contract cannot be transferred or negotiated separately from the contract.

2. The assignee finance company which receives these notes from the seller has no more rights than the merchant, and is responsible for the merchant's obligations under the contract.

Consequently, the Bills of Exchange Act requiring that promissory notes and cheques be marked consumer purchase complements the Quebec Consumer Protection Act. They both serve to warn the assignee finance company that in dealing with a consumer purchase, it will be responsible for the merchant's obligations, and that it will have no greater rights than the merchant against the consumer.

Legal Terminology

consumer	*permits*
merchant	*penalties*
Civil Code	*credit charges*
usurious interest	*credit cards*
product liability	*commercial papers*
Consumer Protection Act	*holder in due course*
credit	*finance company*
itinerant vendors	*instalment sales*
warranty and advertising	*cooling-off period*
Consumer Protection Bureau	*pyramid sales*

credit reports
Department of Consumer
  and Corporate Affairs
unfair trade practices
Combines Investigation Act
mergers

monopolies
resale price maintenance
trade marks
copyright
design
consumer purchases

Questions

1. What is meant by consumer protection legislation?

2. Where may consumer protection legislation be found in the Province of Quebec?

3. What contracts are covered by the Act?

4. Define the following words:

a. consumer

b. goods

c. contract

d. itinerant vendors

e. sale

5. What are the formalities required in making a consumer contract?

6. What contracts are exempt from the provisions of the Consumer Protection Act?

7. What must a contract of loan state?

8. What must a credit card agreement state?

9. What is the rule concerning the issuance of credit cards?

10. What are the rights of the assignee finance company on contracts and notes?

11. What are the rights of a merchant on an instalment sale?

12. What itinerant vendor contracts are exempt from the Act?

13. How can a consumer cancel a contract made with an itinerant vendor?

14. What sales are prohibited under the Act?

15. What warranty is included in a consumer purchase?

16. What obligation does a credit bureau have to the public?

17. What government agency supervises the Act?

18. What is the purpose of the Combines Investigation Act? Illustrate with an example.

19. Name three federal Acts dealing with consumer protection.

APPENDIX

1975

 **LEASE** (1)

LESSOR	BETWEEN _____ (Name) _____ (Address) _____ (Telephone number) hereinafter called the lessor
LESSEE	AND _____ (Name) _____ (Address) _____ (Telephone number) hereinafter called the lessee

SECTION I
DESCRIPTION OF PREMISES, TERM OF THE LEASE AND RENT

DESCRIPTION OF PREMISES

The lessor rents, by this lease, to the lessee the premises situated at _____

_____

known and described as follows: _____

_____

_____

DESTINATION OF PREMISES

The premises will be used as a dwelling

The term of the lease will be _____ months, from the _____ day of _____ 19_____,

TERM

to the _____ day of _____ 19_____.

COPY OF THE LEASE

A signed copy of the lease will be given by the lessor to the lessee within fifteen days of the signing. If the lease is oral, the lessor must, within three days of the agreement, give the lessee a writing reproducing section II of this lease or a non-signed copy of the present lease.

RENT

This lease is made in consideration of the total amount of _____

_____

dollars ($ . . . .), that the lessee will pay to the lessor in equal and consecutive _____

(specify whether monthly, weekly or other) payments of _____

_____

dollars ($ . . . .), each of which will be paid in advance on the first day of each _____

(month, week or other).

(Add here every other clause pertaining to the payment of the rent).

SECTION II
OBLIGATORY PROVISIONS

NOTICE: The Civil Code includes the articles of law applying to a contract of lease (articles 1600 to 1665).

There are two kinds of articles in the Civil Code:

(1) articles which can be waived or amended by mutual agreement between the lessee and the lessor by a clause in the lease;

(2) obligatory articles with which the lessor and the lessee have to comply.

Any clause in a lease which would be inconsistent with an obligatory article of the Civil Code is void as regards the lessor and the lessee.

The following clauses (1 to 43) are the texts of the main obligatory articles found in the Civil Code.

They include the amendments assented by the legislature that have come into force on December 24, 1974.

OBLIGATIONS OF THE LESSOR

GOOD CONDITION AND PEACEABLE ENJOYMENT

1. The lessor shall deliver and maintain the dwelling in a condition fit for habitation and give peaceable enjoyment of it. (Article 1654 C.C.*)

REPAIRS

2. The lessor is obliged to make all repairs imposed on him by law or by a municipal by-law respecting safety or sanitation of the dwelling.

The lessee has the same rights against the lessor in respect of such repairs as if the lessor had undertaken by a lease to make them. (Article 1655 C.C.*)

WITHHOLDING OF RENT WHERE REPAIRS NEGLECTED

3. If the lessor does not make the repairs and improvements to which he is bound, the lessee may, without prejudice to his other rights and recourses, apply by motion to the tribunal to obtain permission to withhold the rent in order to proceed thereto. (Article 1612 C.C.*).

URGENT AND NECESSARY REPAIRS

4. The lessee must suffer urgent and necessary repairs to be made.

He is entitled however to a reduction of rent, according to the circumstances.

He may also demand cancellation of the lease if the repairs are such as to cause him serious prejudice. (Article 1625 C.C.*)

URGENT AND NECESSARY REPAIRS

5. After having informed or attempted to inform the lessor and if the latter does not act in due course, the lessee may undertake urgent and necessary repairs for the preservation or use of the immoveable leased.

Nevertheless, the lessor may at any time intervene to continue the work.

The lessor must reimburse the lessee for reasonable expenses thus incurred. (Article 1644 C.C.*).

Appendix 329

— 2 —

RIGHT TO VISIT

6. The lessee must permit the lessor to ascertain the condition of the thing.

The lessor must exercise this right in a reasonable manner. (Article 1622 C.C.*)

In leases with a fixed term of a year or more, the lessee must, for leasing purposes, allow the premises to be visited and signs to be posted, during the three months preceding the expiry of the lease.

In leases with a fixed term of less than one year, the delay is one month.

Where the lease is for an indeterminate term, the lessee is bound to that obligation from the notice given in accordance with article 1630. (2) (Article 1645 C.C.*)

RIGHT TO VISIT, PREVIOUS NOTICE

7. Except in case of urgency and subject to his right to have a prospective lessee visit the dwelling, under article 1645 (clause number 6), the lessor must give the lessee notice of at least twenty-four hours of his intention to visit the premises in accordance with article 1622 (clause number 6).

The lessor must also give notice of at least twenty-four hours of his intention to have the dwelling visited by a prospective purchaser. (Article 1656 C.C.*)

OTHER RECOURSES OF LESSEE

8. Inexecution of an obligation by the lessor entitles the lessee to demand, in addition to damages:

1. specific performance of the obligation, in cases which admit of it;
2. cancellation of the contract if the inexecution causes him serious prejudice:
3. reduction of the rent. (Article 1610 C.C.*)

OBLIGATIONS OF THE LESSEE

PROPER USE AND CLEANLINESS

9. The lessee must use the dwelling as a prudent administrator and keep it clean. (Article 1657 C.C.*)

GOOD CONDUCT

10. The lessee must so act as not to disturb the normal enjoyment of other lessees of the same immoveable.

He is answerable to the lessor and the other lessees for damage which may result from a violation of this obligation, either on his own part or on that of persons he allows to have access to the immoveable.

Such violation also entitles the lessor to ask for cancellation of the lease. (Article 1635 C.C.*)

RECOURSE OF LESSEE WHEN DISTURBED

11. In the cases provided for in article 1635 (clause number 10), after putting the lessor in common in default, the lessee disturbed in his enjoyment may obtain, if the disturbance persists, a reduction of rent or the cancellation of the lease, according to the circumstances.

He may also recover damages from the lessor in common, unless the latter proves that he acted as a prudent administrator, saving the recourse of the lessor for repayment against the lessee at fault. (Article 1636 C.C.*)

SUBLETTING AND ASSIGNMENT OF LEASE

12. The lessee cannot sublet all or part of the thing or assign his lease without the consent of the lessor, who cannot refuse it without reasonable cause.

If the lessor does not answer within fifteen days, he is deemed to have consented.

The lessor who consents to the subletting or assignment of the lease can only exact the refund of the expenses reasonably incurred. (Article 1619 C.C.*)

DANGEROUS SUBSTANCES

13. The lessee cannot, without the consent of the lessor, use or keep in the dwelling any substance which constitutes a risk of fire and which would have the effect of increasing the insurance premiums of the lessor. (Article 1658 C.C.*)

FIRE

14. In the event of fire in the premises leased, the lessee is not liable for damages unless his fault, or that of persons whom he has allowed to have access thereto, is proved. (Article 1643 C.C.*)

RECOURSE OF LESSEE

15. Inexecution of an obligation by the lessee entitles the lessor to demand, in addition to damages:

1. specific performance of the obligation, in cases which admit of it;
2. cancellation of the contract, if the inexecution causes him serious prejudice. (Article 1628 C.C.*)

AUTOMATIC EXTENSION

16. Every lease for a fixed term of twelve or more months is, at term, extended of right for a term of twelve months.

Every lease for a fixed term of less than twelve months is, at term, extended of right for the same term.

The parties may however agree to a different extension term.

This article does not apply to the lease granted by an employer to his employee accessory to a contract of work. (Article 1659 C.C.*)

NOTICE OF NON-EXTENSION

17. A lessor wishing to avoid the extension of a lease contemplated in article 1659 or wishing to increase the rent or change any other condition for the renewal or extension of such lease must give notice of it in writing to the lessee.

A lessee wishing to avoid the extension of a lease contemplated in article 1659 must give notice of it in writing to the lessor. (Article 1660 C.C.*)

DELAY FOR NOTICE

18. The notice contemplated by article 1660 must be given not later than three months before the expiry of the term in the case of a lease for a fixed term of twelve months or more and one month or one week before the expiry of the term in the case of a lease for a fixed term of less than twelve months according to whether the rent is payable by the month or by the week. If the rent is payable according to another term, the notice must be given with a delay equal to such term or, if it exceeds three months, with a delay of three months.

---

(2) **1630.** A party who intends to cancel a lease for an indeterminate term must give a notice to that effect to the other party.
1631. The delay for the notice is:
1. one month or one week, according to whether the rent is payable by the month or by the week.
If the rent is payable according to another term, the notice must be given with a delay equal to such term or, if it exceeds three months,
with a delay of three months;
2. three days, for moveables.
The notice cannot be otherwise than in writing in the case of a lease of a dwelling.

Such notices cannot be given beyond a delay exceeding twice the delay provided for in the preceding paragraph.

One of the parties may, for reasonable cause, and with the permission of a judge in chambers, give notice after the expiry of the delay provided for in the first paragraph of this article provided that the other party does not suffer serious prejudice therefrom.

In the case of a lease contemplated by the fourth paragraph of article 1659, the lessor must give the lessee notice of at least one month to terminate the lease, whether such lease is for a fixed term or for an indeterminate term. (3) (Article 1661 C.C.*)

CANCELLATION OF LEASE

NON-PAYMENT OF RENT

19. The lessor may demand cancellation of the lease for non-payment of the rent only if the lessee has delayed for more than three weeks. (Article 1663 C.C.*)

UNSAFE PREMISES

20. The lessor may obtain cancellation of the lease when the dwelling is ruinous and becomes dangerous for the public or for the occupants. (Article 1664 C.C.*)

DEATH OF LESSEE

21. The heir or legatee of a deceased lessee may cancell the current lease.

He must send notice thereof to the lessor at least three months before cancellation.

Such notice must be given within six months after the death. (Article 1664b C.C.*)

ABANDONMENT OF PREMISES

22. If the lessee leaves the dwelling before the expiry of the lease, taking his moveable effects, the lessor may make a lease with a new lessee.

The new lease shall entail cancellation of the former, but the lessor retains his recourses for damages against the person who has left the premises. (Article 1664c C.C.*)

PROHIBITIONS

PAYMENT OF RENT AND DEPOSIT

23. The lessor may only exact in advance payment of rent for one term, or, if such term exceeds one month, the payment of one month's rent.

He cannot exact any other amount, in the form of a deposit or otherwise. (Article 1664d C.C.*)

ISSUE OF CHEQUES

24. The lessor cannot exact issue of a cheque or other post-dated instrument for payment of rent except for the final term, or, if such term exceeds one month, for payment of the final month's rent. (Article 1664e C.C.*)

FORFEITURE OF TERM AND CHANGE OF RENT DURING THE TERM OF A LEASE

25. The following are without effect:

1. every clause to forfeit the term for payment of the rent;

2. in a lease for a fixed term of twelve months or less, every clause that would directly or indirectly vary the rent during the term of the lease.

In a lease for more than twelve months, the parties may agree that the rent will be readjusted in relation with any variation of the municipal or school taxes affecting the immoveable, of the unit cost of fuel or electricity in the case of a dwelling heated or lighted at the cost of the lessor and of premiums for fire insurance and liability insurance.

Such readjustment cannot be made during the first twelve months of the lease and cannot occur more than once during each additional period of twelve months.

In case of contestation of the amount of the readjustment, the parties may apply to the tribunal, by way of motion. (Article 1664f C.C.*)

EXEMPTION FROM LIABILITY AND LIABILITY WITHOUT FAULT

26. The following are without effect:

1. every clause of exoneration or limitation of liability in favour of the lessor;

2. every clause intended to render the lessee liable for damage caused without his fault. (Article 1664g C.C.*)

PENAL CLAUSE

27. The following may be annulled or reduced:

1. every penal clause in which the amount provided for exceeds the damage actually sustained by the lessor;

2. every clause which, in the circumstances, is harsh, excessive or unconscionable. (Article 1664h C.C.*)

UNCON-SCIONABLE CLAUSE

DISCRIMINATION

28. Every clause that is discriminatory by reason of the race, creed, sex, color, nationality, ethnic origin, place of birth or language of a lessee or occupant of the dwelling is without effect. (Article 1664i C.C.*)

FAMILY INCREASE

29. Every agreement to alter the rights of the lessee by reason of an increase in the number of members of his family, unless the space of the dwelling warrants it, is without effect. (Article 1664j C.C.*)

PURCHASE OF MOVEABLES ON INSTALMENT PLAN

30. Every agreement by which the lessee obliges himself not to buy moveable effects by instalment purchase is without effect. (Article 1664k C.C.*)

LOCKS

31. Locks allowing access to the dwelling may be changed only with the consent of the parties. (Article 1664l C.C.*)

GOOD CONDITION

32. Every agreement by which the lessee acknowledges that the dwelling is in good condition is without effect. (Article 1664m C.C.*)

OFFENCES

REMITTANCE OF COPY OF LEASE IN WRITING

33. If the parties agree to a written lease, the lessor must, within fifteen days of its making, give the lessee a copy of the lease reproducing, in full and in the manner indicated therein, section II of the form attached as a schedule after article 1665, including the notice, titles and marginal notes. (Article 1664n C.C.*)

(3) Articles 1630 and 1631 apply to a lease made for an indeterminate term. See foot-note (2).

REMITTANCE OF A WRITING FOR ORAL LEASE

34. If the parties agree to an oral lease, the lessor must, within three days of the agreement, give the lessee a writing reproducing, in full and in the manner indicated therein, section II of the form attached as a schedule after article 1665, including the notice, titles and marginal notes. (Article 1664o C.C.*)

LANGUAGE OF THE LEASE

35. The lease and writing contemplated by articles 1664n (clause number 33) and 1664o (clause number 34) shall be drawn up in French or in English, at the option of the lessee. (Article 1664p C.C.*)

TYPE

36. The type used for the lease or writing contemplated by articles 1664n (clause number 33) and 1664o (clause number 34) shall, if printed, be of at least:

1. for marginal notes, for titles and for the word "notice" at the beginning of section II, twelve-point face on thirteen-point body bold-faced capitals;

2. ten-point face on eleven-point body for the remainder of the contract. (Article 1664q C.C.*)

DISCRIMINATION AGAINST CHILDREN

37. No person may refuse to make a lease with a prospective lessee or to maintain a lessee in his rights for the sole reason that he has one or more children, taking into account the space of the dwelling. (Article 1664r C.C.*)

DISCRIMINATION FOR OTHER REASONS

38. No person may refuse to make a lease or may practise discrimination in the making or carrying out of a lease by reason of race, creed, sex, color, nationality, ethnic origin, place of birth or language. (Article 1664s C.C.*)

OFFENCE AND PENALTY

39. Whoever contravenes articles 1664l or 1664n to 1664s (clauses numbers 31 and 33 to 38) is guilty of an offence and is liable, in addition to the costs, to a fine of not more than $500 for each offence. (Article 1664t C.C.*)

OFFENCE AND PENALTY

40. Whoever requires from the lessee any payment other than those authorized by article 1664d or 1664e (clauses numbers 23 and 24) is guilty of an offence and is liable, in addition to payment of the costs, to a fine of not more than $500 for each offence. (Article 1664u C.C.*)

EFFECTS OF OFFENCE

41. Contravention of any of the articles mentioned in articles 1664t and 1664u (clauses numbers 39 and 40) does not allow a person to demand the nullity of the lease. (Article 1664v C.C.*)

PROCEEDINGS

42. Proceedings under article 1664t or 1664u (clauses numbers 39 and 40) are instituted by any person authorized by the Attorney-General in accordance with the Summary Convictions Act (Revised Statutes, 1964, chapter 35) and Part II of such act applies to them. (Article 1664w C.C.*)

REIMBURSE-MENT AND DAMAGES

43. The tribunal condemning a person accused of an offence mentioned in article 1664t or 1664u (clauses numbers 39 and 40) to a fine may, at the request of the victim, order the accused to reimburse him any amount collected without right or to pay him the damages incurred by him from the commission of the offence.

If the accused does not comply with the order within the delay fixed by the tribunal, the victim may have the order referred to the office of the competent civil court.

The order shall then be executed as any judgment of that court. (Article 1665 C.C.*)

---

* C.C.: Civil Code of the Province of Québec.

SECTION III
ADDITIONAL CLAUSES

(Include here any additional clause which may be agreed by the parties; for instance, snow removal, janitor service, heating, description of the premises and of the furniture, if any, etc . . .)

In witness whereof I have signed at _____

this _____ day of _____ 19 _____.

_____   _____
             Lessor   Lessee

_____   _____
        Witness (if required)   Witness (if required)

Distributed by the Information Service of the Ministère de la Justice.
225 est, Grande-Allée, Québec
Palais de Justice, Montréal

Extrait de la Gazette Officielle
Vol 106 No 2   23 janvier 1974
amendé le 24 décembre 1974

Appendix
333

INDEX

Acts of civil status, 33
    birth, 33
    burial, 34
    marriage, 34
Administrative law, 8
Agency, principal and agent, 127-142
    capacity, 130
    definition, 129
    double agent, 136
    obligations of agent, 135, 137
    representation, 130
    special classes of, 131
    termination of, 140
    undisclosed principal, 138
Appearance, 23
Automobiles, 91

Bankruptcy
    assignment, 246
    creditors' meeting, 248
    insolvency, 244
    inspectors, 249, 250
    interim receiver, 247
    ordinary creditor, 254
    petition, 246
    preferred creditor, 253
    proposals, 255-257
    secured creditor, 252
    Superintendent, 244
    tender, 251
    thirty-day goods, 253

    trustee, 250
Bar Association, 16
Bills of exchange
    Bills of Exchange Act, 271-281
    cheque, 274
    consumer sales date, 281
    deferences, 279
    endorsement, 276
    forgery of signature, 277, 280
    good faith defined, 278
    holder in due course, 277
    liability, 277
    postdating, 274
    promissory note, 279
    signature in representative capacity, 282
British North America Act, 6
Bulk sale, 161
Business name, 212
Business organizations
    corporation, 222
    partnership, 214-222
    sole proprietorship, 213

Children, 42
Civil Code, 5
Civil law, 9
Common law, 7
Community of property, 46, 47
Company law
    authorised capital, 232